I0411459

USDA United States
Department of
Agricu ture

Forest Service

Pacific Northwest
Research Station

Genera Technica
Report
PNW-GTR-642
August 2005

Productivity of Western Forests: A Forest Products Focus

TECHNICAL EDITORS

Constance A. Harrington, research forester, U.S. Department of Agriculture, Forest Service, Pacific Northwest Research Station, Forestry Sciences Laboratory, 3625 93rd Ave. SW, Olympia WA 98512, and **Stephen H. Schoenholtz**, associate professor, Department of Forest Engineering, Oregon State University, Corvallis, OR 97331.

Cover Photography by Constance A. Harrington, U.S. Department of Agriculture, Forest Service, Pacific Northwest Research Station, Forestry Sciences Laboratory, Olympia WA 98512

Graphic designer: Jenny Beranek, Beaverton, OR 97006

Papers were provided by the authors in camera-ready form for printing. Authors are responsible for the content and accuracy. Opinions expressed may not necessarily reflect the position of the U.S. Department of Agriculture.

The use of trade or firm names is for information only and does not imply endorsement by the U.S. Department of Agriculture of any product or service.

PESTICIDE PRECAUTIONARY STATEMENT

This publication reports research involving pesticides. It does not contain recommendations for their use, nor does it imply that the uses discussed here have been registered. All uses of pesticides must be registered by appropriate state or federal agencies, or both, before they can be recommended.

CAUTION: Pesticides can be injurious to humans, domestic and wild animals, and desirable plants if they are not handled or applied properly. Use all pesticides selectively and carefully. Follow recommended practices for the disposal of surplus pesticides and pesticide containers.

Productivity of Western Forests: A Forest Products Focus

Constance A. Harrington
and Stephen H. Schoenholtz,
Technical Editors

U.S. Department of Agriculture
Forest Service
Pacific Northwest Research Station
Portland, Oregon
General Technical Report
PNW-GTR-642
August 2005

ABSTRACT

Harrington, Constance A.; Schoenholtz, Stephen H., eds. 2005. Productivity of Western forests: a forest products focus. Gen. Tech. Rep. PNW-GTR-642. Portland, OR: U.S. Department of Agriculture, Forest Service, Pacific Northwest Research Station. 176 p.

In August 20-23, 2004, a conference was held in Kamilche, WA, with the title "Productivity of Western Forests: A Forest Products Focus." The meeting brought together researchers and practitioners interested in discussing the economic and biological factors influencing wood production and value. One of the underlying assumptions of the meeting organizers was that management activities would be practiced within a framework of sustaining or improving site productivity; thus, several papers deal with methods to protect or improve productivity or discuss new studies designed to test the effects of various practices. This proceedings includes 11 papers based on oral presentations at the conference, 3 papers based on posters and 2 papers describing the Fall River and Matlock Long-Term Site Productivity study areas visited on the field tours. The papers cover subjects on forest harvesting activities, stand establishment, silviculture, site productivity, remote sensing, and wood product technologies.

KEYWORDS: Site productivity, forest harvesting, stand establishment, silviculture, forest products, Western forests, LIDAR, log quality, tree quality.

PREFACE

During September 20-23, 2004, we held a conference, "Productivity of Western Forests: A Forest Products Focus," at the Little Creek Hotel and Casino in Kamilche, Washington. The conference was sponsored by Oregon State University College of Forestry, Pacific Northwest Research Station, Western Forestry and Conservation Association, and Northwest Forest Soils Council. The primary goal of the conference was to bring together people interested in managing Western forests for the production of forest products. Many conferences held in recent years have focused on managing forests for wildlife habitat, biodiversity, or other nontimber objectives, but there has been relatively limited current information available on (1) markets for wood products, (2) contemporary harvesting operations, (3) silvicultural practices (especially for stand establishment), and (4) emerging technologies for remote measurement of trees and determination of stand and log characteristics that influence marketability.

The main members of the steering committee were: Stephen Schoenholtz, committee chair, Oregon State University; Bernard Bormann, Pacific Northwest Research Station; David Briggs, University of Washington; Scott Chang, University of Alberta; Mike Curran, British Columbia Ministry of Forests; Randall Greggs, Green Diamond Resource Company; Connie Harrington, Pacific Northwest Research Station; Tim Harrington, Pacific Northwest Research Station; Rob Harrison, University of Washington; Ron Heninger, Weyerhaeuser Company; Bob Powers, Pacific Southwest Research Station; Tom Terry, Weyerhaeuser Company; Eric Turnblom, University of Washington; Joanna Warren, Oregon State University; and Richard Zabel, Western Forestry and Conservation Association. Additional input was provided by Debbie Page-Dumroese, Rocky Mountain Research Station.

Conference organizers wanted to highlight potential effects of forest practices on short- and long-term productivity. This was accomplished through a preconference tour of the Fall River Long-Term Site Productivity Study (west of Chehalis, Washington) and a midconference tour of the Matlock Long-Term Site Productivity Study (west of Shelton, Washington). The midconference tour also visited the Simpson Timber Company small-log mill at Dayton, Washington, and attendees had the opportunity to participate in demonstrations of new equipment for testing wood quality in standing trees and logs.

The conference included 17 invited talks, 10 poster presentations, and 2 tours. Speakers were invited to submit a paper; poster presenters and field-trip organizers were invited to submit an abstract or mini-paper. Eleven speakers, three poster presenters, and two field-trip presenters responded to our invitation to contribute to this proceedings. The papers that follow are organized by topic area in the order that they were presented at the conference, followed by the posters in alphabetical order, and then by summaries of the two field-trip stops at the Fall River and Matlock study sites.

We thank Grace Douglass and Joseph Kraft for assistance in preparing the manuscripts for publication.

This is a product of the Sustainable Forestry Component of Agenda 2020, a joint effort of the USDA Forest Service Research & Development and the American Forest and Paper Association. Funds were provided by the Forest Service Research & Development, Washington Office.

We hope you find the information to be timely and of interest.

Constance A. Harrington
Pacific Northwest Research Station

Stephen H. Schoenholtz
Oregon State University

CONTENTS

PAPERS BASED ON POSTERS

OVERVIEW OF STUDY AREAS ON FIELD TRIPS

METRIC-ENGLISH EQUIVALENTS

HARVESTING

HARVESTING EFFECTS ON SOILS, TREE GROWTH, AND LONG-TERM PRODUCTIVITY

Michael P. Curran[1], Ronald L. Heninger[2], Douglas G. Maynard[3], and Robert F. Powers[4]

ABSTRACT

Soil disturbance related to timber harvesting, reforestation, or stand tending is mainly a result of moving equipment and trees. Compaction and organic matter removal are of primary concern. Severity and extent of disturbance depend on harvest system, soil and climatic conditions. On-site, long-term effects range from permanent loss of growing sites to roads, to more subtle changes in soil properties that ultimately influence site productivity. Off-site effects may include erosion and landslides. Soil disturbance during operations is regulated and monitored to minimize both on- and off-site effects, which can take years or decades to appear. At national and international levels, sustainability protocols recognize forest soil disturbance as an important issue. At the regional level, continual monitoring and testing of standards, practices, and effects, is necessary for the successful implementation of sustainable soil management. In western forests, few studies are old enough to conclusively predict the long-term effects of harvest-induced soil disturbance on tree growth. Results from existing long- and short-term studies have demonstrated a full range of possible productivity outcomes. The net effect depends on which growth-limiting factors have been influenced by disturbance. Refinement of policies will occur as existing studies like the Long-term Soil Productivity (LTSP) network reach critical, predictive stand ages. In the interim, some regional trends are apparent: deeply developed, moderately coarse textured soils appear less sensitive to disturbance. Conversely, shallower and/or finer textured soils appear more sensitive.

KEYWORDS: Criteria and indicators, organic matter depletion, soil disturbance, soil compaction, sustainability protocols.

INTRODUCTION

For forest productivity, sustainable development can be defined as ensuring the biological, chemical and physical integrity of the soil remains for future generations. Sustainability must be addressed throughout all facets of forest management including implementation of individual harvest or stand-tending plans, development of agency or company standards and best management practices (BMPs), and third-party certification. Sustainable development is promoted through reporting procedures required by applicable sustainability protocols, and by having third-party certification of forest practices and products.

Sustainability protocols exist at international and national levels. At the international level, the Montreal Process (MP) includes a Working Group on Criteria and Indicators for the Conservation and Sustainable Management of Temperate and Boreal Forests (Montreal Process Working Group 1997). Some countries have developed their own protocols and procedures designed to track and report progress toward meeting requirements of international protocols such as the MP. For example, the Canadian Council of Forest Ministers recently developed revised criteria and indicators for sustainable forest management (CCFM 2003).

[1] Michael P. Curran, corresponding author, research soil scientist, B.C. Ministry of Forests, Forest Sciences Program, Kootenay Lake Forestry Centre, 1907 Ridgewood Rd , Nelson, BC, Canada, V1L 6K1. (also adjunct professor, Agroecology, University of B.C.). Phone: 250-825-1100. E-mail: mike.curran@gems5.gov.bc.ca

[2] Ronald L. Heninger is a senior scientist, Weyerhaeuser Company, P.O. Box 275, Springfield, OR, USA. 97478-5781

[3] Douglas G. Maynard is a research scientist, Natural Resources Canada, Canadian Forest Service, 506 West Burnside, Victoria, BC, Canada, V8Z 1M5

[4] Robert F. Powers is a program manager, USDA Forest Service, Pacific Southwest Research Station, 2400 Washington Ave., Redding, CA. 96001

Third-party (eco) certification of forest practices and resulting wood products has arisen in response to sustainability protocols and the greening of the global market place. Organizations such as Sustainable Forestry Initiative (American Forest and Paper Association), Canadian Standards Association, Forest Stewardship Council (FSC), and ISO 1400.1 all have documented review processes and procedures for certification. Protecting streams and natural drainage patterns, maintaining slope stability, and regulating soil disturbance are common elements considered. In addition, most require some adaptive management process to ensure continuous improvement of practices on the ground. Compliance with current soil disturbance standards is often used as a proxy for ensuring sustainability. Some call for more restrictive standards than others (e.g., FSC in British Columbia calls for lower disturbance levels than Provincial regulations).

When managing harvest effects on soils, tree growth and long-term productivity at the local level, managers usually focus on reducing soil disturbance from mechanical operations. Soil disturbance occurring at time of harvest can have negative, positive, or no detectable effect on growth or hydrologic function. Soil disturbance at the time of operations is often an indicator used in regulating long-term productivity and hydrologic effects. This is because in many North American ecosystems, we need at least 10 to 20 years of data to draw conclusions about the effects of various practices. In discussing evidence for long-term productivity changes, Morris and Miller (1994) indicated slow-growing stands require 20 or more years of growth before long-term productivity consequences can be ascertained. Soil disturbance is the proxy that we can observe and regulate at the time of harvesting, site preparation, etc. A common approach is needed for describing soil disturbance so that results achieved in different areas are comparable (Curran et al. in prep.).

In this paper, we discuss effects of harvest induced soil disturbance on subsequent tree growth. Long-term productivity implications are explored along with some soil considerations in harvest planning and continuous improvement schemes. More detailed discussion of these effects and practical interpretations are provided in the literature that has been cited, guidebook materials available from government agencies like the B.C. Ministry of Forests (http://www.gov.bc.ca/for), the USDA Forest Service (http://www.fs fed. us/), various University extension websites, and related products like the new Forestry Handbook for B.C. (soils chapter by Krzic and Curran, in press).

HARVESTING EFFECTS ON SOILS

Soil disturbance can be defined as any physical, biological, or chemical alteration of the soil caused by forestry operations. The examples of soil disturbance we provide here are primarily related to harvesting activities. Effects on tree growth may be inconsequential, beneficial or detrimental, depending on the net effect on growth-limiting factors and hydrologic properties. Soil disturbance can be considered in the context of: (1) the necessary permanent access network and (2) disturbance that occurs within individual harvest areas that will be reforested and managed as forest land.

Permanent Access Network (Roads, Trails, Landings)
The permanent access network is part of the infrastructure required to transport timber and manage forest land. Standards are in place for transportation system development because it represents a permanent removal of growing sites from the land base, and can have long-term effects both on- and off-site. Effects can include drainage interception and disruption, as well as erosion and sediment delivery to streams, which can affect other resource values, and can also cause property damage and possibly loss of life in catastrophic events. These are all good reasons to minimize the amount of forest land lost to permanent access.

In-Block Disturbance (Area to be Reforested)
Most in-block soil disturbance is the result of harvest equipment and dragging logs. Effects of soil disturbance depend on harvest method and season of operation. Ground-based harvesting typically creates more disturbance than aerial or cable. Wet season harvest is typically more disturbing than dry season harvest, or winter condition harvest (where that option exists). Severity and extent of in-block disturbance can be controlled or minimized through careful harvest planning and practices. Guidelines, regulations and standards often limit types and extent of disturbance and commonly focus on compaction and displacement.

Fully mechanized harvest activities, where feller-buncher and grapple skidder operations are allowed off main skidtrails, can result in high amounts of soil disturbance. Examples of the type and amounts of soil disturbance that can occur from this type of harvest are shown in figure 1. Total machine traffic coverage on the soil ranged from 49% to 62 %. The amount of concentrated disturbance complied with the guidelines at the time of harvest. Repair of concentrated disturbance is often possible with rehabilitation techniques; however, extensive off-trail disturbance is more problematic if it has damaged the soil. The main concern with off-trail traffic is compaction.

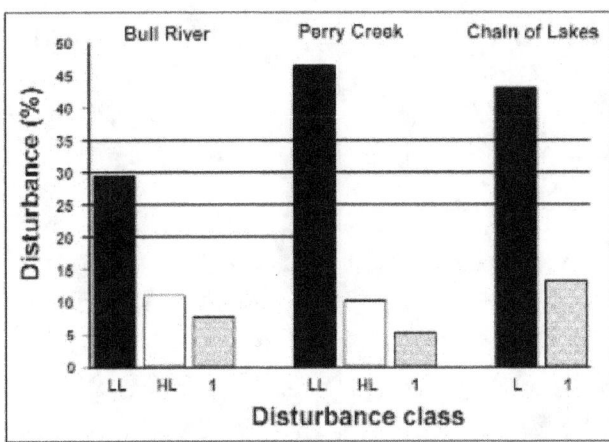

Figure 1—An example of soil disturbance coverage from mechanized harvesting in the Southern Rocky Mountain Trench British Columbia, 1991 (Curran 1999). (LL = light traffic trails; HL = heavy traffic trails – main skid roads; 1 = 5 & 10 cm deep ruts; L at Chain of Lakes includes both LL and HL.)

Figure 2—Close-up of an example of significant compaction from a heavy traffic trail at the Perry Creek site (see Fig. 1). Note the coarse platy structure that often results from heavy compaction of these study soils.

Compaction and Puddling

Compaction and puddling result in alteration and/or loss of soil structure with the affected soil often appearing coarse platy or massive (figure 2). Guidelines define thresholds for compaction severity and spatial extent, beyond which it is generally thought to have a long-term effect on forest productivity or hydrologic function. Compaction results from the weight and vibration of heavy equipment and dragging of logs. Important effects of compaction on forest soils are:

1. Soil density and strength are often increased,
2. Soil macro-porosity is often decreased, and
3. Soil infiltration is often decreased.

Bulk density increases are often measured in terms of total soil or fine fraction bulk density. Neither of these may be a true measure of other effects (e.g., soil porosity and penetration resistance) because trafficking sometimes incorporates considerable amounts of organic matter in the soil. Incorporation of forest floor and other organic material into a soil can result in increased puddling of soils due to clay-sized particles settling under wet conditions, or being smeared by equipment traffic.

Penetration resistance can be a good measure of relative compaction and conditions of high soil strength can restrict root growth. However, penetrometer readings are dependent on soil moisture content at the time and observations are affected by soil texture, and the amount of coarse fragments and roots. Figure 3 shows how compaction increases soil strength as measured by penetration resistance. Soil moisture content often varies between disturbance types due to differences in hydrologic properties (discussed below).

However, while strength is affected by soil moisture and clay content, soils in areas severely disturbed invariably test higher than undisturbed soil, regardless of soil moisture. Figure 3 also demonstrates that most compaction occurs in the top 20 cm. Compaction increases with increasing traffic, and most compaction occurs during the first trips over the same piece of ground; as few as three passes can result in most of the compaction.

Perhaps the most important compaction effect is alteration of soil porosity, due to the collapse or distortion of large macro-pores. Soil compaction increased bulk density on a loam soil resulting in an overall decrease in aeration porosity and slight increases in available and unavailable water (figure 4). Less biological activity occurs as aeration porosity decreases. Once aeration porosity drops below 10% (at 0.01 MPa tension in a standard laboratory test) gas diffusion in the soil is essentially zero (Xu et al. 1992). This is thought to be a result of the tortuous nature of remaining large soil pores and restrictions in the necks between pores.

Another potential result of soil compaction is altered hydrologic function. Saturated hydraulic conductivity can decrease substantially in compacted soils (fig. 5). Infiltration decreases in compacted soil can result in increased surface runoff and consequently less water storage. Soil compaction may or may not impact plant growth detrimentally. Gomez et al. (2002), Powers (1999) and Powers et al. (in review) found that for sandy soils and drier sites, compaction actually improved growth by improving water availability. Interestingly, soil microbial activity may be unaffected by soil compaction. Unless soils are poorly drained, microbial activity probably continues unabated in

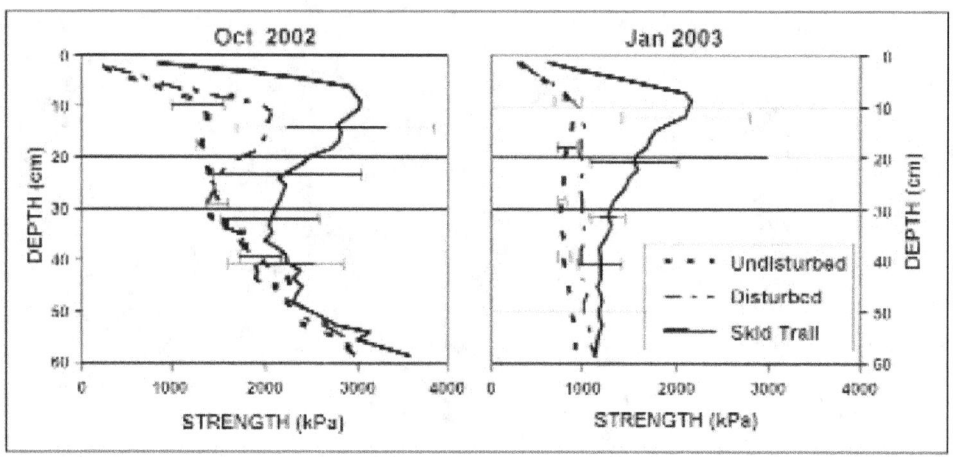

Figure 3—Iron Canyon soil monitoring to determine disturbance severity following second harvest. Penetrometer profiles by disturbance class, October 2002 (21% soil moisture), and January 2003 (45 % soil moisture) (Unpublished data on file at the USFS, PSW Research Station, Redding, California.)

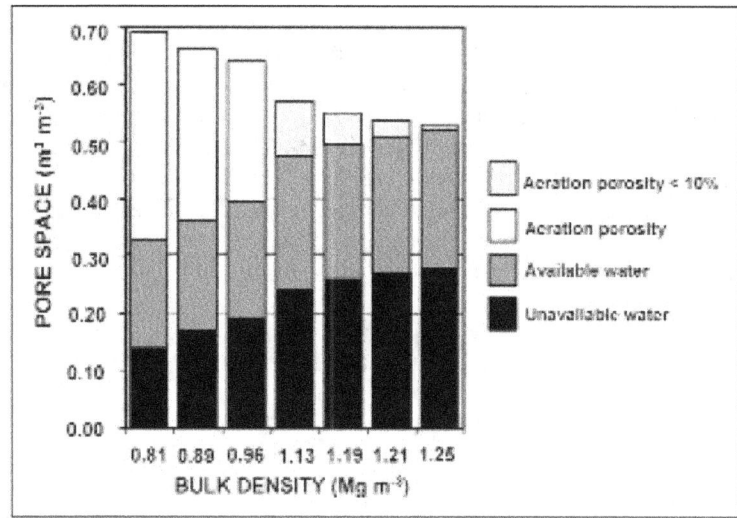

Figure 4—Effect of soil compaction on pore size distribution and water availability, Cohasset Loam studied by Siegel-Issem et al. (2005).

small soil pores and micro-aggregates that are not reduced by compaction (Shestak and Busse 2005).

Severity and extent of compaction are determined by both controlling and manageable factors (modified from Lewis et al. 1989).

Controlling factors are those inherent to the harvest site and include:
- texture,
- coarse fragments,
- forest floor depth/type,
- soil depth, and
- mineralogy.

Manageable factors can be controlled through harvest planning and include:
- machine traffic,
- machine type/dynamic loading,
- seasonal soil conditions (wetness, snow, frozen soil), and
- machine operator awareness, training, and skill.

Various hazard, or risk (hazard times consequence) rating schemes have been developed to evaluate the susceptibility of soils to compaction. One example that focuses on controlling site factors is the B.C. Ministry of Forests compaction hazard key (Curran et al. 2000).

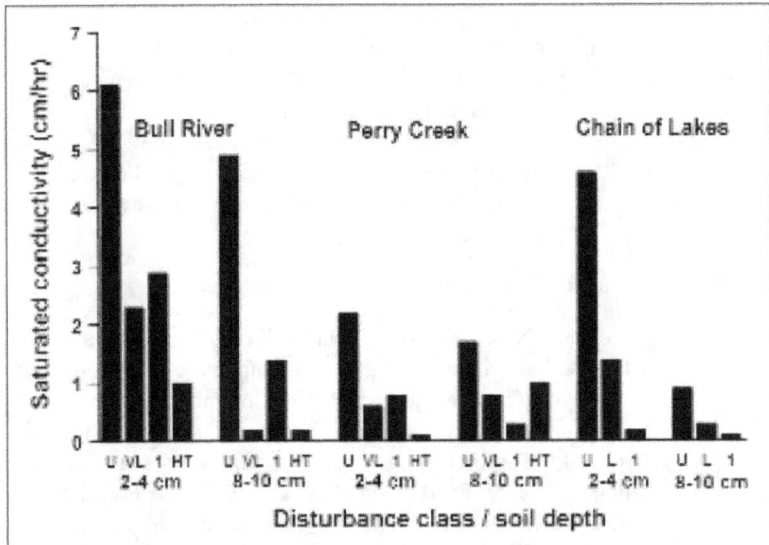

Figure 5—Saturated hydraulic conductivity on soil disturbance types from the mechanized harvesting study shown in Fig. 1 (Curran 1999). (U = undisturbed; VL = light traffic trails; HT = heavy traffic trails – main skid roads; 1 = 5 & 10 cm deep ruts).

Figure 6—Photo of old 1960's era skid trail in the Iron Canyon study site before the recent harvest study. Note lack of tree growth on this trail.

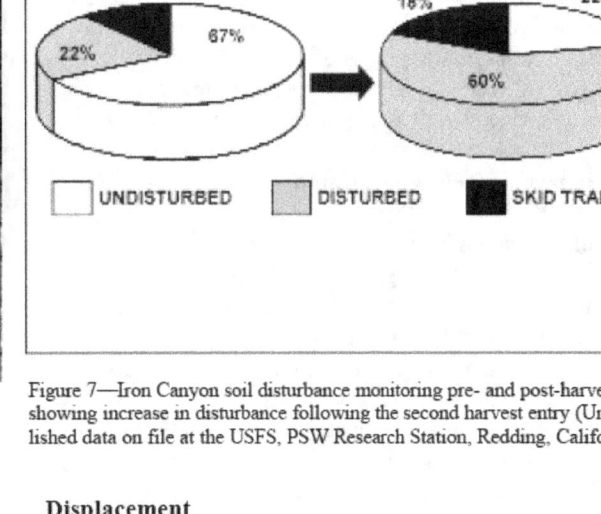

Figure 7—Iron Canyon soil disturbance monitoring pre- and post-harvest showing increase in disturbance following the second harvest entry (Unpublished data on file at the USFS, PSW Research Station, Redding, California.)

Effects of soil compaction can persist for decades (Froehlich et al. 1985), so concern about cumulative effects is important when planning harvest activities. Figure 6 shows there are no trees growing in a heavily used skid trail about 40 years following initial logging. Successive harvest entries can add to already existing compaction and displacement. Figure 7 shows changes from pre- to post-harvest for the area shown in fig. 6. Skid trail coverage nearly doubled, general disturbance increased nearly three-fold, and undisturbed ground fell to one-third its previous extent. Lacking careful supervision, cumulative impacts will occur during ground-based operations.

Displacement

Displacement is the removal of mineral topsoil and forest floor layers from tree-growing sites. It is also a result of machine traffic or dragging of logs. Most organic matter and nutrients needed to sustain plant growth are in the developed topsoil, which varies in depth depending on local soil development. Displacement can result in a loss of available nutrients and effective rooting volume. In addition, it can expose subsoils that are less favourable growing sites (e.g., dense or coarse parent materials). Loss of water-holding capacity, exposure of subsurface seepage, increased runoff, and drainage diversion can also occur and affect off-site values as well. Thus, displacing topsoil an appreciable distance may lower site productivity through loss of available nutrients and effective rooting volume. Dyck and Skinner (1990) found that the overall productivity of a plantation where topsoil had been windrowed was only two-thirds that of an adjacent, non-windrowed plantation.

Severity and extent of displacement are also influenced by controlling and manageable factors (modified from Lewis et al. 1989).

Controlling factors include:
- slope,
- topography,
- soil depth, and
- subsoil type.

Manageable factors include:
- amount and extent of excavation,
- machine size/type,
- seasonal soil conditions (wetness, snow, frozen soil), and
- machine operator awareness, training, and skill.

Few hazard or risk (hazard times consequence) rating schemes are available to evaluate soil susceptibility to displacement. Examples that focus on controlling site factors are the B.C. Ministry of Forests soil displacement and forest floor displacement hazard keys (Curran et al. 2000).

Best Management Practices Components: Harvesting Effects on Soils

Careful planning is required to manage effects of harvest activities on soils. Planning should be based on guidelines and standards that limit specific kinds of soil disturbance and reduce potential for cumulative effects on productivity and hydrologic function. Disturbance from in-block disturbance is often regulated based on inherent sensitivity of the site/soil, with corresponding disturbance criteria and limits that are normally set for temporary access and soil disturbance in the area to be reforested. The most manageable factor may be operator training, awareness, and skill. Managing soil disturbance requires the following best management practice (BMP) components:

BMP components include:
1. site characterization,
2. detailed soil inventory,
3. harvesting strategies to meet soil disturbance standards based on the local soil susceptibility to disturbance,
4. considerations for climatic constraints (e.g., wet soils), or opportunities (e.g., snowpack),

5. monitoring of resulting soil disturbance,
6. restorative treatments for disturbance that is either over prescribed limits or preferably, pre-planned for rehabilitation, and
7. communication and information exchange (feedback loops) amongst the various level above, to enable continuous improvement of standards and practices.

Each of these components is discussed below.

Site characterization (1), and soil mapping of the area (2) are done either during the planning phase for the harvest cycle (e.g., methods in British Columbia described in Curran et al. 2000), or as a ground-checked resource inventory of the entire management area (this is more commonly done in the US Pacific Northwest area). With appropriate interpretations, soil mapping alerts harvesters about the amount of care needed to avoid excessive soil disturbance, when to schedule operations, and what portions of an area are most or least operable in wet weather.

Harvesting strategies (3) have been described for meeting soil disturbance standards under site conditions in western Washington and Oregon by Heninger et al. (1997) and for Interior British Columbia by Curran (1999). The objective is to match equipment capabilities to site sensitivity to disturbance, while providing considerations for climatic constraints (4) (e.g., avoiding wet soils), or opportunities (e.g., using a snowpack to reduce compaction and/or displacement).

Monitoring of resulting soil disturbance (5) follows established methods of measuring the occurrence of specific disturbance types along transects. A working group of the NW Forest Soils Council is currently working towards common disturbance criteria to facilitate comparison and exchange of soil disturbance information (Curran et al. in prep.). Classification systems that are considered to meet desirable criteria, including visually identifiable disturbance types, have been successfully used by the British Columbia Ministry of Forests (Forest Practices Code Act 1995) and Weyerhaeuser Company (Scott 2000), and are currently under developmental use in the U.S. Forest Service Region 6 (Pacific Northwest Region). These classification systems are successfully combined in monitoring protocols to determine severity and areal extent of soil disturbance after operational harvesting (B.C. Ministry of Forests 2001, Heninger et al. 2002).

Restorative treatments for disturbance (6) are required either when disturbance levels are over prescribed limits or preferably, in areas that were pre-planned for rehabilitation.

Figure 8—Decompaction of a logging trail before soil replacement during rehabilitation treatment. (Weyerhaeuser example)

Figure 9—Re-spreading slash onto logging trail as final stage of rehabilitation. (Weyerhaeuser example)

On the right sites, and with appropriate technique, rehabilitation can be an economical and environmentally responsible way to achieve logging efficiency without compromising long-term forest productivity or hydrologic function. (In fact, it can be hard to tell a trail or road existed previously without digging in the soil.) Techniques have been described in the literature, and prescribed in standards or policy guidelines (e.g., B.C. Ministry of Forests 1997), field cards and videos (e.g., Curran 1998). Procedures for successful rehabilitation usually involve both construction and deconstruction phases.

Construction usually includes:
- stockpiling of topsoil for later re-spreading,
- construction of the structure involved out of the subsoil.

Drainage control needs to be considered during construction, to control runoff during harvest but also during and after rehabilitation.

Rehabilitation involves:
- removing large cribbed-in (incorporated) woody debris,
- de-compaction through some form of tillage (e.g., Fig. 8),
- replacement of topsoil layers,
- covering with logging slash similar to the surrounding cutblock area (Fig. 9),
- re-vegetation similar to surrounding cutblock area, and
- use of erosion control mulches or seeding if erosion or sedimentation are concerns.

Rehabilitation of disturbed soils can fully restore the growth potential to that of undisturbed soil, provided the rehabilitation activities are done at the right time. However, not all soils, or all soil disturbances, are conducive to rehabilitation. For example, soil rehabilitation resulted in variable effectiveness in ameliorating compacted soils in a study on Vancouver Island (Maynard and Senyk 2004). In deep, well-drained soils, tilling reduced bulk density to below levels of undisturbed soils and in the short-term improved growth. In contrast, under wetter site conditions rehabilitation decreased survival and growth of seedlings. Other examples where rehabilitation is difficult or very costly include wet clayey-textured soils or where extensive rutting covers the entire harvest area. Rehabilitation is best used as a pre-planned activity for main trails and other temporary access like spur roads and landings that are not needed until the next harvest cycle.

Communication and information exchange (feedback loops) amongst the various levels above, should enable continuous improvement of standards and practices (7 from list on page 8) and be part of an adaptive management system used by each agency responsible for managing soil disturbance and its effects on site productivity and hydrologic function. Strategic databases are needed where disturbance types are tracked in relation to actual tree growth effects on long-term monitoring and research sites. Components for this process are discussed by Curran et al. (in prep.).

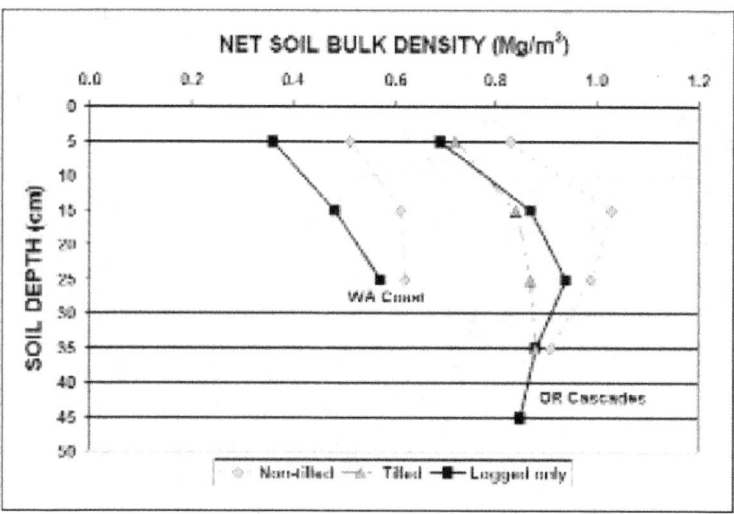

Figure 10—Net soil bulk density (Mg/m³) for a Weyerhaeuser study of tree growth on tilled and non-tilled logging trails (Heninger et al. 2002)

RESULTING TREE GROWTH EFFECTS

Soil disturbance effects on tree growth depend on the growth-limiting factors influencing trees on a given growing site. Disturbance may both positively or negatively influence a tree's growing environment, with the net result being determined by which factor is most limiting to growth.

Growth limiting factors that are often positively influenced by harvesting soil disturbance include:

- competing vegetation,
- soil moisture,
- soil temperature, and/or
- air temperature (frost).

Growth limiting factors that are often negatively influenced include:

- aeration,
- soil penetration resistance,
- soil moisture availability or storage, and/or
- soil nutrients (e.g., nitrogen falling below critical thresholds).

Tree growth effects reflect the tremendous variability of climates and growing sites in the Pacific Northwest and it can be difficult to draw strong conclusions regarding specific types and severity of soil disturbances and tree growth. It is often necessary to monitor sites across the range of management and environmental conditions, and document results in a database used to continually improve guidelines, standards and management practices. Some examples are presented below to illustrate the above statements.

In a Weyerhaeuser study comparing tilled and non-tilled skid trails, bulk density for logged-only, non-tilled, and tilled skid trails by depth and areas (Washington and Oregon) are plotted in figure 10 (Miller et al. 1996 and Heninger et al. 2002). Compared to the logged-only plots, the non-tilled skid trails showed increased bulk density at both geographic locations. The Oregon Cascades tilled skid trails were rehabilitated to almost the same bulk density as the logged-only control for that area. Thus, tillage recovered the bulk density to that of undisturbed soil. There are significant differences between locations in undisturbed soil bulk densities. The next question would be: does this affect tree growth?

In the Washington study, there were no significant differences in Douglas-fir heights among any of the disturbance classes from year 2 through 18 (Fig. 11) (Miller et al. 1996). In the Oregon study, Douglas-fir (Heninger et al. 2002), height growth was reduced on OR skid trails for about 7 years after planting (Fig. 12). Up to age 7 years, the total heights were diverging between treatments. Seedlings on the non-tilled skid trails averaged 15% less in total height. Height growth (slope of line) from year 7 through 10, showed fairly consistent growth rate among the treatments, and was non-significant. Trees on non-tilled skid trail ruts were always shorter than those on logged-only control plots. Trees on tilled skid trails averaged 2% taller than those on logged-only plots. Thus, soil productivity, as measured by total tree height was recovered by tillage. Working through the data, considering time to attain 1.4-m breast height: LO = 4.0 years; NR = 4.7 years; an average difference of 0.7 years to attain breast height. Therefore, trees on the non-tilled skid trails are about one year behind in total height

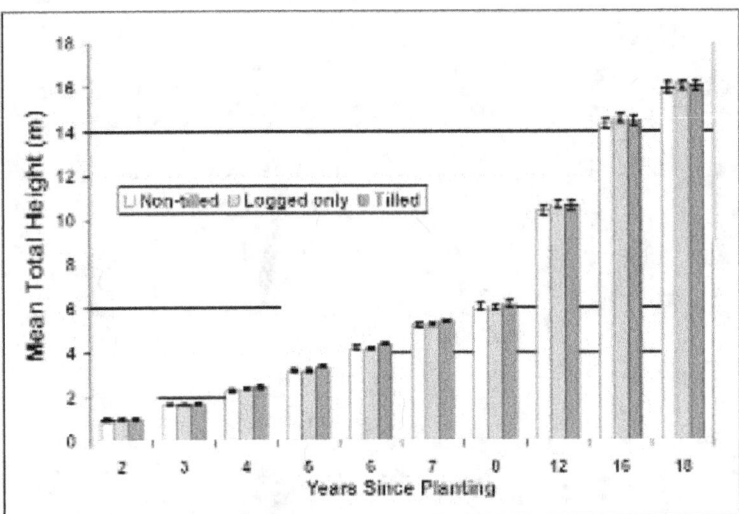

Figure 11—Mean total height of Douglas-fir in Washington for the Weyerhaeuser study of tree growth on till and non-tilled logging trails (Miller et al. 1996).

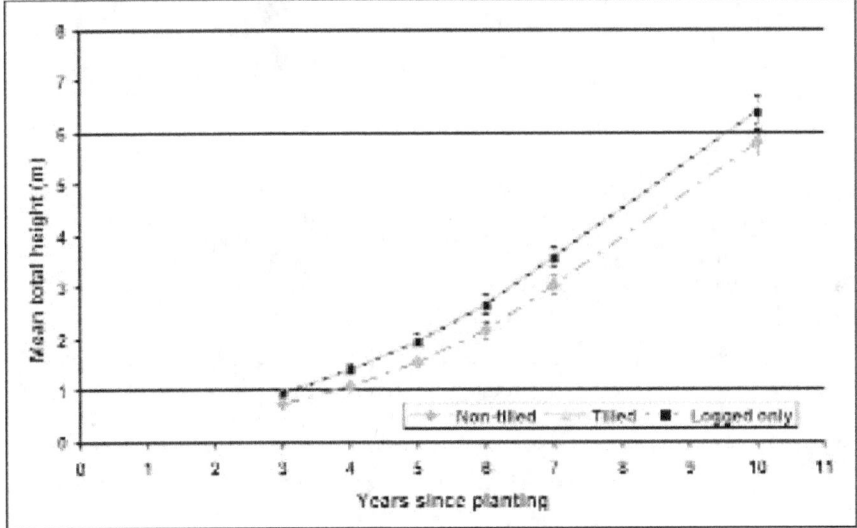

Figure 12—Mean total height of Douglas-fir in Oregon for the Weyerhaeuser study of tree growth on tilled and non-tilled logging trails (Heninger et al. 2002).

and diameter, because it took them one extra year to attain breast height. This difference has been maintained through age 10. The Oregon site has a finer-textured soil than the Washington site and has a longer summer dry period (the effect of the summer dry period is exacerbated by soil compaction). Our hypothesis is that the roots have grown through the compacted skid trail ruts, and are now growing in non-disturbed soil, thus growth rates are now equal. However, the full extent of the impacts on site productivity will surely be magnified if the area in skid trails increases appreciably. Absolute growth will be depressed if roots have little access

to friable soil. So, we need to question how common this trend is and hence whether disturbance criteria need to be modified if longer-term data confirms these apparent trends on these site conditions.

LONG-TERM PRODUCTIVITY

Factors that limit early tree growth and establishment are often different from those that influence long-term productivity. Changes occur as a stand grows and matures, particularly around the time of canopy closure, when the

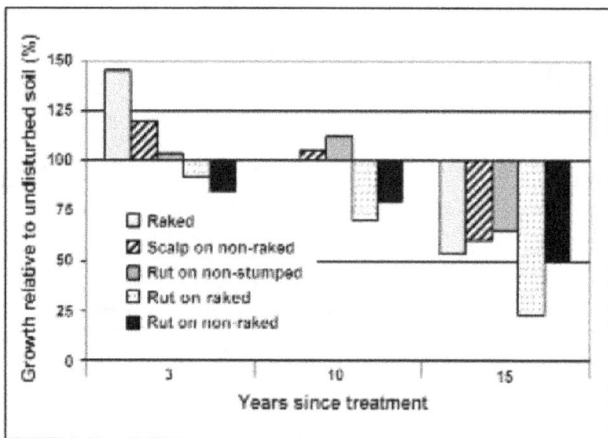

Figure 13—Comparison of relative growth of Douglas-fir on a stump removal trial in southern British Columbia at 3, 10 and 15 years since treatment. All data is relative to the undisturbed condition (adapted from Wass and Senyk 1999.

trees are influenced less by microclimate and competing vegetation, and more by regional climatic conditions and a site's ability to provide adequate nutrients and moisture. Effects that are initially positive or negative may reverse over time. The time required to verify long-term effects on productivity is probably longer in slower growing subalpine or droughty areas. For example, on a relatively clayey site in southeastern British Columbia, short-term growth was enhanced on some disturbance types (Fig. 13). However, in the longer-term (15 years), tree growth was poorer on all soil disturbances compared to the undisturbed areas (Wass and Senyk 1999). It is clear that validation takes time and long-term monitoring/data is essential.

Some trends are becoming apparent. Deeply developed soils in humid climates appear to be less sensitive to disturbance whereas shallow, often younger and drier soils are more sensitive. Volcanic ash-influenced soils are often c o nsidered less sensitive than other soils, but data are still forthcoming.

The actual effects of site disturbances on tree growth depend on many factors, like texture. In British Columbia, our longer-term data currently available are from older studies such as that discussed for figure 13. Figure 14 contrasts 15-year Douglas-fir volume on the Gates Creek site shown in Figure 13 with a less clayey site at Phoenix. Both sites have sandy-loam textures, but clay content varies from 4% at Phoenix to 12% at Gates Creek. This also demonstrates the need for a database that covers the specific soils within the operating area covered by the guidelines. In our example, current compaction hazard ratings for the two sites would be the same, but the soils clearly behaved differently.

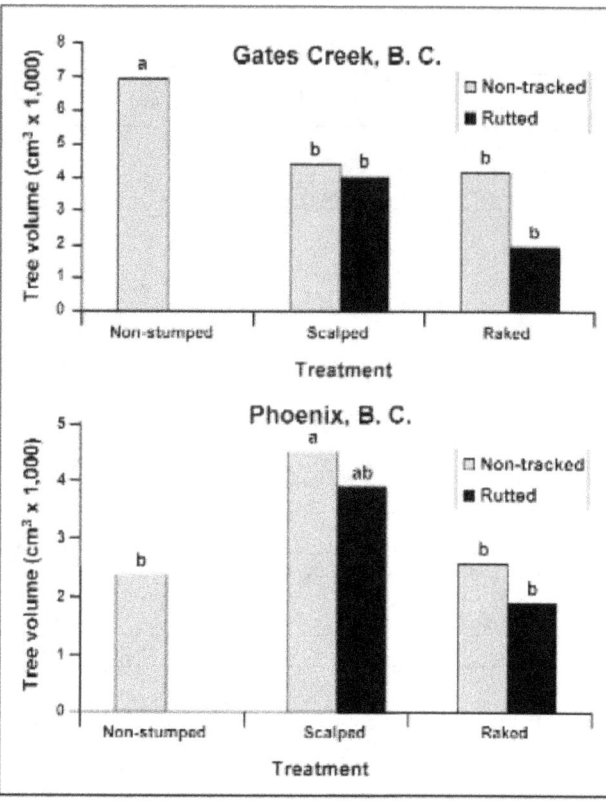

Figure 14—Fifteen-year volume of Douglas-fir seedlings growing in different disturbance types on the Canadian Forest Service Gates Creek and Phoenix stumping trial sites in southern B.C., which are gravelly sandy loam textured with 12% clay at Gates Creek and 4% clay at Phoenix (adapted from Wass and Senyk 1999).

Figure 15 shows the importance of texture in the results from the Long-term Soil Productivity (LTSP) sites in California. In the clayey and loam textured study sites there is clearly a negative affect of compaction on 10-year biomass, whereas on the sandy sites there is actually a positive effect. This is considered to be due to compaction increasing the water-holding capacity on the sandy sites. Ten-year findings from the oldest LTSP sites in California, Idaho, the Lake States, and the Southern Coastal Plain support the conclusion that impacts of soil compaction on tree growth depend mainly on soil texture and degree of soil drought (Powers et al., in prep.). Studies like the LTSP are producing more long-term data every year. Over time, we will have indicators of soil disturbance conditions that affect tree growth under specific conditions.

Long-term productivity is dependent on the amount of permanent access and the net effect of in-block disturbance on future yield. Timber supply modeling takes into account these two factors. However, we need to improve data upon

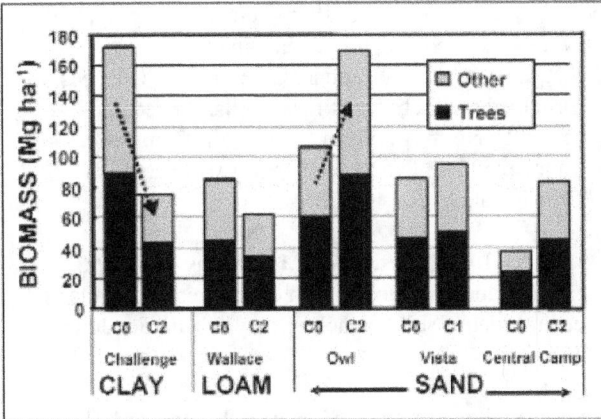

Figure 15—The importance of texture on the LTSP sites in California (C0 = no compaction, C1 = moderate compaction, C2 = severe compaction) (Powers et al. in review).

which in-block soil disturbance projections are based. Many tree growth studies are based on individual tree data from specific disturbance types. Data are needed on an areal (or extent) basis across a cut-block to fully integrate the net effect of on-site disturbance. The LTSP study is an area-based controlled experiment on compaction and organic matter levels that ideally should be paired with operational disturbance types and rehabilitation at each installation. Powers et al. (1998) proposed operationally feasible soil-based indicators for weighing the likely impacts of management on potential site productivity. Among their recommendations were to develop: soil maps highlighting soil types apt to be sensitive to disturbances, soil physical indic a t o r s such as resistance to penetration, and chemical/microbial indicators of nutrient supply, such as mineralizable nitrogen. These indicators need testing and implementation through continued testing, refinement and augmentation of existing soil disturbance standards.

SUMMARY

Harvesting Effects on Soils

Most soil disturbance caused by machine traffic is in the form of compaction and displacement. Compaction often results in increase in bulk density and decreases in penetrability, amount and size of pore space, aeration porosity, infiltration, and hydrologic conductivity. Displacement often results in loss of topsoil and exposure of subsoils. Off-site effects from soil disturbance can include erosion, sediment delivery and loss of life and property loss (not discussed in detail in this paper).

Effects on Tree Growth

Soil disturbance effects on tree growth depend on the nature of the disturbance in relation to the inherent site conditions/sensitivity such as soil texture and climate. Results can range from positive, through no-effect to negative, depending on which growth-limiting factor is affected.

Effects on Long-Term Productivity

Growth-limiting factors change as a stand ages and crown closure occurs. Early effects may reverse over time. Studies like the LTSP will permit better prediction of long-term effects and development of indicators that can be used in managing disturbance at the time of harvesting.

Best Management Practices

A number of soil considerations are required in harvest planning. An adaptive management approach needed to continually improve understanding of management effects on our soils. One needs to:

1. Know the soils upon which operations are planned (through survey of site information),
2. Know what practices should be planned (organize this knowledge based on a soil disturbance classification, and a soil risk rating system),
3. Understand potential effects of these practices (both on- and off-site), and
4. Adapt planned practices (BMPs) over time as more knowledge becomes available.

Site-specific knowledge needs to be part of an adaptive management process for continual improvement of practices (sustainability). A lack of data often results in more restrictive policies, erring on the conservative side. Overly conservative policies and practices cost in terms of economics and social benefit from the forest resource. Conversely, policies that are not conservative enough may cost us in terms of environmental values and long-term productivity and hydrologic function. We need to constantly refine and adapt our guidelines, standards, practices and tools as more information becomes available. To meet these needs, linked databases that track the results of implementation, effectiveness, and validation monitoring are essential.

ACKNOWLEDGEMENTS

We thank Steve Howes, U.S. Forest Service, and Chuck Bulmer, British Columbia Ministry of Forests, for their reviews that have improved this manuscript.

LITERATURE CITED

British Columbia Ministries of Forests. 1997. Soil rehabilitation guidebook. Victoria, BC. Forest Practices Code of British Columbia Guidebook. British Columbia Ministry of Forests. http://www.for.gov.bc.ca/tasb/legsregs/fpc/FPCGUIDE/soilreha/REHABTOC.HTM. (January 2005)

British Columbia Ministries of Forests. 2001. Soil conservation surveys guidebook. 2nd ed. Forest Practices Code of British Columbia Guidebook. Victoria, BC: Forest Practices Branch, British Columbia Ministry of Forests. 63 p. http://www for.gov.bc.ca/tasb/legsregs/fpc/FPCGUIDE/SOILSURV/soilconsurv.pdf. (December 2004)

Canadian Council of Forest Ministers [CCFM]. 2003. Defining sustainable forest management in Canada. Criteria and indicators. Canada. http://www.ccfm.org/2000pdf/CI_Booklet_e.pdf. (November 2003).

Curran, M.P. 1998. Skid trail rehabilitation. Includes: Field cards for summer and winder skid trail construction and rehabilitation. (video). Nelson, BC: British Columbia Ministries of Forests (BCMOF) Research Program. 53min.

Curran, M. 1999. Harvest systems and strategies to reduce soil and regeneration impacts and costs. FERIC Special Report No. SR-133. In: Impact of machine traffic on soil and regeneration: Proceedings of FERIC's Machine Traffic/Soil Interaction Workshop. Edmonton, AB. 75-11.

Curran, M.; Davis, I.; Mitchell, B. 2000. Silviculture prescription data collection field handbook: interpretive guide for data collection, site stratification, and sensitivity evaluation for silviculture prescriptions. [Includes forms FS39A and B]. Land Management Handbook No. 47. British Columbia Ministries of Forests. 156 p. http://www for.gov.bc.ca/hfd/pubs/Docs/Lmh/Lmh47. htm. (December 2004)

Curran, M.; Maynard, D.; Heninger, R. [et al.] [In preparation]. A strategy for more uniform assessment and reporting of soil disturbance for operations, research, and sustainability protocols. Discussion paper from: Conference on Long-term Productivity of Forest Soils. Submitted to Forestry Chronicle 2005.

Dyck, W.J.; Skinner, M.F. 1990. Potential for productivity decline in New Zealand radiata pine forests. In: Gessel, S.P.; Lacate, D.S.; Weetman, G.F.; Powers, R.F., eds. Sustained productivity of forest soils: Proceedings of the 7th North American Forest Soils Conference. Vancouver, BC. Faculty of Forestry, University of British Columbia. 318-332.

Froehlich, H.A.; Miles, D.W.R.; Robbins, R.W. 1985. Soil bulk density recovery on compacted skid trails in central Idaho. Soil Science Society of America Journal 49: 1015-1017.

Gomez, A.; Powers, R.F.; Singer, M.J.; Horwath, W.R. 2002. Soil compaction effects on growth of young ponderosa pine following litter removal in California's Sierra Nevada. Soil Science Society of America Journal 66: 1334-1343.

Heninger, R.L.; Terry, T.; Dobkowski, A.; Scott, W. 1997. Managing for sustainable site productivity: Weyerhaeuser's forestry perspective. Biomass and Bioenergy. 13(4/5): 255-267.

Heninger, R.L.; Scott, W.; Dobkowski, A.; [et al]. 2002. Soil disturbance and 10-year growth response of coast Douglas-fir on non-tilled and tilled skid trails in the Oregon Cascades. Canadian Journal of Forest Research 32: 233-246.

Krzic, M.; Curran, M.P. [In press]. Forest soils and tree nutrition. In: Forestry Handbook for British Columbia. Vancouver, B.C: Faculty of Forestry, University of British Columbia. 353-389

Lewis, T., and Timber Harvesting Subcommittee. 1991. Developing timber harvesting prescriptions to minimize site degration. BC Min. Forests Land Management Report No. 62.

Maynard, D.G.; Senyk, J.P. 2004. Soil disturbance and five-year tree growth in a montane alternative silvicultural systems (MASS) trial. Forestry Chronicle 80: 573-582.

Miller, R.E.; Scott, W.J.; Hazard, W. 1996. Soil Compaction and conifer growth after tractor yarding at three coastal Washington locations. Canadian Journal of Foresr Research. 26:225-236.

Montréal Process Working Group, 1997. First approxi-
mation report on the Montréal Process, 1997. Ottawa,
ON: The Montréal Process Liaison Office, Canadian
Forest Service.

Morris, L.A.; Miller, R.E. 1994. Evidence for long-term
productivity changes as provided by field trials. In:
Dyck, W.J; Cole, D.W.; Comerford, N.B., comps., eds.
Impacts of Forest Harvesting on Long-Term Site
Productivity. London; Chapman and Hall: 41-48.

Powers, R.F.; Alban, D.H.; Miller, R.E. 1990. Sustaining
site productivity in North American forests: problems
and prospects. In: Gessel, S.P.; Lacate, D.S.; Weetman,
G.F.; Powers, R.F., eds. Sustained Productivity of Forest
Soils: Proceedings of the 7th North American Forest
Soils Conference. Vancouver, BC: Faculty of Forestry,
University of British Columbia: 49-79.

Powers, R.F. 1999. On the sustainable productivity of
planted forests. New Forests 17: 263-306.

Powers, R.F.; Scott, D.A.; Sanchez, F.G. [et al.] [In
preparation]. The North American long-term soil productivity experiment. Findings from the first decade of
research.

Shestak, C.J.; Busse, M.D. 2005. Compaction alters physical but not biological indices of soil health. Soil
Science Society of America Journal 69:236-246.

Scott, W. 2000. A soil disturbance classification system.
Internal Report Forest Res. Tech. Note, Paper #00-1,
Federal Way, WA: Weyerhaeuser Company. 12 p.

Siegel-Issem, C.M.; Burger, J.A.; Powers, R.F. [et al.]
2005. Seedling root growth as a function of soil density
and water content. Soil Science Society of America
Journal 69: 215-226.

USDA Forest Service. [Draft] 2003. National report
on sustainable forests – 2003. U.S. Department of
Agriculture, Forest Service FS-766. http://www fs.fed.
us/research/sustain/ (November, 2003).

Wass, E.F.; Senyk; J.P. 1999. Tree growth for 15 years
following stumping in interior British Columbia.
Technology Transfer Note 13. Victoria, BC: Canadian
Forest Service, Pacific Forestry Center.

Xu, X.; Nieber, J.L.; Gupta, S.C. 1992. Compaction
effect on the gas diffusion coefficient in soils. Soil
Science Society of America Journal 56: 1743-1750.

HARVEST PLANNING TO SUSTAIN VALUE ALONG THE FOREST-TO-MILL SUPPLY CHAIN

Glen Murphy and Paul W. Adams[1]

ABSTRACT

During the relatively few days it takes to harvest a stand of trees in a forest, more cost is incurred, more revenue is earned, and potentially greater environmental impacts occur than in all of its prior decades of management combined. Careful design, management and follow-up of the harvesting operation can help to maximize current net revenues (gross revenues minus costs) while protecting future timber productivity.

Net-value recovery from a given piece of land is a function of volume, gross value and costs. These can be affected by a wide range of factors that relate to stand, terrain, markets, company policies, harvest systems, operating conditions and practices, etc.

Harvest planning is a design process aimed at matching equipment and crew capabilities to the operating environment while meeting production goals–one solution does not fit all design situations. To do this effectively the planner needs information on such factors as topography, soil characteristics, tree characteristics, and areas to be preserved/protected. The planner can specify such things as equipment selection, skid-trail layout, felling patterns, operating season, road spacing, harvest opening size, utilization level, duff and slash management, delimbing/processing location, log suspension, post-harvest treatments, and standing tree protection.

To effectively protect or enhance future productivity, a forest manager has to continuously improve current harvesting practices based on lessons learned from monitoring the effects of past practices—sometimes over long periods. Where possible, the effects should be measured directly rather than indirectly, e.g., monitoring not only the soil disturbance but also its effect on tree volume and quality. Such observations are likely to show that not all disturbance and soil changes from harvest operations are equal in their effects on site productivity and net value recovery, i.e., they can range from negative to insignificant to positive.

KEYWORDS: Harvesting, value recovery, soil disturbance, costs, productivity.

INTRODUCTION

Forest managers spend decades creating potential value in each tree. At harvest time more costs are incurred, more revenue is generated, and more environmental impacts can occur than at any other time during the rotation. An important challenge for the harvest planner is to maximize current net value recovery, while sustaining future net value recovery. We prefer to use net value recovery, rather than productivity, as a performance measure in this paper since it ties together the impacts of harvesting and management activities on volume production, values and costs.

*Net value recovery = Volume * (Gross Value – Costs)*

Between seedling and sawmill, there are many ways in which net-value recovery can be sustained or lost along the

[1] Glen Murphy and Paul W. Adams are both professors, Forest Engineering Department, Oregon State University, Corvallis, OR 97331. Email contact for the corresponding author is glen.murphy@oregonstate.edu

forest-to-mill supply chain. Value recovery can be maximized through:

- improved inventory systems which allow better understanding of the resource in terms of quantity, quality and location,
- optimal scheduling of stands and allocation of logs to markets,
- planning of harvest layout,
- selection and scheduling of appropriate equipment and practices,
- improved log segregation and processing practices,
- optimal truck scheduling and log stocks management,
- improved process manufacturing, and
- improved post-harvest monitoring and treatment.

In this paper we will briefly look at: is there a need for harvest planning in the Pacific Northwest (PNW), what factors affect gross value recovery and harvesting costs, what is harvest planning, what information is needed, what can the planner specify, and finally the importance of monitoring performance and continuous improvement.

Is There a Need for Harvest Planning?

Good harvest planning generally leads to greater productivity, reduced costs, improved worker safety, and fewer environmental impacts.

Today, many forest companies, including those in the PNW, operate in a worldwide marketplace facing increasing global competition from other timber producers. Competition is coming, however, not only from other wood producers but also from (1) other industries, such as steel, aluminum, plastics, and composites that are competing successfully with the forest industry in traditional markets, and (2) alternative uses for the investors' dollars. To be globally competitive, forest companies need to control costs, sort and allocate logs to the most appropriate markets, and maximize the value of the forest at the time of harvest. Harvest planning is vital for meeting these economic requirements in the short and long term.

Forest soil compaction has been studied for over 50 years in the PNW (Garrison and Rummel 1951). It has been found that most PNW soils are susceptible to compaction, compaction occurs in both dry and moist soils, large areas may be compacted, and compaction can persist for decades (Wronski and Murphy 1994). Soil compaction sometimes, but not always, leads to reduced tree growth, and effects may vary with soil type and other site conditions. For example, a study of compaction effects on seedling growth on three

sites in northern California with clay, loam, and sandy loam soils found reduced, insignificant, and increased stem volume growth, respectively (Gomez et al. 2002). Causal factors for observed growth impacts have become clearer, e.g., Powers et al. (1998) found that sandy loam soils compacted by mechanized thinning had soil strengths that were limiting to root growth during the summer months. They conclude that such a seasonal soil strength increase may effectively shorten the growing period for impacted trees.

PNW forest managers are not alone in their interest in the impacts of harvesting systems on the site. Research on the impacts of soil disturbance on tree growth in radiata pine plantations at four sites, with different soil characteristics, in New Zealand has shown that planted seedling survival was not affected, stem malformation was affected on two of the sites, and selection for pruning and for final crop was affected on all four sites. Volume growth was also affected, particularly for the heavily disturbed areas (Firth and Murphy 1989, Murphy and Firth 2004). Other New Zealand research has shown that, while the impacts of heavy soil disturbance (topsoil removal and subsoil compaction) on volume production may be large (e.g., up to a 40% reduction) the impacts on net value recovery are likely to be even greater (e.g., up to 65% reduction) due to stems having to be cut into lower value products because of size and quality constraints (Murphy et al. 2004).

Even without planning, harvesting operations create a mosaic of disturbance classes so these volume and value reductions are not seen over the whole harvest site. However, harvest planning can effectively reduce the impacts that do occur. Moreover, economic analyses have shown that volume losses from compaction can justify a significant investment in planning and other measures to avoid or reduce these impacts (Stewart et al. 1988, Murphy et al. 2004).

Factors Affecting Gross Value Recovery

Many factors affect the gross value recovery coming off a given piece of land (Murphy et al. 1991, Conradie et al. 2004). These include among other things:

- the proportion of the land area allocated to timber production—land allocated to non-timber uses, such as reserves, is likely to reduce gross value recovery
- the volume per hectare of productive area and the tree species planted on that area
- the tree size—usually, though not always, larger trees are more valuable than smaller trees both on a per tree basis and a unit volume basis
- the quality of the wood and the treatments the stand has undergone—stems with rot or malformation are less valuable than well formed, rot-free stems; pruned

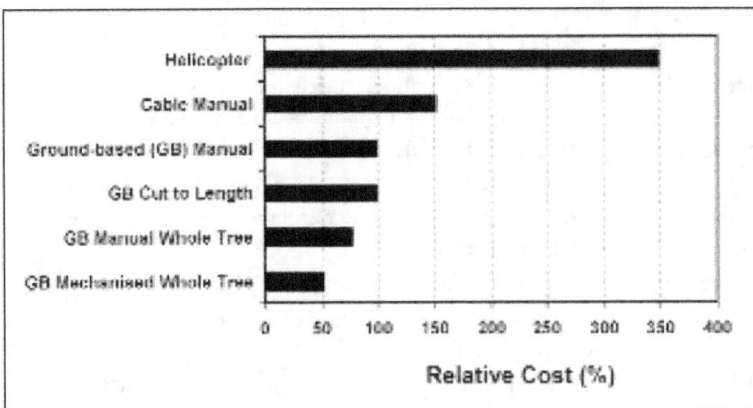

Figure 1—Standing-tree-to-truck costs for a range of harvesting systems (costs are expressed relative to costs of ground-based manual operations).

stems are generally more valuable than unpruned stems; older, high density wood is usually more valuable than young, low density wood, etc.

- the markets available for the wood, the prices the markets are prepared to pay, and how well the wood has been allocated to those markets
- the premium the markets are prepared to pay for "environmentally friendly" products—there are mixed signals from consumers on how large a premium will generally be paid for environmentally friendly products, ranging from nil to less than 10%
- gains or losses in productivity and stem quality due to soil disturbance related to forest operations
- thinning-damage—the few studies that quantify thinning damage in terms of value recovery indicate that losses range from 1 to 2% of the value of the stand at the time of final harvest
- felling practices—8% to 12% of the value of a stem can be lost through poor manual falling practicesextraction breakage—up to 1% of the potential value may be lost through extraction breakage
- bucking tools and practices—bucking can have one of the largest impacts on value recovery. Losses of up to 30% of potential value recovery have been recorded for manual operations and up to 70% for mechanized operations.
- loading and transport damage—little research has been done on value recovery losses due to loading and transport. Damage is likely to result in losses of less than 1%. Mis-sorting and loading of logs for the wrong destination sometimes is of bigger concern.
- harvest system selection—mechanized harvesting systems have value recovery advantages over conventional systems with mechanized felling (due to lower

stumps and less breakage) but tend to incur lower value recovery during bucking.

- equipment selection—mechanized felling equipment that is too small for the tree size it is operating in can result in unacceptable value losses from stem breakage, and butt damage. Soil disturbance can be high if inappropriate equipment is selected.
- operator skills and training—studies of many types of operations indicate that a third of the variation in performance is often related to the human factor.

Factors Affecting Harvesting Cost

Many factors affect the harvesting costs for timber coming off of a given piece of land (Conway 1976). These include among other things:

- the size of the harvest unit—all harvest units generally incur the same fixed move-in, move-out costs. Unit volume costs are therefore likely to be greater for small harvest units than large harvest units.
- harvest system selection (see Figure 1 for relative costs per unit of volume)
- harvesting equipment selection—even for the same harvesting system, differences in costs can result from the type of equipment selected. Not all equipment has the same features, purchase price, repairs and maintenance requirements, etc.
- piece size—harvesting can generally be classed as a piece handling problem; it takes a similar amount of resources to handle a small piece as it does a big piece. Harvesting small trees, or big trees cut into small pieces, tend to result in higher costs than harvesting bigger trees. Costs rise rapidly once piece size falls below about 1 m^3 (200 bf).
- stand treatment—thinning generally results in higher costs (~ 10%) than clearfelling for the same piece

19

size. The size of this increase depends largely on the number of stems per hectare removed.

- operating practices—for example, requiring a mechanized harvester to cover forwarder trails with a running bed of limbs and tops may lower harvester productivity and increase costs
- operator skills and training—see comment on value recovery
- terrain and soil type—steep terrain is generally more expensive to harvest than gentle terrain. Some soil types can limit harvesting activity, particularly when they are wet, resulting in a shorter operating season. Fixed costs, therefore, have to be spread across fewer operating days. Some soils can result in significant wear on harvesting equipment, e.g., sands or volcanic ashes.
- weather conditions—can limit the length of the operating season or reduce productivity on days when harvesting can be undertaken.
- extraction distance—generally harvesting costs increase as the distance the timber has to be extracted increases. One of the exceptions to this is for cable logging systems where very short extraction distances can result in frequent shifting of cables and a lot of unproductive time.
- market complexity—the more complex the market (as measured by the number of log sorts) the higher the harvesting cost. This can be due to an increase in time required for sorting, a reduction in average piece size, larger landings required, etc.
- distance to markets—transport from landing to mill can account for up to 50% of stump-to-mill harvesting costs. The greater the distance to the mill, the higher the transport costs.
- environmental protection requirements—such as riparian area protection, use of designated/old skid trails, etc.

What Is Harvest Planning and What Information Is Needed to Implement It?

Harvest planning is a process whereby equipment and crew capabilities are matched to social, environmental and economic requirements so that production goals can be met. One solution does not fit all design situations. As noted earlier, an important goal is to sustain net value recovery along the forest-to-mill supply chain.

Information required by harvest planners to effectively carry out their job includes among other things:
- data on the terrain–contour maps, digital elevation models, aerial photos,

- applicable rules and regulations related to the project area,
- detailed information on existing infrastructure; e.g., road locations and conditions, bridge weight limits, sortyard locations, etc.,
- harvest schedule for area-level tactical planning (e.g., how will this harvest area relate to past and future harvest areas?),
- soils maps and soil descriptions,
- location of problem areas; e.g., unstable slopes,
- special on-and off-site requirements; e.g., archeological sites, riparian zones, reserves, viewsheds,
- inventory data; volume per hectare, tree size and stem characteristics,
- markets; what log grades and lengths are stems likely to be cut into,
- available equipment and skills in the region.

What can the Harvest Planner Specify?

There are many things the harvest planner can specify that will affect soil disturbance and net value recovery. Some of these include:

1. System selection—the selection of the harvesting system can affect costs, gross value recovery, and soil disturbance. A wide range of systems are available—helicopters, single-span skyline, multi-span skyline, skidder logging, excavator logging, cut-to-length systems, motor-manual systems, fully mechanized systems, etc., —but only a limited number of these will result in an economically viable harvest operation for a specific unit.

2. Equipment selection—equipment design, track and wheel size, and suspension type can all effect duff integrity and soil disturbance. Murphy (1982) found that equipment design could cause a two- to three-fold difference in the number of passes made by ground-based extraction equipment before topsoil removal and subsoil compaction occurred on skid trails.

3. Skidtrail layout—planned skid trails can result in less soil disturbance overall, compared with the logger's choice of travel, by designating where ground-based equipment travels (Froehlich et al. 1981). Providing the distance between skid trails is not too great (requiring large amounts of time to pull winch-line to hook on the logs), costs can also be reduced because of faster travel times from stump to landings.

4. Felling pattern—timber felling patterns can influence the degree of soil disturbance generated, and the amount of breakage and damage to the residual crop. Felling stems

parallel to each other, and in a herring-bone pattern in relation to the extraction skid trail or skyline corridor, helps to minimize disturbance, breakage and damage (Garland 1983, Garland and Jackson 1997).

5. Operating season—limiting the operating season to times when the soils are less susceptible to disturbance may reduce the impacts of harvesting on future site productivity. Identifying effective limits is challenging, however, given the wide range of site conditions and soil and machine types that exist. For example, loaded machines and travel on slopes can result in much greater vehicle ground pressures than the static values more often reported (Lysne and Burditt 1983). Limiting the operating season will also result in higher harvesting costs as fixed costs have to be spread across fewer operating days and harvest volume production.

6. Road and landing location and spacing—as well as taking land out of productive use for timber production, forest roads and skid trails can be important sources of runoff and sediment. However, only a fraction of all roads and skid trails usually cause problems. Some of the key factors determining whether they are a problem are their length, location, design, use and maintenance history. Road spacing can also affect harvesting system selection, harvesting productivity (closer road spacings usually result in faster cycle times and lower extraction costs), and road construction costs (Sessions 1992).

7. Utilization level (bole-only or full-tree) and processing location—short-term net value recovery can be increased (or decreased) by increasing the level of biomass utilization (Murphy et al. 2003). Nutrient removal from the site, however, may or may not have significant impacts on long-term value recovery. Processing stems at the stump versus at roadside can have different effects on costs, value recovery, and nutrient concentration. (Murphy 1987, Smidt and Blinn 1995).

8. Standing tree protection—damage to standing trees during thinning operations can result in future gross value losses due to reduced growth and quality impacts (e.g., scarring) (Han et al. 2000). The potential for damage can be greater near designated skid trails and skyline corridors where traffic flow is concentrated. Providing protection for standing trees comes at a cost but may result in net value recovery gains.

9. Duff and slash management—delimbing at the stump keeps nutrient resources dispersed. Slash on skid trails acts as a cushion between heavy equipment and the soil. Maintaining or increasing slash on skid trails has been shown to help reduce compaction and disturbance (Allen et al. 1997).

10. Log suspension—harvesting operations can be designed to reduce soil disturbance by providing greater log lift. However, this sometimes has a negative impact on costs and gross value recovery. Log suspension can be achieved by providing greater lift (e.g., using helicopters, multi-span systems, forwarders instead of skidders, etc.) or by cutting the stem into shorter logs.

11. Post-harvest treatments—runoff and erosion can be minimized by including water bars, or slash-filter and sediment traps in the design of skid trails and roads. Limbs and tops, removed at the landing, can be spread out over the harvest unit.

12. Riparian area protection—delineation of riparian areas can affect harvest system productivity, costs and net value recovery as well as the amount of sediment reaching streams.

13. Tillage of skid trails and large landings—is useful for clearfell sites when compaction is unavoidable; tillage of thinned sites may result in damage to the root system of the residual crop, but the impact of such damage has not been widely studied. Various implements have been used for tilling compacted forest soils, and cost-effectiveness can vary significantly (Andrus and Froehlich 1983). Where moisture is limiting, the tree productivity benefits of tillage may be masked by lack of weed control. Tillage can also be extended to treat areas compacted by earlier machine operations.

Continuous Improvement and Monitoring

To effectively protect or enhance future productivity and net value recovery, a forest manager has to continuously improve current harvesting practices based on lessons learned from monitoring the effects of past practices—sometimes over long periods. For example, until quite recently it was thought that soil compaction was invariably bad and was a problem serious enough to merit major operational changes.

Where possible, the effects of harvesting practices should be measured directly rather than indirectly; a detailed study of the soil is not always needed to identify soil productivity concerns. Soil productivity is reflected directly in tree growth, form and health. When coupled with indirect monitoring of soil productivity (mapping and quantifying the problem visually, with bulk density measurements, with penetrometers, etc.), a much clearer picture of cause and effect relationships and the situations that merit attention should emerge.

CONCLUSIONS

The impacts of soil disturbance on volume production can range from negative to insignificant to positive. Productivity measures, however, need to include a quality component and be long-term. Net value recovery is a useful alternative performance measure to productivity.

Sustaining net value recovery along the forest to mill supply chain means managing activities that affect not only productivity (i.e. volume production) but also gross value recovery and costs. To sustain net value recovery, future impacts as well as current impacts need to be considered when harvesting operations are being planned. Harvest planners have a wide range of alternative solutions at their disposal. One solution does not fit all design situations.

Forest managers looking to continuously improve their practices, and their net value recovery, need to manage gross value recovery and costs associated with their operations. They also need to monitor and evaluate the impacts of c u rrent operations on the trees, in addition to the soils.

ACKNOWLEDGEMENTS

The authors acknowledge the valuable comments made by Han-Sup Han and John Firth in helping to improve this paper.

LITERATURE CITED

Allen, M.M.; Adams, P.W.; Kellogg, L.D. 1997. Soil bulk density and penetrometer cone index after harvester and forwarder traffic over different slash depths in the Oregon Cascades. Weyer- haeuser Foundation Report. Corvallis, OR: Forest Engineering Department, Oregon State University. 42 p.

Andrus, C.W.; Froehlich, H.A. 1983. An evaluation of four implements used to till compacted forest soils in the Pacific Northwest. Res. Bulle. 45. Corvallis, OR: College of Forestry, Oregon State University. 12 p.

Conradie, I.; Greene, W.D.; Murphy, G.E. 2004. Value recovery with harvesters in southeastern USA pine stands. Forest Products Journal 54(12): 80-84.

Conway, S. 1976. Logging practices. Miller Freeman Publications, USA. 416 p.

Firth, J.; Murphy, G.E. 1989. Skidtrails and their effect on the growth and management of young *Pinus radiata*. New Zealand Journal of Forestry Science 19(1): 22-8.

Froehlich, H.A.; Aulerich, D.E.; Curtis, R. 1981. Designing skid trail systems to reduce soil impacts from tractor logging machines. Res. Pap. 44. Corvallis, OR: Forest Research Laboratory, Oregon State University.

Garland, J.J. 1983. Designated skid trails minimize soil compaction. Extension Circ. 1110. Corvallis, OR: Extension Service, Oregon State University. 6 p.

Garland, J.J.; Jackson, D. 1997. Felling and bucking techniques for woodland owners. Extension Circ. 1124. Corvallis, OR: Extension Service, Oregon State University. 16 p.

Garrison, G.A.; Rummell, R.S. 1951. First-year effects of logging on ponderosa pine forest range lands of Oregon and Washington. Journal of Forestry 49: 708-713.

Gomez, A.; Powers, R.F.; Singer, M.J.; Horwath, W.R. 2002. Soil compaction effects on growth of young ponderosa pine following litter removal in California's Sierra Nevada. Soil Science Society of America Journal 66: 1334-1343.

Han, H.-S.; Kellogg, L.D.; Filip, G.M.; Brown, T.D. 2000. Scar closure and future timber value losses from thinning damage in western Oregon. Forest Products Journal 49(11/12): 9 p.

Lysne, D.H.; Burditt, A.L. 1983. Theoretical ground pressure distributions of log skidders. Transactions of the American Society of Civil Engineers (ASAE) 26: 1327-1331.

Murphy, G.E. 1982. Soil damage associated with production thinning. New Zealand Journal of Forestry Science 12(2): 281-92.

Murphy, G.E. 1987. An economic analysis of final log manufacturing locations in the steep terrain radiata pine plantations of New Zealand. College of Forestry, Oregon State University. Ph.D. thesis. 420 p.

Murphy, G.E.; G.P. Cossens; Twaddle, A.A. 1991. How to improve value recovery from plantation forests: research and practical experience in New Zealand. In: Proceedings: Forestry operations in the 1990's: challenges and solutions. Namaimo, BC: Council on Forest Engineering.

Murphy, G.E.; Siren, M.; O'Brien, S. 2003. Potential use of slash bundling technology is western US stands. In: Proceedings: Council on Forest Engineering. Bar Harbor, ME.

Murphy, G.E.; Firth, J. 2004. Soil disturbance impacts on early growth and management of radiata pine trees in New Zealand. Western Journal of Applied Forestry 19(2): 109-116.

Murphy, G.E.; Firth, J.; Skinner, M.F. 2004. Long-term impacts of forest harvesting related soil disturbance on log product yields and economic potential in a New Zealand forest. Silva Fennica 38(3): 279-289.

Powers, R.F.; Tiarks, A.E.; Boyle, J.R. 1998. Assessing soil quality: practicable standards for sustainable forest productivity in the United States. In: Davidson, E. and others, eds. The contribution of soil science to sustainable forest management. SSSA Special Pub No. 53. Madison, WI: Soil Science Society of America. Chap. 3.

Smidt, M.; Blinn, C.R. 1995. Logging for the 21st century: protecting the environment. FO-06518. Extension Service, University of Minnesota.

Sessions, J. 1992. Proceedings of Computer Supported Planning of Roads and Harvesting Workshop., ed. IUFRO S3.05., S3.06. Feldafing, Germany: University of Munich. 316 p.

Stewart, R.; Froehlich, H.; Olsen, E. 1988. Soil compaction: an economic model. Western Journal of Applied Forestry 3(1): 20-22.

Wronski, E.B.; Murphy, G.E. 1994. Responses of forest crops to soil compaction. In: Soane, B.D.; van Ouwerkerk, C., ed. Soil compaction in crop production. Elsevier Science Publishers, Amsterdam: 317-342.

STAND
ESTABLISHMENT

SILVICULTURAL TECHNOLOGY AND APPLICATIONS FOR FOREST PLANTATION ESTABLISHMENT WEST OF THE CASCADE CREST

Timothy B. Harrington[1] and Jeff Madsen[2]

ABSTRACT

Research and operational trials have identified methods of forest plantation establishment that promote high rates of survival and early growth of tree seedlings in the Pacific Northwest. Primary reasons for this success are the intensive control of competing vegetation provided by herbicide treatments and the planting of high quality seedlings. This paper discusses the current state of the art in forest plantation establishment in Oregon and Washington west of the crest of the Cascade Range. It considers technologies developed in the last two decades that currently have widespread application on lands managed primarily for wood products. The focus of this review is on even-aged silviculture of conifer seedlings, especially coastal Douglas-fir (*Pseudotsuga menziesii* (Mirb.) Franco var. *menziesii*), but other species, silvicultural systems, and regions are considered where appropriate.

KEYWORDS: Vegetation management, nursery technology, tree planting, Douglas-fir.

BACKGROUND

In western Oregon and Washington (i.e., the "Westside"), nearly half of all timberland is publicly owned. The federal government owns 38% and state agencies control 11% of all timberland in this region. Remaining ownership is dominated by industrial (34%) and other private landowners (17%), including various tribal ownerships (Bolsinger et al. 1997, Alig et al. 2003, Haynes 2003, Campbell et al. 2004). Each of these landowner classes differs strongly in their management philosophies and constraints. In the last decade, federal forestry agencies have had to operate within a litigious environment, and as a result, their timber harvest currently is focused on salvage from fire and insect disturbances (Malmsheimer et al. 2004). State-managed forest lands work under a range of constraints and objectives including those of a federal Habitat Conservation Plan for lands of the Washington State Department of Natural Resources, various land trust concerns, and economic mandates (Coyner and Coyner 2004, OSDF 2004a, Washington DNR 2004).

With the exception of tribal owners, private landowners operate under state Forest Practices Laws, the federal Clean Water Act, and the Endangered Species Act. The Sustainable Forestry Initiative includes additional self-imposed regulations by forest industry (SFB 2004). As a result of these various conditions and constraints, most of the timber harvest on the Westside comes from private land (87%). Only 2% of the harvest comes from federal lands with the remaining 11% from state-managed timberlands (Larsen and Nguyen 2004, OSDF 2004b).

The private forest industry faces increasing regulatory restrictions as urban and suburban interfaces move ever closer to its land. Increasing property values from real estate development are shifting land investment away from traditional forestry practices in some areas (Alig et al. 2003). Facing global competition for wood products, Westside industrial landowners are pushed towards intensive silviculture and lower rotation ages as they continue to protect public resources and control treatment costs (Talbert 2004).

[1] Timothy B. Harrington is Research Forester, USDA Forest Service, PNW Research Station, Forestry Sciences Laboratory, 3625 93rd Avenue, Olympia, WA 98512.

[2] Jeff Madsen is Forestry Manager, Port Blakely Tree Farms LP, 8133 River Drive SE, Tumwater, WA 98501.

PREDOMINANT LIMITING FACTORS

Much of the forest land on the Westside is classified as the Western Hemlock (*Tsuga heterophylla* (Raf.) Sarg.) Zone because of the species' potential to establish and ultimately dominate most forest plant communities (Franklin and Dyrness 1973). Douglas-fir is the primary crop species, with occasional planting of western hemlock, western redcedar (*Thuja plicata* Donn ex D. Don), and red alder (*Alnus rubra* Bong.) (Briggs and Trobaugh 2001). Forest site quality is determined largely by soil depth, soil texture and rainfall (Steinbrenner 1981). Nitrogen is the macronutrient most limiting to forest productivity (Heilman 1981).

Douglas-fir seedlings require moderate to high levels of sunlight for optimal development. Mailly and Kimmins (1977) found that seedlings need at least 40% of full sunlight to ensure survival and continued morphological development, although maximum growth rate occurs under full sunlight conditions (Drever and Lertzman 2001). In contrast, western redcedar seedlings require only 10% of full sunlight to survive (Wang et al. 1994), and their maximum growth rate occurs at 30% of full sunlight (Drever and Lertzman 2001).

Experiments throughout the region testing two-aged and uneven-aged silvicultural systems have identified significant reductions in conifer seedling growth from overstory shade and other resource limitations (Brandeis et al. 2001, Mitchell 2001, York et al. 2004). Such multi-cohort methods of regeneration can be challenging to establish and maintain; thus, most of the wood-producing industrial forests on the Westside are managed using even-aged silvicultural systems with clearcutting the dominant method of regeneration (Smith et al. 1997).

Competing Vegetation
Perhaps the most important biological constraint to establishment of Westside forest plantations is competition for limited resources from competing vegetation. Intense shade and early-season depletion of soil moisture occur when development of competing vegetation goes unchecked. For at least five decades, forest managers have been aware of the competitive pressure that results from tall-growing hardwoods and shrubs. Reductions in Douglas-fir height growth have been directly related to the amount of shade at or above half of the tree's height (Ruth 1956, Howard and Newton 1984, Wagner and Radosevich 1991a). In addition, severe competition for soil water can result from as little as 20% crown cover of woody vegetation (Oliver 1984, Shainsky and Radosevich 1986, White and Newton 1989).

About fifteen years ago, Westside foresters became keenly aware of the importance of competition from herbaceous vegetation (Newton and Preest 1988, Petersen et al. 1988, White and Newton 1989, Hughes et al. 1990, Wagner 2000). Many of the common grass and forb competitors invade recently harvested sites by wind dispersed seed. During the first three years of plantation establishment they compete strongly with conifer seedlings for soil water, sometimes depleting available supplies early in the growing season (Newton and Preest 1988).

Invasive species of all types are a continual threat to ecosystems throughout the United States (National Biological Information Infrastructure 2004). Recent changes in Westside plant communities resulting from invasion by non-native species may intensify the competitive pressure that already exists for conifer seedlings during plantation establishment. Species such as Scotch broom (*Cytisus scoparius* (L.) Link.), Himalayan blackberry (*Rubus discolor* Weihe & Nees), and Japanese knotweed (*Polygonum cuspidatum* Sieb. & Zucc.) establish soon after a site disturbance such as clearcutting. Once established, their seed or bud banks can survive for extended periods of time, making them long-term residents of Westside forest communities. Other species, such as English holly (*Ilex aquifolium* L.), English ivy (*Hedera helix* L.), and false-brome (*Brachypodium sylvaticum* (Huds.) Beauv.), are shade tolerant and capable of establishing in a wide range of light environments. Thus, they may already be present in a forest community at the time of timber harvest and able to quickly increase their abundance in response to the disturbance.

Wildlife Damage
Damage to conifer seedlings from black-tailed deer (*Odocoileus hemionus columbianus* Richardson), Roosevelt elk (*Cervus canadensis roosevelti* Merriam), and mountain beaver (*Aplodontia rufa pacifica* Merriam) can be particularly devastating during establishment of Westside forests (Black et al. 1979). Their effects on early growth of Douglas-fir seedlings are so significant that often silvicultural studies must be fenced to eliminate confounding of tree responses from animal damage. Western redcedar is particularly vulnerable to browsing by deer and elk because of its high palatability, whereas western hemlock is generally avoided. Brandeis et al. (2002) found that, when browsed for three consecutive years, cedar had only 56% of the stem volume of non-browsed seedlings

Root and Foliage Pathogens
The common root disease of Westside forests, laminated root rot (*Phellinus weirii* (Murr.) Gilb.), is generally considered a site-specific problem that impacts yield but does

not destroy entire stands (Thies and Sturrock 1995). Since 1990, the foliage disease, Swiss needle cast (*Phaeocryptopus gaeumannii*), has reached epidemic status and caused significant growth losses in coastal Douglas-fir (Maguire et al. 2002). However, recent aerial surveys suggest that the Swiss needle cast epidemic may be stabilizing or even subsiding (Kanaskie et al. 2004). Sudden oak death (*Phytophthora ramorum*) is a potential future threat to forest stands because of its wide variety of plant hosts and ability to invade through either the stem or foliage, depending on the host.

Environmental Regulations

Although these biological constraints can pose some unique challenges to plantation establishment, often the overriding constraints to management activities are environmental regulations imposed by government agencies or self-imposed by forest industry. National and state environmental protection laws impact reforestation activities significantly. In addition, a relatively recent development in forest management is the emergence of an activist citizenry that has the time and resources to challenge specific management activities of public and private landowners. National Forests are often involved in years of administrative appeals prior to final adoption of management plans (Teich et al. 2004; Malmsheimer et al. 2004). These laws and/or social pressures can directly influence the entire range of forest management activities.

For example, new forest practices laws for riparian zones (to safeguard threatened fish species) have significantly increased the area that is non-managed or managed at low intensity. Adjacency constraints in the Sustainable Forestry Initiative and state Forest Practices Laws can determine the location of future timber harvests and even reduce a landowner's planned harvest levels. Adjacency constraints also encourage managers to make large investments in silvicultural treatments to accelerate the development of young stands so they will meet the "green-up" requirements that enable the harvest of an adjacent stand. Air quality ("smoke management") rules have almost eliminated the use of broadcast burning for site preparation on the Westside.

TECHNOLOGY APPLICATIONS

A wide variety of research programs within universities, government laboratories, and private industry have developed successful approaches for regenerating Westside forests given the challenges posed by competing vegetation, animal damage, and pathogens. These techniques are contributing to an ever-increasing intensity of silviculture that accelerates the rate at which forest plantations become merchantable.

Vegetation Management

A considerable amount of research on plantation establishment has contributed to a conceptual framework of "crop" seedling responses to vegetation management. Many of these concepts have been borrowed from the agricultural literature (Cousens 1987) and applied successfully to forestry. The following are three major contributions to this conceptual framework.

(1) Competition thresholds-(Wagner et al. 1989, Monleon 1999) quantify the "breakpoints" in relationships of crop seedling performance to abundance of competing vegetation. The breakpoints signify large changes in seedling response, and therefore, dictate the abundance at which competing vegetation should be managed to ensure a reasonable return on investment from vegetation management.

(2) Critical-period thresholds-(Wagner et al. 1999, Wagner 2000, McDonald and Fiddler 2001, Rose and Rosner 2004) define the time period when competing vegetation should be controlled (i.e., duration of weed control) in order to prevent reductions in crop seedling performance.

(3) Minimum area of vegetation control-(Dougherty and Lowery 1991, Rose et al. 1999) quantifies the portion of a crop seedling's growing space that must be kept free of competing vegetation to maximize its performance. If the minimum area is less than 100%, a spot treatment can be prescribed that will potentially provide a cost-saving relative to a broadcast treatment.

Intensive control of competing vegetation early in stand establishment is being attempted on some forest sites as a means of maximizing productivity and accelerating the rate of stand development. Larger-scale use of backpack sprayer crews is providing forest managers with the flexibility to conduct vegetation management treatments in local problem areas. Pre-harvest herbicide applications are being used successfully in southwestern Oregon and northwestern California to provide more effective control of evergreen woody vegetation than from conventional post-harvest methods (Fredricksen 2005). While herbicides are a critical tool for Westside plantation establishment, all of the new products now in use have much lower toxicity to mammals and fish compared to older products. In addition, most of the newer products are effective at extremely low application rates (e.g., sulfometuron herbicide typically is applied at 3 ounces or less of active ingredient per acre).

Herbicide technology has improved considerably over the last two decades. Experimental comparisons have demonstrated the effectiveness of thinline applications of imazapyr or triclopyr ester herbicides for controlling bigleaf maple (*Acer macrophyllum* Pursh.), a rapidly growing and difficult-to-control competitor (Wagner and Rogozynski 1994). When added to fall site preparation sprays of imazapyr or glyphosate herbicides, sulfometuron provides effective control of herbaceous vegetation throughout the following growing season (Ketchum et al. 1999), thus, eliminating the need for an additional treatment in the spring. One of the newer herbicides, clopyralid, provides selective control of broadleaf herbs without injuring neighboring Douglas-fir seedlings.

Pre-emergent herbicides have the potential to prevent germination and suppress growth of shrub and hardwood competitors. For example, a greenhouse study demonstrated that hexazinone herbicide reduced germination and suppressed growth of varnishleaf ceanothus (*Ceanothus velutinus* Dougl.), deerbrush ceanothus (*C. integerrimus* H. & A.), and thimbleberry (*Rubus parviflorus* Nutt.) (Rose and Ketchum 2002b). Similarly, hexazinone reduced the survival and growth of seedlings of the invasive shrubs, Scotch broom and Portuguese broom (*Cytisus striatus* Hill) (Ketchum and Rose 2003). Figueroa (1994) found that sulfometuron significantly reduced germination of red alder seedlings.

Non-herbicide methods for controlling competing vegetation also are being developed. After two decades of research on methods for controlling red alder with cutting treatments, Belz (2003) concluded that the greatest mortality occurred when trees were cut at six to seven years of age and 13 to 15 weeks after budbreak, presumably when carbohydrates reserves were at their lowest level. Tappeiner et al. (1996) observed reductions in crown volume and area of bigleaf maple sprout clumps if the parent trees were cut at 1-ft height one or two years before stand harvest. Mulches are being used successfully to both conserve soil water and reduce abundance of competing vegetation adjacent to conifer seedlings (McDonald and Helgerson 1990). Mulching is most effective when the material has high longevity and is applied early in the growing season before soil water has been depleted.

The timing, intensity, and duration of competing vegetation control are essential features to consider for any vegetation management treatment because often they determine treatment cost-effectiveness. Wagner et al. (1999) found that the duration of vegetation control resulting in a continued increase in stem volume index varied among conifer species from two to four years. Manually removing competing vegetation around ponderosa pine (*Pinus ponderosa* Dougl. ex Laws.) seedlings provided similar tree growth responses regardless of whether the treatment occurred in years 1-3, years 4-6, or years 1-6 after planting (McDonald and Fiddler 2001). Ten-year growth of Douglas-fir was similar when grown with densities of varnishleaf ceanothus of 0 to 2700 plants/acre, but it decreased by 41% when density exceeded 6070 plants/acre (Monleon et al. 1999). However, regardless of ceanothus density, Douglas-fir growth increased following removal of herbaceous vegetation. Rose et al. (1999) found that Douglas-fir growth increased with area of vegetation control, with maximum values occurring when either 60% (one site) or 100% (two sites) of growing space was treated. Reporting on a large study that compared various levels of vegetation control in western Oregon, Rose and Rosner (2004) found that increases in stem volume were proportional to the total number of years of control for all four conifer species tested. Seedling growth after four years of control resulted in 3- to 18-fold increases in stem volume relative to non-treated seedlings.

Seedling Quality

Quality of Douglas-fir planting stock has improved greatly in the last two decades. These improvements have been prompted by studies attesting to the benefits of large planting stock (Wagner and Radosevich 1991b, Roth and Newton 1996, Rose and Ketchum 2003). In addition, the "target seedling concept," which links specific morphological and physiological traits with field performance, has improved methods of plantation establishment by defining tangible seedling characteristics for nursery managers to cultivate and for foresters to select (Rose et al. 1990). The plug+1 and 1+1 bareroot stock-types are currently accepted standards for plantation establishment on the Westside and have replaced the mainstay of the 1980's, the 2+0 bare root. Exponential nutrient loading is a relatively new concept for nursery fertilization regimes (Timmer 1996) in which fertilizer is applied at an exponentially increasing rate to maintain seedling nutrient content at a constant level, and therefore free from nutrient stress. This approach has been used effectively in forest productivity research to test the upper limit of tree growth responses to fertilization (Powers and Reynolds 1999).

Planting Techniques

Given the current focus on large seedlings, planting is almost entirely done with a planting shovel, replacing the former planting tool of choice, the hoedad. The shovel enables planters to set the roots of large stocktypes in a hole of adequate width and depth, thereby avoiding potential problems associated with shallow planting and deformity of the taproot. Although use of careful planting methods continues to be recommended, (Rose and Morgan 2000), taproot deformity at planting may not cause significant problems to the developing plantation. Surprisingly, Haase et al. (1993) did not find any differences in 10-year survival and growth of Douglas-fir seedlings planted with straight, "L"-shaped, or "J"-shaped root systems. Planting in the fall, as opposed to the winter or early spring, has been used in coastal areas to take advantage of warm soil temperatures in the fall that should translate into increased root growth following planting; however, the authors are not aware of any published research on the benefits of this practice.

Planting Density

Although planting density continues to be an item of debate, most plantations are established at 400 to 500 seedlings/acre. Recent research has indicated that higher planting densities (up to 1200 trees/ac) may stimulate short-term increases in both diameter and height growth of Douglas-fir (Scott et al. 1998; Flewelling et al. 2001). This effect may be the result of a phytochrome response that modifies seedling allometry (Ritchie 1997). Because the growth stimulation associated with high initial densities is relatively short-lived, and reverses after several years, pre-commercial thinning must follow soon thereafter if potential benefits are to be captured. It remains to be seen if these early growth gains due to higher initial densities justify the cost of planting more trees per acre and the need for early pre-commercial thinning.

Genetic Improvement

Possibly more resources have been directed towards genetic improvement of conifers on the Westside than any other yield-improvement treatment. Regional tree improvement cooperatives are now well into second generation testing and breeding efforts. Nearly all large private landowners and some public agencies utilize various levels of genetically improved seed in their regeneration efforts. A recent realized genetic gain study in Oregon estimated a 28% stem volume gain for Douglas-fir (St. Clair et al. 2004). Greater genetic gains than this may be achievable with increased selection differentials (Jayawickrama and Ye 2004). Current programs select for wood quality and stem form factors in addition to increased growth rates. Although the genetic source of seedlings can significantly contribute to stand productivity, research on ponderosa pine indicates this may only happen when they are grown without competing vegetation (McDonald et al. 1999). In the absence of competing vegetation, full-sibling families averaged 1.3 ft taller than "woods-run" families six years after planting;

whereas, their heights were not significantly different in the presence of competing vegetation.

Seedling Fertilization

Seedling fertilization is being considered as a technique for accelerating juvenile growth of Douglas-fir. New, slow-release products have been developed that can be combined with the soil medium of container stock or placed directly into the planting hole. Rose and Ketchum (2002a) found that fertilization of Douglas-fir seedlings resulted in increased growth only on sites having adequate soil water. The growth increases associated with fertilization were smaller and more transient than those from control of competing vegetation, probably because the latter is associated with increases in both soil water and nutrients. Roth and Newton (1996) reported decreases in Douglas-fir survival following fertilization with 200 lbs N/ac, a response they attributed, in part, to N-stimulated increases in the abundance of competing vegetation. Powers and Reynolds (1999) found that stem growth responses of ponderosa pine to competing vegetation control and repeated fertilization varied according to the inherent fertility and soil water availability of a given site, with greater responses to fertilization occurring on the less droughty sites.

Treatment Combinations

Various combinations of treatments have been tested during plantation establishment to determine whether they interact to produce synergistic, antagonistic, or simple additive responses of crop seedlings. Synergistic responses indicate that the combined effect of two or more treatments is greater than the sum of responses to the individual treatments applied alone. Antagonistic responses indicate that the combined effect is less than the sum of individual treatment responses, while additive responses occur when the combined effect is equal to the sum of the responses. For example, the addition of repeated fertilization to a sustained vegetation control regime caused neutral, additive, or synergistic responses of ponderosa pine growth, depending on whether the dominant factor limiting tree growth was soil water or fertility (Power and Reynolds 1999; R.F. Powers, personal communication). Rose and Ketchum (2002a, 2003) detected only additive responses of Douglas-fir growth to combinations of seedling size, fertilization, and area of vegetation control. Growth increases from fertilization were greatest on sites with adequate soil moisture, similar to the findings of Powers and Reynolds (1999), but these responses were short-lived as opposed to the sustained responses to vegetation control. Roth and Newton (1996) found that N fertilization had no effect on first-year survival and growth of Douglas-fir when the treatment was combined with control of competing vegetation, but in the absence of vegetation control it reduced seedling performance.

Alternative Crop Species

A wide range of factors are motivating forest managers to consider alternative crop species to Douglas-fir. Among many, these include development of new markets, declining availability of certain raw materials, and increased incidence of forest diseases. The widespread outbreak of Swiss needle cast has prompted increased interest in planting western hemlock on sites formerly planted with Douglas-fir. A survey of all major Westside forest landowners conducted by Briggs and Trobaugh (2001) showed the percentage of western hemlock planted either in mixture with Douglas-fir or by itself began a steady increase in 1999.

Previous research has shown how Douglas-fir, a species of moderate to low shade tolerance, tends to occur in the upper canopy while western hemlock, capable of living in lower light conditions, will occur in the lower canopy of natural stands (Oliver and Larson 1996, Lewis et al. 2000). The ability of these species to occupy different niches suggests that mixtures of them may be more productive than pure stands (Vandermeer 1989). Recent research assessing the differences between Douglas-fir and western hemlock growing in pure and mixed plantations has shown that only at high densities (700 trees/acre) will the cubic volume of mixed stands exceed that of pure stands of either species. Lower densities – 200 and 450 trees/ac – did not show productivity increases from the mixture (Amoroso et al. 2004).

Red alder has become a viable species for plantation silviculture on the Westside. Seed collection, nursery, and planting guidelines have been developed (Hibbs and Ager 1989, Ahrens et al. 1992). Recent interest has developed for planting hybrid poplar (hybrid of *Populus trichocarpa* Torr. & Gray and *P. deltoides* Bartr. ex Marsh.) on farmland in the Willamette Valley of Oregon because of its rapid growth and high yield on poorly drained clay soils (Hibbs et al. 2003). Such stands have produced up to 4000 ft³/acre in six years on soils considered poor for agriculture.

Minimizing Browse Damage

Although a variety of barrier products exist for protecting conifer seedlings from deer and elk browse (Schaap and DeYoe 1986), many of these can restrict and deform shoot growth if not maintained properly. Gourley et al. (1990) compared growth of tall (2 ft) Douglas-fir seedlings following six methods of protection with or without control of competing vegetation. Control of competing vegetation had

the dominant effect, increasing fifth-year height an average of 1 ft regardless of method of protection. In plots where vegetation was controlled, the methods of protection had neutral or negative effects relative to seedlings receiving no protection. It is likely that smaller seedlings, as well as those growing under intense competition, may benefit from protection because their smaller initial size may prolong the time period when they are susceptible to being browsed.

Protecting Soil Productivity

A better understanding of the effects of soil disturbance on forest productivity has been developed (Miller et al. 2004). For example, research in northern California has shown that soil compaction effects on seedling growth can be negative, neutral, or even positive depending on soil texture and soil water regime (Gomez et al. 2002). Reductions in Douglas-fir growth from soil compaction following ground-based harvesting have been shown to last as little as two years in coastal Washington and up to seven years in the Oregon Cascade Mountains (Heninger et al. 2002).

FUTURE NEEDS

Many of the advances in Westside silviculture have been the result of research aimed at providing greater understanding of the mechanisms of tree responses. In following with this approach, areas of research likely to advance the technology of Westside plantation establishment include:

(1) Species- and site-specific competition thresholds- How do tree responses to competing vegetation vary with species and site characteristics? Can models predicting these responses be used to refine vegetation management prescriptions and improve their cost-effectiveness?

(2) Seedling fertilization- What are the reasons for the limited responses of planted seedlings to fertilization, and what are methods that can be used to overcome these limitations?

(3) Minimizing animal damage- While considerable research has gone into developing various products and practices that protect seedlings from animal damage, very few have been shown to be cost-effective. Continued research and development is needed in this area to develop products or practices that reduce these growth losses.

(4) Silvicultural treatment interactions- Can treatment responses be predicted according to the limiting factors on a given site? A general model is needed that links seedling resource needs with the resource supplying power of the site and of specific silvicultural treatments.

(5) Predicting young stand development-New yield models and plantation site index equations are needed to forecast the differential growth rates resulting from various silvicultural treatments during plantation establishment.

(6) Plantation silviculture for alternative crop species-Advanced technology exists for establishing Douglas-fir plantations, yet basic information on seedling responses to treatment is still lacking for western hemlock, western redcedar, and red alder. These information gaps must be filled if intensive management is to be applied to these alternative crop species.

ACKNOWLEDGMENTS

The authors are grateful to M. Newton, R. Deal, and K. Puettmann for reviewing an earlier version of this paper and providing many helpful comments.

LITERATURE CITED

Ahrens, G.G.; Dobkowski, A.; Hibbs, D.E. 1992. Red alder: guidelines for successful regeneration. Special publication 24. Corvallis, OR: Oregon State University, Forest Research Laboratory. 11 p.

Alig, R.J.; Plantinga, A.J.; Ahn, S.E.; Kline, J.D. 2003. Land use changes involving forestry in the United States: 1952 to 1997, with projections to 2050. Gen. Tech. Rep. PNW-GTR-587. Portland, OR: U.S. Department of Agriculture, Forest Service, Pacific Northwest Research Station. 92 p.

Amoroso, M.M.; Turnblom, E.C.; Briggs, D.G. 2004. Growth and yield of Douglas-fir and western hemlock in pure and mixed planted stands: results at age 12 from the SMC type III trials. SMC Working Paper No. 3, Seattle, WA: Stand Management Cooperative, College of Forest Resources, University of Washington.

Belz, D. 2003. Severing red alder: timing the cut to achieve the best mortality. Western Journal of Applied Forestry 18(3): 199-201.

Black, H.C.; Dimock, E.J., II; Evans, J.; Rochelle, J.A. 1979. Animal damage to coniferous plantations in Oregon and Washington. Part I: a survey 1963-1975. Res. Bulle. 25. Corvallis, OR: Forest Research Laboratory, Oregon State University. 44 p.

Bolsinger, C.L.; McKay, N.; Gedney, D.R.; Alerich, C. 1997. Washington's public and private forests. Resour. Bulle. PNW-RB-218. Portland, OR: U.S. Department of Agriculture, Forest Service, Pacific Northwest Research Station. 144 p.

Brandeis, T.J.; Newton, M.; Cole, E.C. 2001. Underplanted conifer seedling survival and growth in thinned Douglas-fir stands. Canadian Journal of Forest Research 31: 302-312.

Brandeis, T.J.; Newton, M.; Cole, E.C. 2002. Biotic injuries on conifer seedlings planted in forest understory environments. New Forests 24: 1-14.

Briggs, D.; Trobaugh, J. 2001. Management practices on Westside industrial forest lands, 1991-2000: with Projections to 2005. SMC Working Paper No. 2. Seattle, WA: Stand Management Cooperative, College of Forest Resources, University of Washington. 71 p.

Campbell, S.; Dunham, P.; Azuma, D. 2004. Timber resource statistics for Oregon. Resour. Bulle. PNW-RB-242. U.S. Department of Agriculture, Forest Service, Pacific Northwest Research Station. 67 p.

Cousens, R. 1987. Theory and reality of weed control thresholds. Plant Protection Quarterly 2: 13-20.

Coyner, B.; Coyner C. 2004. Drinking from a fully-charged fire hose. Evergreen. http://www.evergreen-magazine.com/index2 html. (8 Dec.).

Dougherty, P.M.; Lowery, R.F. 1991. Spot-size of herbaceous control impacts loblolly pine seedling survival and growth. Southern Journal of Applied Forestry 15(4): 193-199.

Drever, C.R.; Lertzman, K.P. 2001. Light-growth responses of coastal Douglas-fir and western redcedar saplings under different regimes of soil moisture and nutrients. Canadian Journal of Forest Research 31: 2124-2133.

Flewelling, J., Collier, R., Gonyea, B., Marshall, D., Turnblom, E. 2001. Height-age curves for planted Douglas-fir with adjustments for density. Stand Management Coop. SMC Working Party Paper No. 1. Seattle, WA: Stand Management Cooperative, College of Forest Resources, University of Washington.

Franklin, J.F.; Dyrness, C.T. 1973. Natural vegetation of Oregon and Washington. Gen. Tech. Rep. PNW-GTR-8. Portland, OR: U.S. Department of Agriculture, Forest Service, Pacific Northwest Research Station. 417 p.

Figueroa, P. 1994. Control of red alder seed germination using pre-plant broadcast herbicide applications: four-year status report. Proceedings of Western Society of Weed Science.

Fredrickson, E. [In press]. Pre-harvest control of competing vegetation. Redding, CA: Proceedings: 25th Annual Forest Vegetation Management Conference.

Gomez, A.; Powers, R.F.; Singer, M.J., Horwath, W.R. 2002. Soil compaction effects on growth of young ponderosa pine following litter removal in California's Sierra Nevada. Soil Science Society of America Journal 66(4): 1334-1343.

Gourley, M.; Vomocil, M.; Newton, M. 1990. Weeding reduces the effect of deer-browsing on Douglas-fir. Forest Ecology and Management 36: 177-185.

Haase, D.L; Batdorff, J.H.; Rose, R. 1993. Effect of root form on 10-year survival and growth of planted Douglas-fir trees. Tree Planters' Notes 44: 53-57.

Haynes, R., tech. coord. 2003. An analysis of the timber situation in the United States: 1952 to 2050. A technical document supporting the 2000 USDA Forest Service RPA assessment. Gen. Tech. Rep. PNW-GTR-560. Portland, OR, U.S. Department of Agriculture, Forest Service, Pacific Northwest Research Station. 254 p.

Heilman, P. 1981. Minerals, chemical properties, and fertility of forest soils. In: Heilman, P.E.; Anderson, H.W.; Baumgartner, D.M. Forest soils of the Douglas-fir region. Pullman, WA: Cooperative Extension Service, Washington State University. 121-136.

Heninger, R.L.; Scott, W.; Dobkowski, A.; Miller, R.; Anderson, H.; Duke, S. 2002. Soil disturbance and 10-year growth response of coast Douglas-fir on nontilled and tilled skid trails in the Oregon Cascades. Canadian Journal of Forest Research 32: 233-246.

Hibbs, D.E.; Ager, A.A. 1989. Red alder: guidelines for seed collection, handling, and storage. Special Publication 18. Corvallis, OR: Oregon State University, Forest Research Laboratory. 6 p.

Hibbs, D.; Withrow-Robinson, B.; Brown, D.; Fletcher, R. 2003. Hybrid poplar in the Willamette Valley. Western Journal of Applied Forestry 18(4): 281-285.

Howard, K.M.; Newton, M. 1984. Overtopping by successional Coast-Range vegetation slows Douglas-fir seedlings. Journal of Forestry 82(3): 178-180.

Hughes, T.F.; Tappeiner, J.C.; Newton, M. 1990. Relationship of Pacific madrone sprout growth to productivity of Douglas-fir seedlings and understory vegetation. Western Journal of Applied Forestry 5: 20-24.

Jayawickrama, K.J.S.; Ye, T. 2004. Predicted genetic gains for first-generation Douglas-fir programs: summaries and within-zone geographic trends. Portland, OR: Northwest Tree Improvement Cooperative.

Kanaskie, A.; McWilliams, M.; Sprengel, K.; Overhulser, D. 2004. In: Swiss Needle Cast Cooperative, Annual report. Mainwaring, D., ed. Corvallis, OR: Oregon State University, Department of Forest Science. 7-11.

Ketchum, J.S.; Rose, R.; Kelpsas, B. 1999. Weed control in spring and summer after fall application of sulfometuron. Western Journal of Applied Forestry 14(2): 80-85.

Ketchum, J.S.; Rose, R. 2003. Preventing establishment of exotic shrubs (*Cytisus scoparius* L. (Link.) and *Cytisus striatus* (Hill)) with soil active herbicides (hexazinone, sulfometuron, and metsulfuron). New Forests 25: 83-92.

Larsen D.N.; Nguyen, Q. 2004. Washington timber harvest 2002. Olympia, WA: Washington State Department of Natural Resources. 75 p. http://www.dnr.wa.gov/base/publications html. (25 Nov.).

Lewis, J.D.; McKane, R.B.; Tingley, D.T.; Beedlow, P.A. 2000. Vertical gradients in photosynthesic light response within an old-growth Douglas-fir and western hemlock canopy. Tree Physiology 20: 447-456.

Maguire, D.A.; Kanaskie, A.; Voelker, W.; Johnson, R.; Johnson, G. 2002. Growth of young Douglas-fir plantations across a gradient in Swiss needle cast severity. Western Journal of Applied Forestry 17(2): 86-95.

Mailly, D.; Kimmins, J.P. 1997. Growth of *Pseudotsuga menziesii* and *Tsuga heterophylla* seedlings along a light gradient: resource allocation and morphological acclimation. Canadian Journal of Botany 75: 1424-1435.

Malmsheimer, R.W.; Keele, D.; Floyd, D.W. 2004. National Forest Litigation in the U.S. Court of Appeals. Journal of Forestry 102(2):20-25.

McDonald, P.M.; Helgerson, O.T. 1990. Mulches aid in regenerating California and Oregon forests: past, present, and future. Gen. Tech. Rep. PSW-123. Berkeley, CA: U.S. Department of Agriculture, Forest Service, Pacific Southwest Research Station. 19 p.

McDonald, P.M.; Mori, S.R.; Fiddler, G.O. 1999. Effect of competition on genetically improved ponderosa pine seedlings. Canadian Journal of Forest Research 29: 940-946.

McDonald, P.M.; Fiddler, G.O. 2001. Timing and duration of release affect vegetation development in a young ponderosa pine plantation. Res. Pap. PSW-RP-245. Redding, CA: U.S. Department of Agriculture, Forest Service, Pacific Southwest Research Station. 15 p.

Miller, R.E.; Colbert, S.R.; Morris, L.A. 2004. Effects of heavy equipment on physical properties of soils and on long-term productivity: a review of literature and current research. Tech. Bulle. 887. Research Triangle Park, NC: National Council for Air and Stream Improvement. 76 p.

Mitchell, A.K. 2001. Growth limitations for conifer regeneration under alternative silvicultural systems in a coastal montane forest in British Columbia, Canada. Forest Ecology and Management 145: 129-136.

Monleon, V.J.; Newton, M.; Hooper, C.; Tappeiner, J.C., II. 1999. Ten-year growth response of young Douglas-fir to variable density varnishleaf ceanothus and herb competition. Western Journal of Applied Forestry 14(4): 208-213.

National Biological Information Infrastructure. 2004. Invasive Species Information Node. Available at: http://invasivespecies.nbii.gov/. (12 Dec.).

Newton, M; Preest, D.S. 1988. Growth and water relations of Douglas-fir (*Pseudotsuga menziesii*) seedlings under different weed control regimes. Weed Science 36: 653-662.

Oliver, C.D.; Larson, B.C. 1996. Forest stand dynamics. Update ed. McGraw-Hill, New York, NY. 467 pp.

Oliver, W.W. 1984. Brush reduces growth of thinned ponderosa pine in northern California. Res. Pap. PSW-172. Berkeley, CA: U.S. Department of Agriculture, Forest Service, Pacific Southwest Research Station.

OSDF (Oregon State Department of Forestry). 2004a. Oregon Department of Forestry Strategic Plan: 2004-2011. http://www.odf.state.or.us/DIVISIONS/resource_policy/resource_planning/StrategicPlan/ASP.pdf?id=20101. (8 Dec.).

OSDF (Oregon State Department of Forestry). 2004b. Annual timber harvest report- 2003 http://www.odf.state.or.us/DIVISIONS/resource_policy/resource_planning/Annual_Reports/Default.asp. (25 Nov.).

Petersen, T.D.; Newton, M.; Zedaker, S.M. 1988. Influence of *Ceanothus velutinus* and associated forbs on the water stress and stemwood production of Douglas-fir. Forest Science 34(2): 333-343.

Powers, R.F.; Reynolds, P.E. 1999. Ten-year responses of ponderosa pine plantations to repeated vegetation and nutrient control along an environmental gradient. Canadian Journal of Forest Research 29: 1027-1038.

Ritchie, G.A. 1997. Evidence for red: far red signaling and photomorphogenic response in Douglas-fir (*Pseudotsuga menziesii*) seedlings. Tree Physiology 17: 161-168.

Rose, R.; Carlson, W.C.; Morgan, P. 1990. The target seedling concept. Gen. Tech. Rep. RM-200. Fort Collins, CO: U.S. Department of Agriculture, Forest Service, Rocky Mountain Forest and Range Experiment Station: 1-8.

Rose, R.; Ketchum, J.S.; Hanson, D.E. 1999. Three-year survival and growth of Douglas-fir seedlings under various vegetation-free regimes. Forest Science 45(1): 117-126.

Rose, R.; Ketchum, J.S. 2002a. Interaction of vegetation control and fertilization on conifer species across the Pacific Northwest. Canadian Journal of Forest Research 32: 136-152.

Rose, R.; Ketchum, J.S. 2002b. The effect of hexazinone, sulfometuron, metsulfuron, and atrazine on the germin a-tion success of selected *Ceanothus and Rubus* species. Western Journal of Applied Forestry 17(4): 194-201.

Rose, R.; Ketchum, J.S. 2003. Interaction of initial seedling diameter, fertilization, and weed control on Douglas-fir growth over the first four years after plant-ing. Annals of Forests Science 60: 625-635.

Rose, R.; Morgan, P. 2000. Guide to reforestation in Oregon. Oregon Dept. of Foresty and College of Forestry, Oregon State Univ., Corvallis. 50 p.

Rose, R.; Rosner, L. 2004. Effects of up to five consecu-tive years of weed control and delayed weed control on Douglas-fir and other PNW conifer species. In: Vegetation Management Research Cooperative 2003-2004 annual report. Corvallis, OR: Oregon State University. 44 p.

Roth, B.E.; Newton, M. 1996. Survival and growth of Douglas-fir relating to weeding, fertilization, and seed source. Western Journal of Applied Forestry 11(2): 62-69.

Ruth, R.H. 1956. Plantation survival and growth in two brush-threat areas in coastal Oregon. Res. Pap. 17. PNW-RP- 17. Portland, OR: U.S. Department of Agriculture, Forest Service, Pacific Northwest Forest and Range Experiment Station. 14 p.

Schaap, W.; DeYoe, D. 1986. Seedling protectors for preventing deer browse. Res. Bulle. 54. Corvallis, OR: Forest Research Laboratory, Oregon State University. 12 p.

Scott, W.; Meade, R.; Leon, R.; Hyink, D.; Miller, R. 1998. Planting density and tree-size relations in coast Douglas-fir. Canadian Journal of Forest Research 28: 74-78.

Shainsky, L.J.; Radosevich, S.R. 1986. Growth and water relations of *Pinus ponderosa* seedings in competitive regimes with *Arctostaphylos patula* seedlings. Journal of Applied Ecology 23: 957-966.

Smith, D.M.; Larson, B.C.; Kelty, M.J.; Ashton, P.M.S. 1997. The practice of silviculture: applied forest ecology. 9th ed. New York, NY: John Wiley and Sons, Inc. 301-315.

St. Clair, J.B.; Mandel, N.L.; Jayawickrama, K.J.S. 2004. Early realized genetic gains for coastal Douglas-fir in the northern Oregon Cascades. Western Journal of Applied Forestry 19(3): 195-201.

Steinbrenner, E.C. 1981. Forest soil productivity relation-ships. In: Heilman, P.E.; Anderson, H.W.; Baumgartner, D.M. Forest soils of the Douglas-fir region. Pullman, WA: Cooperative Extension Service, Washington State University. 199-229.

SFB (Sustainable Forestry Board). 2004. 2002-2004 Sustainable Forestry Initiative (SFI) Program. http://www.aboutsfb.org/sfi.htm. (25 Nov.).

Talbert, C. 2004. Plantation productivity under current intensive silvicultural practices: results from research and operations. In: Proceedings: Intensive Plantation Forestry in the Pacific Northwest. Portland, OR: Oregon State University. http://outreach.cof.orst.edu/plantation/agenda htm. (8 Dec.).

Tappeiner, J.C., II; Zasada, J.; Huffman, D.; Maxwell, B.D. 1996. Effects of cutting time, stump height, parent tree characteristics, and harvest variables on develop-ment of bigleaf maple sprout clumps. Western Journal of Applied Forestry 11(4): 120-124.

Teich, G.M.R.; Vaughn, J.; Cortner, H.J. 2004. National trends in the use of Forest Service administrative appeals. Journal of Forestry 102(2): 14-19.

Thies, W.G.; Sturrock, R.N. 1995. Laminated root rot in western North America. Gen. Tech. Rep. PNW-GTR-349. Portland, OR: U.S. Department of Agriculture, Forest Service, Pacific Northwest Research Station. 32 p.

Timmer, V.R. 1996. Exponential nutrient loading: a new fertilization technique to improve seedling performance on competitive sites. New Forests 13: 275-295.

Vandermeer, J.H. 1989. The ecology of intercropping. Cambridge, UK: Cambridge University Press. 237 pp.

Wagner, R.G.; Petersen, T.D.; Ross, D.W.; Radosevich, S.R. 1989. Competition thresholds for the survival and growth of ponderosa pine seedlings associated with woody and herbaceous vegetation. New Forests 3: 151-170.

Wagner, R.G.; Radosevich, S.R. 1991a. Neighborhood predictors of interspecific competition in young Douglas-fir plantations. Canadian Journal of Forest Research 21: 821-828.

Wagner, R.G.; Radosevich, S.R. 1991b. Interspecific competition and other factors influencing the performance of Douglas-fir saplings in the Oregon Coast Range. Canadian Journal of Forest Research 21: 829-835.

Wagner, R.G.; Rogozynski, M.W. 1994. Controlling sprout clumps of bigleaf maple with herbicides and manual cutting. Western Journal of Applied Forestry 9(4): 118-124.

Wagner, R.G.; Mohammed, G.H.; Noland, T.L. 1999. Critical period of interspecific competition for northern conifers associated with herbaceous vegetation. Canadian Journal of Forest Research 29: 890-897.

Wagner, R.G. 2000. Competition and critical-period thresholds for vegetation management decisions in young conifer stands. Forestry Chronicle 76(6): 961-968.

Wang, G.G., H. Qian, and K. Klinka. 1994. Growth of *Thuja plicata* seedlings along a light gradient. Canadian Journal of Forest Research 72: 1749-1757.

Washington DNR (Washington State Department of Natural Resources). 2004. Strategic plan for the Department of Natural Resources. http://www.dnr.wa.gov/htdocs/obe/budgetstrategy/budgetstrategy05_07.pdf. Accessed: (8 Dec.).

White, D.E.; Newton, M. 1989. Competitive interactions of whiteleaf manzanita, herbs, Douglas-fir and ponderosa pine in southwest Oregon. Canadian Journal of Forest Research 19: 232-238.

York, R.A.; Heald, R.C.; Battles, J.J.; York, J. 2004. Group selection management in conifer forests: relationships between opening size and tree growth. Canadian Journal of Forest Research 34: 630-641.

STATE-OF-THE-ART SILVICULTURAL TECHNOLOGY AND APPLICATIONS FOR FOREST STAND ESTABLISHMENT IN INTERIOR BRITISH COLUMBIA

John McClarnon[1] and R. Allan Powelson[2]

ABSTRACT

As part of the pressure to be competitive in international softwood markets, the British Columbia forest industries' post-harvest management objective has become the establishment of acceptable free growing stands at the lowest possible cost in the shortest timeframe. To achieve this objective, it is critical to understand, at a site-specific level, when and where to apply any given silviculture intervention and how effective it will be. As well, it is important to understand the costs versus benefits of different treatment options. Studies and operational experience in British Columbia, and especially in the sub-boreal spruce and black and white boreal spruce zones, indicate that the survival and early growth of conifer seedlings can be substantially improved through deployment of select seed, selection of appropriate species and stock type combinations, and through appropriate site preparation and brushing treatments.

KEYWORDS: Stand establishment, technology applications, limiting factors.

INTRODUCTION

In British Columbia, where approximately 95% of the forestland is publicly owned Provincial Forest, the government has the ultimate stewardship role and sets overall resource management objectives. Under an overarching legislative framework, harvesting rights and forest management responsibilities, including the mandatory achievement of government approved free growing stocking standards, are provided to the forest industry through an array of different agreements. In British Columbia, a "free growing stand" is defined as a stand of healthy trees of a commercially valuable species, the growth of which is not impeded by competition from plants, shrubs or other trees (BC Gov. 2004). The achievement of free-growing status is satisfied by attaining pre-determined standards for crop trees within a specified time period; height, height-above-competing brush, density, inter-tree spacing, and species composition (BCMOF 2000a).

Due to the intense pressure to remain competitive in international softwood markets, one of the overriding post-harvest stand management objectives for the British Columbia forest industry has become the establishment of acceptable free-growing stands at the lowest possible cost in the shortest timeframe. In this context, critical issues impacting even-aged stand establishment and management of lodgepole pine (*Pinus contorta* Dougl. var. *latifolia* Engelm.) in the Sub-Boreal Spruce biogeoclimatic zone (SBS) and white spruce (Picea glauca [Moench] Voss) in the Boreal White and Black Spruce biogeoclimatic zone (BWBS) in interior British Columbia are reviewed.

PREDOMINANT LIMITING FACTORS

In the central and northern interior and higher elevations of British Columbia, combinations of any of the following limiting factors may be encountered; cold soil temperature, wet soils in spring, over-winter damage, severe frost events, very short growing seasons, late access to sites in the spring, deep snow packs and snow press (Meidinger and Pojar

---

[1] John McClarnon is regeneration specialist, Silviculture Practices Section, British Columbia Ministry of Forests, PO Box 9513 Stn Prov Govt, Victoria, BC, V8W9C2.

[2] R. Allan Powelson is forester/ecologist, ALTRA Forestry Ltd., P.O. Box 125 Pender Island, B.C. V0N 2M0.

1991, Krasowski 1996). Damage from ungulates, hares, voles, cattle, porcupine, spruce leader weevil, pine stem rusts, and armillaria and tomentosus root diseases may be locally significant limiting factors (Meidinger and Pojar 1991). To provide examples of the application of silviculture technology in interior British Columbia, this paper focuses on sites within the SBS and BWBS zones where the predominant growth limiting factors are either cold soil temperature, spring soil saturation, summer drought conditions, a preponderance of vegetation competition from aspen (*Populus tremuloides* Michx.), hard pine stem rusts such as western gall rust (*Endocronartium harkenssii* (J.P. Moore) Y. Hirat) or a combination of any of these (Meidinger and Pojar 1991, McDowell 1998a, McDowell 1998b, Bedford et al. 2000, Bedford and Sutton 2000). In order to manage the impacts of these many limiting factors, forest practitioners in British Columbia have to use a variety of technologies and systems.

TECHNOLOGY APPLICATIONS

Biogeoclimatic Classification System

Successful site management begins with accurate identification and description of site characteristics. The Biogeoclimatic Ecosystem Classification (BEC) system, which integrates climate, soil and site features, and indicator plant species to group ecosystems (Meidinger and Pojar 1991), provides a "common language" to describe forest sites and is utilized by all forest practitioners throughout the province as the basis for silviculture prescriptions (http://www. for.gov.bc.ca/hre/becweb/). The classification system provides ecosystem specific recommendations for ecologically appropriate tree species rated on the basis of productivity, feasibility and reliability. Region specific field guides provide silviculture treatment recommendations, predictions of competing vegetation potential, and ecosystem specific recommendations for site preparation. Local hazards are communicated through ecological footnotes as microsite limitations (e.g., elevated microsites are preferred), mesosite limitations (e.g., restricted to southerly aspects), geographic restrictions (e.g., restricted to lower elevations of biogeoclimatic unit), pest limitations (e.g., risk of heavy browsing by moose), and abiotic limitations (e.g., risk of snow damage).

Improved Seed

Legislation has mandated that improved seed (that which has a genetic worth of five percent or greater and has desirable traits) must be used for reforestation when it is available and requires that all seed, either natural or improved, must be used in compliance with seed transfer guidelines. In British Columbia, the tree seed improvement program is a provincially co-ordinated co-operative venture between government and industry (FGC 2004). Program goals are to increase the average volume gain of select seed used for Crown land reforestation to 20% by the year 2020 and to increase select seed use to 75% of total provincial sowing by 2013 (FGC, 2004). In 2003, the deployment in British Columbia of seedlings grown from improved seed included planting 49 million interior spruce, 10 million lodgepole pine, 4.3 million western larch, and 1.1 million western white pine seedlings. Increasing genetic worth and the production of improved seed are leading to wider availability of faster growing seedlings.

Site Preparation

In the past, site preparation was applied extensively in interior British Columbia reaching a maximum of 101,009 ha in 1992/1993 (BCMOF 2000b). However, in recent years as the amount of area site prepared in interior British Columbia has dropped to 51,088 ha in 2002 (BCMOF 2003) (table 1), direct planting into appropriate micro-sites in undisturbed forest floor materials with minimal screefing has become a widespread practice (Heineman 1998). The suitability of this practice, however, depends on the sites limiting factors. For direct forest-floor planting to be a success in interior British Columbia, planting should occur: as soon after harvest as possible, on sites with adequate moisture throughout the growing season, on sites with reasonable soil temperatures, and only on sites that have low to moderate levels of competing vegetation unless viable options exist for vegetation management. (Heineman1998). Site preparation to reduce planting shock and improve survival and early seedling growth remains critical on sites with cold wet soils, very dry soils, growing season frost and/ or significant competing vegetation particularly where herbicides are not an option (Krasowski 1996, Sutton et al. 2001). Mechanical site preparation accounted for 75% of the 51,088 hectares treated in interior British Columbia in 2002. M o u n ding and disc trenching are the two most commonly employed site preparation methods. Other site preparation techniques include drag scarification to promote lodgepole pine natural regeneration, prescribed burning, and patch scarification.

In the SBS, direct forest-floor planting did not result in significantly lower lodgepole pine seedling survival (Bedford and Sutton 2000, Macadam et al. 2001). Similarly, white spruce exhibited the same general trends in the BWBS (Bedford et al. 2000) and the SBS (Sutton et al. 2001). While there may be little improvement in seedling survival with site preparation in the SBS and BWBS, there are significant early growth benefits (Krasowski, 1996, Bedford and Sutton 2000, Bedford et al. 2000, Byman 2000, Sutton

Table 1—Preparing sites for planting and natural regeneration on interior British Columbia Crown land in 2002/2003 (BCMOF 2003).

Treatment	Area in hectares
Biological	48
Burn	5,917
Chemical - air	0
Chemical - ground	232
Grass seeding	77
Manual	5978
Mechanical	38,836
Not specified	18
Total	51,088

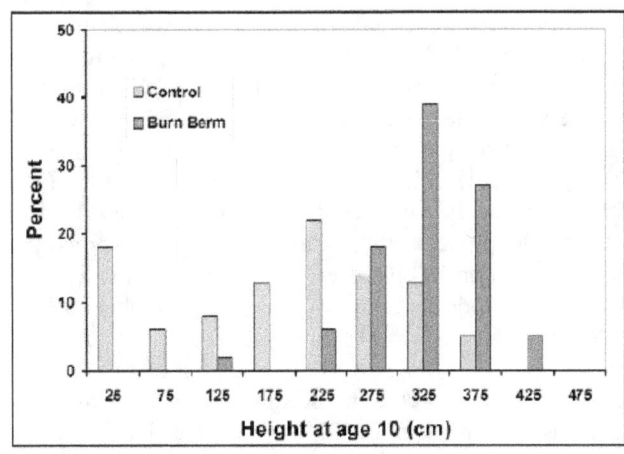

Figure 1—Height frequency distribution on unprepared vs. prepared sites.

Table 2—Effect of site preparation on time to free growing^a condition and meeting green-up^b requirements.

Treatment	Species	Years to free growing (2 m)		Years to green-up (3 m)
Untreated	Spruce	7		16
Herbicide	Spruce	6		11
Breaking plow	Spruce	5		10
		Well stocked	Minimum Stocking	
Untreated	Pine	7	11	9
Disc trench	Pine	6	7	8
Burn	Pine	5	7	7

^{a} A free growing stand means a stand of healthy trees of a commercially valuable species, the growth of which is not impeded by competition.

^{b} Stands are required to meet "green up", generally a height of 3 to 3.5 m of dominant trees of a commercial tree species, before adjacent stands or cutblocks can be harvested.

et al. 2001). These growth performance differences attributed to site preparation, however, diminished with time (Bedford and Sutton 2000, Bedford et al. 2000). Site preparation has also been shown to reduce the potential for over-winter injury resulting from freeze-desiccation (Krasowski 1996). Treatments that increased the root zone temperature of young seedlings reduced the potential for over-winter injury and damage (Krasowski 1996). As the root systems of established seedlings expand and exploit areas outside of the area of site preparation, growth of seedlings unimpeded by competing vegetation, is largely independent of micro-site and growth increments become uniform across treatment types (Bedford and Sutton 2000).

Another beneficial aspect of site preparation is the potential for uniformity of growth over the entirety of the growing site. Seedling establishment is more likely to occur on similar micro-sites after site preparation. This uniformity of micro-site selection results in greater uniformity of growth performance of seedlings across the growing site (fig. 1).

Uniformity of seedling performance across the growing site can result in earlier achievement of the seedling characteristics necessary for the statutory free growing obligations in British Columbia (table 2) (Bedford and Sutton 2000).

This improved growth performance, however, should not be expected to be maintained for extended time periods into the rotation of the stand.

Seedlings

Due to significant reductions in the use of herbicides, broadcast burning and mechanical site preparation, p r o m p t planting of high quality seedlings has become the primary

41

tool in addressing site-limiting factors. In British Columbia, approximately 85% of the harvested area is planted (BCMOF, 2003). Regeneration is primarily focused towards conifers with the exception of the boreal region where aspen and mixedwood stand regeneration is more c o m m o n . Tree planting densities are usually in the range of 1200 to 1600 stems per hectare. Very low densities are prescribed in some fire prone natural disturbance ecosystems or where wildlife management objectives (e.g., continuous g r i z z l y bear forage production) take precedence over timber objectives.

Development of container seedling techniques evolved in British Columbia in the 1970s. Continuous improvement since that time has resulted in large-scale production of high quality seedlings in a diversity of stocktypes (BCMOF 1998). Lodgepole pine and interior spruce account for 47% and 31%, respectively, of the approximately 234 million seedlings sown in British Columbia in 2004 (SPAR 2004). Greater than 90% of the sowing is to produce one-year-old container stock and the 410-styroblock container size (cavity volume of 80 ml) accounts for 40% (SPAR 2004) of the production. The majority of seedlings (80%) are planted in the spring window (to June 21st), with close to 20% as summer plant, and a small remainder as fall plant (SPAR 2004). While approximately 24% of the sowing (mostly lodgepole pine) is in copper treated container stock (SPAR 2004), little to no gain in survival and growth has been demonstrated from this treatment (Jones et al. 2002). The microsite that healthy seedlings are placed into is more important in affecting growth than the nursery treatment they were subjected to prior to planting (Jones et al. 2002).

Vegetation Management

Forest practitioners in the British Columbia interior may encounter any one of a multitude of vegetation complexes. These include the fireweed (BCMOF 1997c), fern (BCMOF 2002), ericaceous shrub and subalpine herb (BCMOF 1997b), pinegrass (BCMOF 1997e), reedgrass (BCMOF 2000c), dry alder (BCMOF 1997a), wet alder (BCMOF 1997f), aspen, and mixed broadleaf shrub complexes (BCMOF 1997e). A web-based stand establishment decision aid is now available to provide practitioners with access to the latest available information on vegetation management of different complexes. The key to minimizing and justifying expenditures is determining the appropriate situations, timing, and treatment types for vegetation management.

Approximately 60% of the 53,637 hectares brushed annually in interior British Columbia is done with manual techniques, including brush saws, chain saws, girdling tools,

Table 3—Brushing on interior British Columbia Crown land in 2002 and 2003 (BCMOF, 2003).

Treatment	Area in hectares
Biological	1,858
Chemical air	14,204
Chemical Ground	6,276
Manual – not specified	1,515
Manual – non-motorized	17,996
Manual – motorized	13,052
Mechanical	5
Not specified	191
Total	53,637

and manual stem snapping (table 3). Aerial spraying and ground based herbicide application account for approximately 25 and 15% of the brushing program respectively (BCMOF 2003). A widespread lack of public acceptance of the use of herbicides in British Columbia has limited the number of herbicides available, the situations where they can be used, and the methods of application that can be deployed.

In the SBS and BWBS, aspen is one of the main competitors limiting coniferous growth potential. Strategies to reduce the impacts of aspen have been to leave it standing during harvest and girdle some of the residual stems so that approximately 5m^2/ha remain to reduce sprouting, post-harvest foliar spray, cut-stump, and hack-and-squirt applications of glyphosate; basal bark and cut-stump applications of triclopyr; hand-snapping in mid-summer below the lowest live limb, cutting stems below the lowest live limb, and 2 entry manual brushings that retain sufficient aspen stems in the first entry to maintain conifer tree growth but reduce aspen coppicing.

Determining the amount of broadleaved basal area that can be retained without significantly reducing growth performance of the target crop species is essential in developing effective mixed-wood management stand establishment prescriptions and to determine acceptable levels of broadleaf components in free growing coniferous stands to maintain biodiversity and ecological functioning (Comeau et al. 1999, Comeau et al. 2003.). Species dependant factors such as leaf shape, size, orientation, and opaqueness impact light availability below broadleaf canopies (fig. 2) and light availability increases rapidly with height in a broadleaf canopy, even in dense stands where understory light availability is low (Comeau et al. 2003). Interest by forest managers in retaining either crop or non-crop broadleaved stems

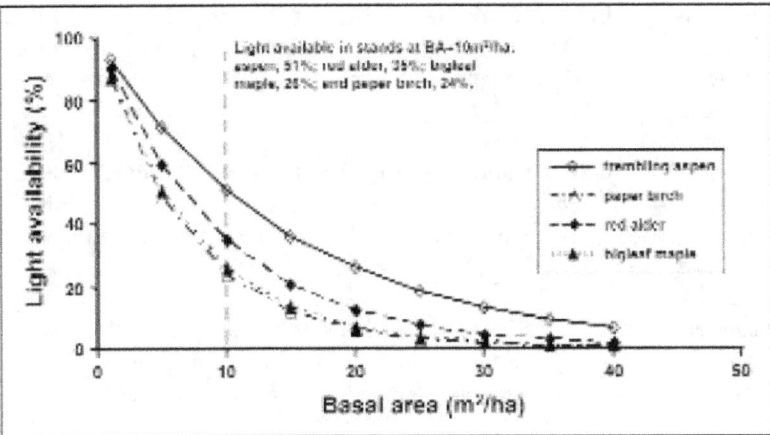

Figure 2—Light availability under broadleaf canopies.

in stands targeted for coniferous regeneration has led to the development of predictive models for aiding in the determination of the amount of broadleaf stems to be retained (Comeau et al. 2003).

Forest Health

Western gall rust is one of the significant growth limiting factors of lodgepole pine in both the SBS and BWBS zones (Fink et al. 1993, Reich 2002). Conducting forest health overview studies has identified fairly specific ecosystems where western gall rust will have a higher likelihood of impacting the regenerating stand (Reich 2002). Current management strategies for minimizing the impacts of hard pine stem rusts are the establishment and maintenance of high stand densities (Reich 2002). Stand establishment regimes being employed that can result in high densities on these sites include the encouragement of high natural regeneration levels (e.g. stump processing and chain-dragging), direct seeding (e.g., aerial, hand, or direct spot seeding), or high density planting (Reich 2002).

Costs

Cost of the technologies applied to achieve a free growing stand, as is legislatively required in British Columbia, varies widely (table 4). While individually some treatment costs may appear to be high, forest practitioners have to weigh this cost against the potential reductions in time to achieve the legislative growth obligations (table 2) that may be possible with the various combinations of these treatments. By fully understanding the growing site and its limitations, the goal of maximizing growth performance while minimizing total cost may be achievable.

Table 4—Range of current costs for silvicultural treatments in Interior British Columbia.

Treatment	Cost Range ($CAD/ha)
Broadcast burning	400 – 2000
Excavator mounding	700 – 900
Disk trench	180 – 220
Chain drag	180 – 250
Seed (B vs. A class)	16 – 84
Seedlings	186 – 545
Planting (no site prep.)	336 – 420
Planting (site prepared)	238 – 322
Direct seed/site prepared	400 – 550
Aerial herbicide spray	225 – 275
Backpack herbicide	300 – 700
Sheep grazing	260 – 400
Brush saw	450 – 500
Manually brush (1-m radii)	500 – 600
"Snap" aspen	250 – 350
Thinning	450 – 600
Pruning	550 – 900

Future directions

Future directions may include the development of approaches to assessing the free growing requirement that are linked to growth and yield objectives and assess achievement of the free growing objectives at a landscape level rather than at the individual cutblock level. Tools are required to predict appropriate mixtures of broadleaves and conifers for different crop objectives. Results in interior British Columbia remain variable with respect to seedling response following fertilization at time of planting or nutrient loading in the nursery and further work is required to improve consistency of response. Widespread loss of plantations to drought and fire in 2003 combined with large-scale forest health outbreaks (e.g., mountain pine beetle) suggests that climate change may become one of the most significant factors influencing future stand establishment.

SUMMARY

Studies and operational experience in British Columbia, including the SBS and BWBS zones, indicate that the survival and early growth of conifer seedlings can be substantially improved through deployment of select seed, selection of appropriate species and stock type combinations, and appropriate site preparation and brushing treatments. Choice of treatments that do not improve survival or growth or treatments that exacerbate the growth-limiting factors present on a site will fail to achieve the growth performance objectives in a timely manner and will lead to higher expenditures when trying to achieve the free growing obligations.

LITERATURE CITED

Bedford, L.; Sutton, R.F. 2000. Site preparation for establishing lodgepole pine in the sub-boreal spruce zone of interior British Columbia: the Bednesti trial, 10 years results. Forest Ecology and Management 126: 277-238.

Bedford, L.; Sutton, R.F.; Strodeur, L.; Grismer, M. 2000. Establishing white spruce in the boreal white and black spruce zone: Site preparation trials at Wonowon and Iron creek, British Columbia. New Forests 20: 213-233.

British Columbia Ministry of Forests [BCMOF]. 1997a. Operational summary of vegetation management: dry alder complex. Victoria, BC: Forest Practices Branch. 11 p.

British Columbia Ministry of Forests [BCMOF]. 1997b. Operational summary of vegetation management: ericaceous shrub complex. Victoria, BC: Forest Practices Branch. 11 p.

British Columbia Ministry of Forests [BCMOF]. 1997c. Operational summary of vegetation management: fireweed complex. Victoria, BC: Forest Practices Branch. 11 p.

British Columbia Ministry of Forests [BCMOF]. 1997d. Operational summary of vegetation management: mixed shrub complex. Victoria, BC: Forest Practices Branch. 11 p.

British Columbia Ministry of Forests [BCMOF]. 1997e. Operational summary of vegetation management: pinegrass complex. Victoria, BC: Forest Practices Branch. 11 p.

British Columbia Ministry of Forests [BCMOF]. 1997f. Operational summary of vegetation management: wet alder complex. Victoria, BC: Forest Practices Branch. 11 p.

British Columbia Ministry of Forests [BCMOF]. 1998. Provincial seedling stock type selection and ordering guidelines. Victoria, BC: Forest Practices Branch.

British Columbia Ministry of Forests [BCMOF]. 2000a. Establishment to free growing guidebook: revised edition [May]. Victoria, BC: Forest Practices Branch.

British Columbia Ministry of Forests [BCMOF]. 2000b. Just the facts: a review of silviculture and other forestry statistics. Victoria, BC: Forest Practices Branch.

British Columbia Ministry of Forests [BCMOF]. 2000c. Operational summary of vegetation management: reedgrass complex. Victoria, BC: Forest Practices Branch. 8 p.

British Columbia Ministry of Forests [BCMOF]. 2002. Operational summary of vegetation management: fern complex. Victoria, BC: Forest Practices Branch. 8 p.

British Columbia Ministry of Forests [BCMOF]. 2003. 2002/2003 Annual service plan report: detailed statistical tables for 2002/03. Victoria.

Byman, P. 2000. Response of lodgepole pine seedlings to Donaren mounding. Prince George, BC: University of Northern British Columbia. M.S. thesis. 55 p.

Comeau, P.G.; Biring, B.S.; Harper, G.J. 1999. Conifer response to brushing treatments: a summary of British Columbia data. Extension Note 41. Victoria, BC: British Columbia Ministry of Forests, Research Branch. 12 p.

Comeau, P.; McClarnon, J.; Heineman, J.; Kazems, R. **2003.** Predicting light availability in broadleaf stands: a tool for mixedwood management. Victoria, BC: British Columbia Ministry of Forests, Forest Practices Branch. 22 p.

Fink, K.E.; Humphreys, P.; Hawkins, G.V. **1989.** Field guide to pests of managed forests in British Columbia. FRDA report 16. Victoria, BC: British Columbia Ministry of Forests, Protection Branch. 188 p.

Forest Genetics Council of British Columbia [FGC]. **2004.** Forest genetics council of British Columbia strategic plan 2004 – 2008. Victoria, BC: Forest Genetics Council of British Columbia. 9 p.

Heineman, J. **1998.** Forest floor planting: a discussion of issues as they relate to various site limiting factors. Silviculture note #16. Victoria, BC: Forest Site Management Section: British Columbia Ministry of Forests, Forest Practices Branch. 11 p.

Jones, M.D.; Kiiskila, S.; Flanagan, A. **2002.** Field performance of pine stocktypes: two-year results on interior lodgepole pine seedlings grown in Styroblocks, Copperblocks, or Airblocks. B.C. Journal of Ecosystems and Management. Forest Research Extension Partnership. British Columbia Journal of Ecosystems and Management. Vol. 2 (online at http://www forrex.org/jem/2002/vol2/ no1/art5.pdf) Vol. 2.

Krasowski, M.J. **1996.** Measures to reduce overwinter injury to planted spruce in the boreal forest of British Columbia. FRDA report 254. Victoria, BC: British Columbia Ministry of Forests Research Branch, Canadian Forest Service. 18 p.

Macadam, A., Sutton, R.F., Bedford, L. **2001.** Site preparation for establishing lodgepole pine on backlog sites in the sub-boreal spruce zone. Silviculture note #27. Victoria, BC: Silviculture Practices Section, British Columbia Ministry of Forests, Forest Practices Branch. 5 p.

McDowell, J.A. **1998a.** The ecology of the sub-boreal spruce zone. Victoria, BC: British Columbia Ministry of Forests, Research Branch. 6 p.

McDowell, J.A. **1998a.** The ecology of the boreal white and black spruce zone. Victoria, BC: British Columbia Ministry of Forests, Research Branch. 6 p.

Meidinger, D.; Pojar, J. **1991.** Ecosystems of British Columbia. Special Report Series 6. Victoria, BC: British Columbia Ministry of Forests, Research Branch. 330 p.

Province of British Columbia [BC Gov.]. **2004.** Forest and Range Practices Act. Victoria, BC.

Reich, R. **2002.** Forest health issues: options and decision aids for managing hardpine stem rusts in F.L.A. 18162 of the Nechako forest. [place of publication unknown].

Seed Planning and Registry System [SPAR]. **2004.** Seed planning and registry system on-line report. Victoria, BC: British Columbia Ministry of Forests.

Sutton, R.F.; Bedford,L.; Strodeur, L.; Grismer, M. **2001.** Site preparation for establishing interior spruce in British Columbia: trials at Upper Coalmine and Mackenzie. Western Journal of Applied Forestry 16: 9-17.

STAND ESTABLISHMENT AND TENDING
IN THE INLAND NORTHWEST

Russell T. Graham[1], Theresa B. Jain[1], Phil Cannon[2]

ABSTRACT

The moist, cold, and dry forests of the Inland Northwest occupy approximately 144 million acres. Ponderosa pine, lodge-pole pine, western white pine, western larch, and Douglas-fir are usually the preferred commercial species of the area. These early-seral species are relatively resistant to endemic levels of insects and diseases. They tend to grow rapidly and in general produce commercial products at a young age, especially using focused management actions packaged in silvicultural systems that are documented in silvicultural prescriptions. Even-aged systems (clearcut, seed-tree, and shelterwood) are the most appropriate for growing commercial products. In limited circumstances uneven-aged systems may be appropriate on sites where ponderosa pine is the late seral-species. Planting of improved, site adapted trees usually offer the greatest control over the amount, kind, and establishment of plantations. The control of competing vegetation during the site preparation and tending phases of the silvicultural system is usually extremely beneficial in enhancing tree growth and product development. The forest soils of the Inland West are generally deficient in nitrogen and, in some settings, also potassium deficient. The organic and mineral surface layers, often containing ash and loess soils, are vulnerable to compaction, displacement, or damage from fires (prescribed and wild) or mechanical forest operations. Therefore, soil and its conservation should be integral to all activities included in a silvicultural system. For production forestry, herbicides offer an alternative that can maintain the soil resource yet control competing vegetation and most often yield excellent results when properly applied. Cleanings, weedings and thinnings are integral parts of the silvicultural system. These and all parts of silvicultural systems designed to produce commercial products can be readily quantified, displayed, and visualized (spatially explicit) through time using the Forest Vegetation Simulator.

KEYWORDS: Forest products, silvicultural systems, regeneration, stand tending, fertilization, site preparation, forest management.

FORESTS OF THE INLAND NORTHWEST

The Inland Northwest (144.2 million ac) forest region is defined by the Bitterroot, Selkirk, Cabinet, Salmon River, Lemhi, Steens, Purcell, Cascade, and Blue mountain ranges with many having elevations over 5,000 ft. This rough and complex topography results in a variety of forest settings ranging from steep slopes in narrow V-cut canyons to gentle rolling slopes in wide river valleys. During the Pleistocene, alpine glaciers shaped many of the canyons and valleys throughout the area. Now these glaciated landscapes are covered with a mantle of glacial till often compacted on the valley floors. Much of the fine silt outwashed by the glaciers was redeposited by winds leaving deep layers of loess deposits over many landscapes. Some 15,000 to 12,000 years ago, Glacial Lake Missoula repeatedly filled and emptied, flooding much of northern Idaho and eastern Washington removing topsoil and redistributing the surface sand, silt, and gravels. The eruption of pre-historic Mt. Mazama (Crater Lake, OR) about 7,000 years ago deposited a fine textured layer of ash up to 25 inches thick across the area. The granitic and metasedimentary rocks, ash, and

[1] Russell T. Graham, Theresa B. Jain are Research Foresters, USDA Forest Service, Rocky Mountain Research Station, 1221 South Main, Moscow, ID, 83843.

[2] Phil Cannon is Corporate Silviculturist, Boise Corporation, 1111 West Jefferson Street, P.O. Box 50 Boise, ID 83728.

loess deposits throughout the area are continually being modified by disturbance events giving rise to a wide variety of soils (Jain and Graham 2005, Quigley et al. 1996).

Moist marine air originating from the Pacific Ocean moderates temperatures within the Inland Northwest, while continental dry and cold air from the east brings cold weather in winter and hot weather in the summer. Dry Arctic air brings damaging frosts in winter and cool periods in summer and the interaction of the marine and continental masses brings convective precipitation and lightning in summer and warm wet periods in the winter. These air masses, along with the heterogeneous and rugged topography, create a highly variable climate, which in turn, supports mosaics of compositionally and structurally diverse forests. Historically (1850 to 1900), 19 percent (27.4 million acres) of the Inland Northwest (144.2 million acres) was covered by dry forests, with 30 percent of them occurring below 4,000 feet and the remainder occurring at higher elevations. Moist forests covered 18 percent (25.9 million acres) of the region. The cold forests historically made up 10 percent of the area with 99 percent of them growing at elevations exceeding 4,000 feet (Hann et al. 1997).

Moist Forests

Moist forests of the Inland Northwest occur in two locations, the eastern Cascade Mountains (east of the Cascade Crest in Washington and Oregon) and the Northern Rocky Mountains (northeastern Washington and Oregon, northern Idaho, and western Montana) (fig. 1). They grow at elevations ranging from 1,500 to 5,300 feet and occasionally occur at elevations up to 6,000 feet (Foiles et al. 1990, Graham 1990, Packee 1990, Schmidt and Shearer 1990, Hann et al. 1997) (fig. 1). These forests are influenced by a maritime climate with wet winters and dry summers. Most precipitation occurs during November through May, with amounts ranging from 20 to 90 inches (Foiles et al. 1990, Graham 1990, Packee 1990, Schmidt and Shearer 1990). Precipitation comes as snow and prolonged gentle rains, accompanied by cloudiness, fog, and high humidity. Rain-on-snow events are common January through March. A distinct warm and sunny drought period occurs in July and August with rainfall in some places averages less than one inch per month. Soils that maintain these forests include, but are not limited to, Spodosols, Inceptisols, and Alfisols. A defining characteristic of the Northern Rocky Mountains is the layer of fine-textured volcanic ash (up to 25 inches thick) that caps the residual soils.

For both locations, the vegetation complexes range from early- to late-seral, and occur within a landscape mosaic possessing all possible combinations of species and seral

stages. Potential vegetation type (PVT) is a classification system based on the physical and biological environment characterized by the abundance and presence of vegetation in the absence of disturbance (Daubenmire and Daubenmire 1968, Hann et al. 1997, Smith and Arno 1999). They are defined by and named for indicator species that grow in similar environmental conditions (Hann et al. 1997). The PVTs in the Northern Rocky Mountains include western redcedar (*Thuja plicata*), western hemlock (*Tsuga heterophylla*) and grand fir (*Abies grandis*) with western white pine (*Pinus monticola*), western larch (*Larix occidentalis*), lodgepole pine (*Pinus contorta*), Douglas-fir (*Pseudotsuga menziesii*) and ponderosa pine (*Pinus ponderosa*) as the early- and mid-seral species (Daubenmire and Daubenmire 1968, Hann et al. 1997). The eastern Cascades PVTs include western redcedar, western hemlock, grand fir, white fir (*Abies concolor*), and noble fir (*Abies procera*). The early- and mid-seral species include lodgepole pine, Douglas-fir, and ponderosa pine while western white pine and western larch are less abundant when compared to forests in the Northern Rocky Mountains (Franklin and Dyrness 1973, Lillybridge et al. 1995).

Lush ground-level vegetation is the norm in the moist forests. The vegetation complexes are similar to those occurring on the west-side of the Cascade Mountains and in some Pacific coastal areas. Tall shrubs include vine maple, (*Acer circinatum),* Rocky Mountain maple (*Acer glabrum*), Sitka alder (*Alnus sinuata*), devil's club (*Oplopanax horridum*), rose (*Rosa* spp.), gooseberry (*Ribes* spp.), huckleberry (*Vaccinium* spp.,) and willow (*Salix* spp.). Forbs include baneberry (*Actaea rubra*), pathfinder (*Adenocaulon bicolor*), wild ginger (*Asarum caudatum*), queencup beadlily (*Clintonia uniflora*), bunchberry dogwood (*Cornus canadensis*), and golden thread (*Coptis occidentalis*) (fig. 2).

Throughout the moist forests, native disturbances (snow, ice, insects, disease, and fire) singly, and in combination, created heterogeneity in patch sizes, forest structures, and compositions. Ice and snow created small gaps and openings, thinning forest densities and altering species composition. Native insects (e.g., pine beetle [*Dendroctonus* spp.]) and diseases (e.g., root rots [*Armillaria* spp.]), mistletoe (*Arceuthobium* spp.) infected and killed the very old or stressed individuals which tended to diversify vegetation communities (Hessburg et al. 1994, Atkins et al. 1999). Fires played a role in creating a mosaic of forest compositions and structures. Non-lethal fires (low intensity and severity surface fires that cleaned the forest floor, killed and/or consumed small trees and shrubs, and killed lower branches of overstory trees while leaving them alive) occurred at relatively frequent intervals (15 to 25 yrs) in a

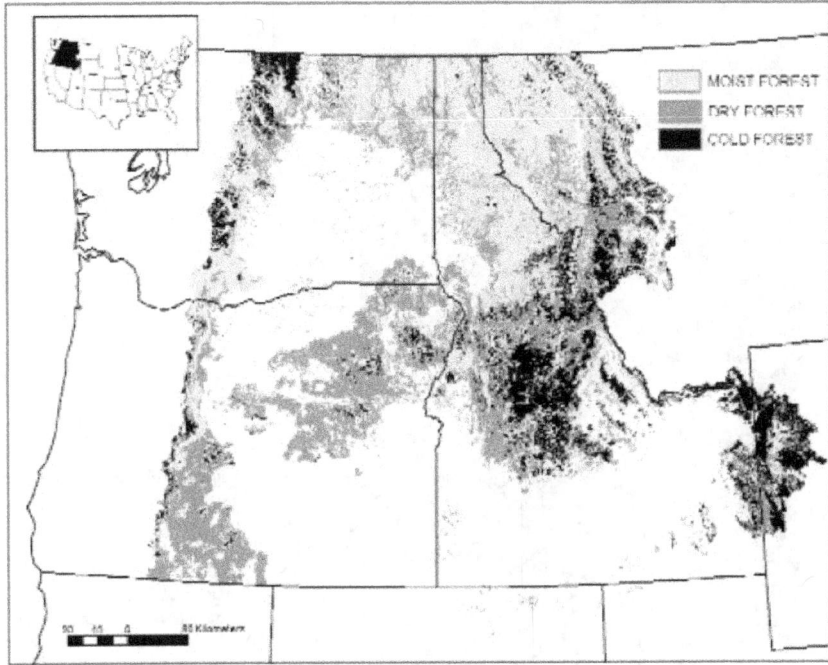

Figure 1—Extent of the forests of the Inland Northwest (144.2 million acres). The cold forests containing subalpine fir and Engelmann spruce potential vegetation types (PVTs) occupy 14.4 million acres (10%) of the area, the dry forests containing ponderosa pine, Douglas-fir, and dry grand fir PVTs occupy 27.4 million acres (19%), and the moist forests containing the moist grand fir/white fir, western redcedar, and western hemlock PVTs occupy 25.9 million acres (18%) (Hann et al. 1997).

quarter of the area. Lethal fires (intense and severe crown fires that killed and/or consumed the vegetation in all canopy layers) burned about a quarter of the area at intervals of 20 to 150 years but occasionally extended to 300 years. The mixed-fire regime (a combination of lethal and non-lethal fires) occurred across the rest of the moist forests at 20 to150 year intervals. Fires typically started burning in July and were usually out by early September when the weather changed (Hann et al. 1997). Although fire exclusion played a role in altering the moist forests of the Northern Rocky Mountains, introduction of a European stem rust, white pine blister rust (*Cronartium ribicola*) in 1910, caused the greatest change (Neuenschwander et al. 1999, Fins et al. 2001). The rust infects all five-needle pines, and subsequently decimated the abundant western white pine (fig. 3). Because the rust killed so many trees, the majority of surviving pines were harvested under the assumption they too would succumb to the rust (Ketcham et al. 1968).

Cold Forests

Within the Inland Northwest, cold forests occur at high elevations occupying about 10 percent of the area. They occur primarily in northern Idaho, central Idaho, and in the Northern Cascades Mountains of Washington (fig. 1). Growing seasons in cold forests are short, ranging from approximately 90 days at the lower elevations to just a few weeks at the higher elevations, and frosts can occur any time of the year. These forests are limited by poorly developed soils, and limited by moisture in some areas. Nearly

Figure 2—A young (100-year-old) stand of western white pine exhibiting a lush layer of ground-level vegetation located north of Wallace, Idaho.

Figure 3—Western white pine blister rust (A), an introduced disease from Europe, in the early 1900s devastated much of the native western white pine. However through breeding programs and natural resistance, western white pine is once again a viable commercial species (B). This stand of first-generation blister rust-resistant pines is ≈ 50 years old, ≈100 to 120 feet tall, and ≈ 18 to 22 inches in diameter.

all (99 percent) of the cold forests occur over 4,000 feet, but cold air drainage allows some cold forests to extend below 4,000 feet (Hann et al. 1997).

On settings dominated by subalpine fir (*Abies lasiocarpa*), mean annual temperatures range from 25° to 40° F. Precipitation generally ranges between 24 and 75 inches with the majority falling in the form of snow and sleet. Snow comes early and stays late and can reach depths over 500 inches on settings in the Cascade Mountains with lesser amounts where lodgepole pine persists (central Oregon and central Idaho) (Alexander et al. 1990). The soils supporting the cold forest are relatively young. They were covered by extensive mountain glaciers during the Pleistocene and have been free of ice less than 12,000 years. At the higher elevations, most soil parent material is alluvium or glacial tills, but soil surfaces range from very weakly weathered (cobbly with no organic layers) to thick soils composed primarily of organic materials.

Like the moist forests, lush ground-level vegrtation is the norm for most settings in the cold forests. Tall shrubs include false huckberry (*Menziesia ferruginea*) and Sitka alder while the dominant medium and low shrubs are often huckleberries. Pinegrass (*Calamagrostis rubescens*), blue-joint reedgrass (*Calamagrostis canadensis*), and elk sedge (*Carex geyeri*) typify the graminoids occurring in the cold forests. Some of the most commonly occuring forbs include beargrass (*Xerophyllum tenax*), round-leaved violet (*Viola orbiculata*), and queencup beadlily (Cooper et al. 1991).

The PVTs dominating the cold forests include subalpine fir and subalpine fir/Engelmann spruce (*Picea Engelmannii*). Western larch and lodgepole pine are early-seral species in the subalpine fir/Engelmann spruce PVT, Douglas-fir and western white pine are mid-seral species, and grand fir, Engelmann spruce, and subalpine fir are late-seral species (fig. 4). The mixes of these species occurring in the subalpine fir/Engelmann PVT are highly dependent on elevation (and associated climate), and disturbance frequency and type.

Depending on the physical setting, the cold forests of the Inland Northwest historically (1850-1900) burned at 25 to 100 year intervals. Approximately 10 percent of these forests were burned by non-lethal surface fires, every 30 to 100 years. Lethal crown fires burned 25 to 30 percent of the cold forests every 30 to 100 years with the longer intervals occurring in moist areas. During the short fire season (≈ 60 days), a mixed fire regime burned about 60 percent of the cold forests at 25- to 100-year intervals, with occasional large fires occurring every 100 years (Hann et al. 1997).

Figure 4—A thinned stand of lodgepole pine (an early-seral species) growing on a subalpine-fir potential vegetation type.

Figure 5—A young (70-year-old) ponderosa pine stand being maintained by a low intensity surface fire. Note the presence of some ground-level vegetation.

Dry Forests

Dry forests occur across a wide range of elevations in northeastern Washington, northeastern Oregon, central and southern Idaho, and south-central Oregon (fig. 1) (Hann et al. 1997). Soil parent materials include granites, metasedimentaries, glacial tills, and basalts. Vegetation in these forests is usually limited by water availability and often is subject to drought. Nutrient deficiencies develop in eroded areas that can limit forest development. Douglas-fir, ponderosa pine, and dry grand fir/white fir (PVTs) dominate these settings (Hann et al. 1997). When western larch is present in dry forests it is always an early-successional species (dominant after disturbance). Grand fir/white fir or Douglas-fir are late-successional species that are usually more shade-tolerant than the early-seral species they succeed, while ponderosa pine can play both roles, depending on the PVT (Daubenmire and Daubenmire 1968, Hann et al. 1997). Surface vegetation in the dry forests includes shrubs (kinnikinnick (*Arctostaphylos uva-ursi*), *Ceanothus* spp., snowberry (*Symphoricarpos albus*), ninebark [*Physocarpus malvaceus*]), grasses (pine grass) e.g., bromes (*Bromus* spp.), and sedges (*Carex* spp.) (Foiles et al. 1990, Hermann and Lavender 1990, Oliver and Ryker 1990) (fig. 5).

Fire, insects, diseases, snow, ice, and competition thinned these forests, and surface fires provided opportunities for plant regeneration (Pearson 1950, Foiles et al. 1990, Hermann and Lavender 1990, Oliver and Ryker 1990). In concert, these disturbances historically maintained a variety of structural and successional stages. Fire exclusion, harvesting, and changes in fire regime altered the composition and structure of the dry forests (Hann et al. 1997). The area burned currently by non-lethal surface fires is estimated to be less than 50 percent of the dry forests and the mean interval of these fires is estimated to be to 40 to 80 years. Mixed-fires are estimated to burn 35 percent of the dry forests with a mean interval of 45 to 60 years and lethal fires are estimated to burn 20 percent of the dry forests at mean intervals of 45 to 60 years (Hann et al. 1997).

FOREST SOIL

Soil is the foundation of a forest ecosystem and its character is a major contributor to site productivity (Harvey et al. 1987). In general, nitrogen (N) is the most limiting nutrient in most forests (Moore 1988, Moore et al. 1991). However, there is evidence that potassium (K) also plays a key role, especially in relation to disease and insect infestation (Moore et al. 1994). As stated earlier, much of the Inland Northwest is covered by rich loess and ash soils.

These materials, along with the weathering of the parent materials (granitics, basalts, meta-sediments), all contributed to the productivity of the forest. Therefore, conservation of the soil resource is essential to maintain and sustain forest productivity.

The character of the litter, humus, soil wood, and surface mineral layers of forest soils are critical when developing silvicultural systems (Harvey et al. 1987, Jurgensen et al. 1997). These soil layers are most easily and commonly disturbed by silvicultural activities, yet they are crucial to forest productivity. Depending upon the setting, organic matter (OM) is generally concentrated near the soil surface. Organic matter maintains the nitrogen cycle in soils through its decomposition and by facilitating N fixation (the process of making elemental N into a form that plants can use) and N storage of N (Jurgensen et al. 1979). Physical properties and nutrition are very important soil attributes but the biological component is integral for maintaining forest productivity. In particular, ectomycorrhizae (fungi that have a symbiotic relationship with the plants) and their environment are critical for maintaining soil productivity. Ectomycorrhizae establish on the root systems of trees and facilitate the uptake of both water and nutrients by the tree, which in turn supplies nutrients to the fungi (Harvey et al. 1981, Harvey et al. 1987).

Woody Residues

Although they are not a soil component, the quantity, quality, and disposition of coarse woody debris (CWD) can influence forest soils (Harvey et al. 1987, Jurgensen et al. 1997). The quantity of downed material can vary dramatically, depending on site, forest conditions, and forest treatments (Brown and See 1981). Physically, woody residues protect soil from erosion, displacement and compaction. Residues provide shade and protection from wind and snow and can protect newly established seedlings from livestock (Edgren and Stein 1974, Graham et al. 1992). However, falling or rolling logs can damage regeneration and fuel loadings can threaten forests by increasing the fire hazard (Brown et al. 2003). Decaying logs, especially those with the incipient and advanced forms of decay, are excellent substrates for non-symbiotic nitrogen fixation and if nitrogen-fixing plants such as ceanothus (*Ceanothus* spp.), buffaloberry (*Shepherdia canadensis*), or leguminous forbs are not present, non-symbiotic forms of nitrogen fixation can be significant.

In addition to CWD, organic input to forest soils comes from many other sources. Grasses, shrubs, root turnover, needle fall, etc. contribute to soil OM. In general, CWD

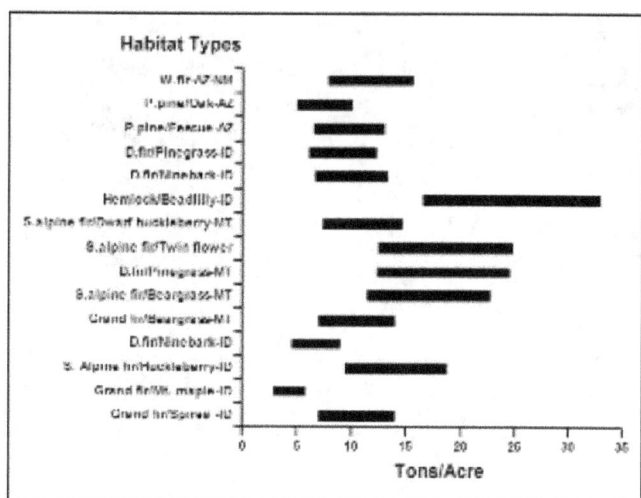

Figure 6—The amount of coarse woody debris suggested by Graham et al. (1994) for maintaining soil productivity in the forests of the Rocky Mountains. A=Arizona, I=Idaho, M=Montana for the habitat types where the recommendations apply.

comes from tree boles and limbs over three inches in diameter (smaller material is usually considered a fire hazard). Accumulation of CWD on the forest floor depends upon the amount of decomposition occurring on a site and the frequency and severity of wildfires that burn a forest (Brown and See 1981, Brown 1983). In general, those forests that were frequently burned by low intensity surface fires tended to accumulate and use less CWD than the cold and moist forests with long fire-return intervals (Graham et al. 1994a, Hann et al. 1997). The amount of CWD suggested for maintaining soil productivity ranges from 3 tons per acre on ponderosa pine settings to over 30 tons per acre on western hemlock settings in moist forests (fig. 6) (Graham et al. 1994a).

Litter

Unconsolidated and undecomposed litter directly provide both N and ectomycorrhizae habitat for soil function. This material is composed of organic materials from trees, shrubs, grasses, forbs, and other plant material. Litter is not usually important for ectomycorrhizal activity, but if moisture is maintained in these layers, ectomycorrhizae can be present (Harvey et al. 1987). However, through its decay, litter becomes a greater soil contributor. Litter can vary widely in amount, composition, and structure depending on forest type and PVT, as well as fire-return interval and decomposition rate. Litter protects the soil from erosion and retains moisture in the lower layers (Pannkuk and Robichaud 2003.) and protects soils from compaction (Lull 1959). Litter can be an impediment to both natural and artificial tree regeneration. If the litter layer is thick, which often

Figure 7—A large accumulation of brown cubical rotten wood occurring in a lodgepole pine stand near Butte, Montana. In these forests, this material can be a major component of the surface soil.

occurs in ponderosa pine forests where decomposition is slow and fire has been excluded, tree seeds falling on this layer germinate, but root elongation may not keep pace with litter drying (Haig et al. 1941, Pearson 1950). On the other hand, if litter remains moist during germination and early seedling growth (a situation that may be found in many moist forests), establishment of tree seedlings on organic layers is quite common (Minore 1972). Because this most often occurs in the moist and cold forests with late seral species, the desired mix of species for commodity production is not often realized.

Humus

Even though the humus (decomposed material in which plant parts are indistinguishable) soil layer may be very thin (i.e. < 0.25 in), it can be a prime site for both N and ectomycorrhizae. For example, in the surface 12 inches of a Douglas-fir/ponderosa pine forest soil, over 20 percent of the total N can occur in the humus and over 30 percent of the ectomycorrhizae (Harvey et al. 1987). In addition, it often has high moisture contents and is rich in calcium, potassium, and magnesium. This layer often represents the transition between organic layers and the mineral soil and, when it is burned over, it is a superb site for seed germination and seedling establishment (Haig et al. 1941).

Soil Wood

A component of forest soils that is often over looked is soil wood which is highly decomposed wood incorporated into mineral soil horizons and is usually in the form of brown cubicle rot (fig. 7) (Harvey et al. 1987). As it ages and further decomposes, it can take on a much finer texture. As with the other organic components of soil, the quantity and character of soil wood can be quite variable. For example, the amount of soil wood in the surface 12 inches of a forest soil is 20 percent in cold forests, 22 percent in Douglas-fir forests, and over 26 percent in moist forests (Harvey et al. 1987). Soil wood does not usually occur as a layer within soil but rather occurs in deep pockets created by buried logs and decaying stumps (Reinhardt et al. 1991). Soil wood protects soils from compaction, provides OM to the mineral soil, is also an important source of N ($\approx$20 percent of the amount in surface 12 inches of soil) and is an excellent substrate for ectomycorrhizae ($\approx$50 percent of the amount in surface 12 inches of soil) (Harvey and others 1987). Because of its water-holding availability and nutritional, biological, and physical characteristics, soil wood is often prime habitat for rooting. In the cold forests, these materials, intermingled with exposed parent material, can constitute the majority of the soil (Graham et al. 1994a). Forests dominated by pines and Douglas-fir develop brown cubical rotten wood products that are deposited on the forest floor and are subsequently incorporated into the mineral soil. These products can persist in soils for hundreds of years and during that time provide soil structural and nutritional benefits. In contrast, grand fir/white fir develop white rotten wood products that are dispersed in soil relatively rapidly (decades), thus shortening their contribution to soil productivity (Larsen et al. 1980, Harvey et al. 1987).

Surface Mineral Soil

The surface 6 to 12 inches of mineral soil is derived from the deposits and parent materials of the site, but is also highly influenced by vegetation, surface organic layers and disturbance history inherent to the PVT. The OM incorporated into shallow mineral horizons carries important properties into the mineral soil. Mineral soil with robust OM amounts has better nutrition, water-holding capacity, and structure than soils with small amounts of OM. In addition, OM-rich mineral soils are excellent sites for nitrogen fixation and ectomycorrhizae (Harvey et al. 1987). Surface mineral layers are highly susceptible to compaction and displacement and soils with high volcanic ash content are particularly sensitive to forest operations (Harvey et al. 1989b).

Figure 8—When fires are excluded from ponderosa pine forests, organic layers tend to accumulate and tree roots, ectomycorrhizae, and nutrients tend to concentrate in these layers. Note the contrast between the amount of organic material on the forest floor when General Custer came through the Black Hills in 1874 and the amount that has accumulated around the rocks by 2000. Photos courtesy of Paul Horsted/custertrail.com (Grafe and Horsted 2002).

Altered Forest Soils

Soils in many forests are different from those that occurred historically. Soils have been altered through species changes (within shrub, tree, or forb components), organic material accumulation on the forest floor, and by soil compaction and displacement. These changes have been the result singly, or in combination of fire exclusion, timber harvesting, animal grazing, and climate shifts. There is a gradual shift in the proportion of soil nitrogen reserves and OM in mineral layers of pine forests to surface organic layers in fir forests. Accumulation of both above-and below-ground biomass from roots, needles, and boles in fir forests is accelerating activities of decomposers by increasing and changing the basic substrate they utilize (Harvey 1994). Associated with these changes in litter type and quantity is a likely change in soil surface chemistry, including allelopathic substances with the potential to alter a variety of microbial activities (Rose et al. 1983). Forests dominated by grand fir tend to concentrate both nitrogen and potassium in their foliage; these forests often have live crowns extend down to the soil surface (Mika and Moore 1990, Moore et al. 1991). In general, this combination of a low

canopy structure with nutrients and microbial activities concentrated in or near the soil surface make both of these critical ecological resources susceptible to mechanical and fire destruction (fig. 8).

GROUND-LEVEL VEGETATION

In the forests of the Inland Northwest, ground-level vegetation is highly diverse with the cold and moist forests containing lush and diverse shrub, grass, and forb communities (fig. 2) (Daubenmire and Daubenmire 1968, Pfister et al. 1977, Cooper et al. 1991). Each plant in these communities has a different strategy for reproducing and surviving disturbances (Noste and Bushey 1987). Ground-level vegetation can also play many roles such as maintaining nutrients on a site after a disturbance, providing OM to the forest floor, protecting soils from erosion, and facilitating nutrient cycling (Yarie 1980, Pannkuk and Robichaud 2003). These plants tend to turnover a greater percentage of their biomass each year through litter fall than do trees. Therefore, they tend to cycle nutrients and OM more readily than trees.

54

Ground-level vegetation often aggressively responds to canopy openings and forest floor disturbances. Species that may not be present before a disturbance can proliferate after a disturbance. For example, canopy removal and prescribed fire can facilitate robust development of *Ceanothus* spp. especially in the cold and moist forests even though none was present pre-disturbance. Seeds of *Ceanothus* spp. lie in wait in the forest floor for scarification through heat to germinate; these species can rapidly occupy a site after disturbance (Noste and Bushey 1987). Other ground-level vegetation, such as alder, willow, and maple, are aggressive resprouters from the root crown, rhizome or above-ground stem. Some species are exceptional at resisting or enduring disturbances. For example, pine grass in the dry and moist forests and bear grass in the cold forest readily survive disturbances.

When it comes to producing forest crops, ground-level vegetation often competes aggressively with the establishment and growth of conifers (Baumgartner et al. 1986, Boyd 1982). In all forests, the forb, shrub, and grass layers can present formidable competition for nutrients, water, and light with tree seedlings. In addition, it can interfere with conifer development by occupying sites with roots, even though the area appears to be unoccupied and, even though ground-level vegetation may be dead, its root systems can interfere with tree planting. Also, ground-level vegetation can be allelopathic, that is emitting toxins both when the plant is alive and dead, interfering with seed germination and tree development (Ferguson 1991). Indirectly, ground-level vegetation can supply habitat for damaging animals, facilitating trampling, browsing and girdling damage on plantations (Kingery and Graham 1991, Graham et al. 1992, Ferguson 1999).

SILVICULTURAL SYSTEMS

In general, silviculture can be defined as the art and science of controlling the establishment, growth, competition, health, and quality of forests and woodlands to meet the diverse needs and values of landowners and society on a sustainable basis (Helms 1998). The processes silviculturists use to manipulate forest vegetation are included in a silvicultural system and documented in a silvicultural prescription. A silvicultural system outlines a series of treatments over the life of a stand to fulfill a set of values or interests for a particular landowner (Schlich 1906). The prescription is the formulation of a silvicultural strategy using biological, managerial, and economic knowledge to meet stand management objectives (Smith et al. 1997,

Nyland 2002). This plan should ensure that future yields of goods are conserved while harvesting or utilizing currently available goods (Smith et al. 1997). Most often, the early- and mid-seral species are the fastest growing and most tolerant of endemic diseases and insects and are readily managed using well-honed silvicultural systems so, therefore, they are the preferred species for timber and fiber production.

Even-Aged Silvicultural Systems

Even-aged silvicultural systems usually create and maintain stands with trees representing one age class, or a narrow range of age classes. Historically, lethal fires created forests containing even-aged stands. In general, clearcut, shelterwood, and seed-tree systems can emulate these stand-replacing events but these tend to perpetuate early-seral or relatively intolerant (e.g., shade, canopy closure, competition) trees.

With the exception of the clearcut, the other even-aged silvicultural systems (seed-tree and shelterwood systems) include some high forest cover during a portion of the system development. Overstory density and the species prescribed in seed-tree and shelterwood systems depend on the site and desired forest structure and composition. The number of overstory trees prescribed in a shelterwood depends on how much shelter is required to successfully regenerate a desired tree species. As canopy cover increases, the amount of shade-tolerant (e.g., grand fir, hemlock) regeneration will also increase.

Clearcut Method

The clearcut regeneration method is easy to apply and is often well suited for situations where disease and/or insect problems exist. Disposal of hazard fuels and site preparation can readily be accomplished using prescribed fire, mechanical means, or chemical application. In addition, the planting of improved stock from tree improvement programs is facilitated by the clearcut method. Clearcutting is most applicable on sites and PVTs in which biophysical conditions present without canopy cover provide suitable conditions for seedling establishment and development (e.g., western hemlock and subalpine fir PVTs, northerly slopes etc.) (fig. 9). The optimum size and orientation of the clearcut is also predicated on the biophysical setting and the species and kind of regeneration desired (Burns 1983). If natural regeneration is planned, then ample seed and dispersal will need to be available from neighboring seed walls (clearcut edge) or within the tops of the trees left after harvesting.

Figure 9—A clearcut regenerated with western white pine located near Coeur d'Alene, Idaho. Note the well-defined seed wall (clearcut edge).

Seed-Tree Method

The seed-tree method can be applied on all slopes and aspects but needs to be tailored to the forest PVT and biophysical setting. Vigorous, wind-firm trees should be left as seed trees and selected for their phenotypic traits (Hoff et al. 1976). On most settings, four to six trees per acre are adequate for seed production for most preferred species. For example, 7 to 12 trees/acre might be prescribed for a poor seed-producing species (western larch), whereas 3 to 7 seed trees/acre might be utilized with a prolific seed-producing species (western white pine). If possible, site preparation should coincide with a seed crop in the overstory. The seed trees should be removed as soon as possible after regenerationbecomes established. Stocking control is usually needed to maintain the desired number and species composition in the regenerated stand (Schmidt 1988). The seed-tree method is ideal where seed dispersal could be problematic from adjacent seed walls if the clearcut method was applied. This often occurs with ponderosa pine because it has heavy seeds that are dispersed shorter distances compared to some of the mid- and late-seral species such as grand fir and Douglas-fir (Haig et al. 1941, Burns 1983) whose seeds disperse longer distances.

Shelterwood Method

The shelterwood regeneration method is applicable on all aspects and slopes, but is especially suited to steep, dry slopes where regeneration would benefit from protection. Dominant overstory densities used in this method range from 15 to 40 trees per acre depending on species. The greater the number of trees left in the overstory, the greater the proportion and number of shade-tolerant species regenerated (Haig et al. 1941). Because of the wide range in fire resistance of the species occurring on these sites, slash disposal and site preparation may be difficult and expensive depending on species and slope. Vigorous trees should be left in the overstory to withstand the shock of release, stand through weather events (e.g., snow, wind) and act as good seed producers. When an adequate regeneration is achieved, the overstory should be promptly removed (Burns 1983).

Application of Even-Aged Systems

In the cold forests, the clearcut and seed-tree methods are very appropriate for producing even-aged stands of early-seral species (e.g., western larch, Douglas-fir). Lodgepole pine is the most frequently managed species within the cold forests because it readily germinates and develops using clearcuts on the subalpine fir PVTs (Schmidt and Alexander 1985) (fig. 4). Serotiny in lodgepole pine usually ensures the presence of viable seed in the unopened cones present in the slash left after harvesting. However, diligence is needed when disposing of slash and preparing sites to insure the seed stored in the cones is not removed or destroyed. Cone serotiny is variable in lodgepole pine; therefore the presence of unopened cones should be verified prior to relying on this characteristic to supply seed for regeneration (Lotan 1973).

Western larch is often a preferred early-seral species in the cold forests and it also regenerates and develops well using the clearcut system (Schmidt and Shearer 1990). Douglas-fir is more intermediate in response to clearcutting in these

Figure 10—A shelterwood system was used to regenerate western white pine. Rust-free shelter trees were chosen. The seedlings regenerated using this method could exhibit up to 19% resistance to blister rust (Hoff et al. 1976).

settings but it also responds better to the open conditions of a clearcut than spruce and subalpine fir, species that are late-seral associates in these cold forests. In portions of the dry forests, especially those on the more moist PVTs such as the drier grand fir/white fir settings, clearcutting has been successfully used to perpetuate ponderosa pine (Ryker and Losensky 1983).

Clearcutting is very applicable for use in the moist forests (fig. 9). The preferred early-seral species, western white pine, western larch, and Douglas-fir, all regenerate and develop readily using this method. In addition, because of the large amounts of fuel that can be created when harvesting, clearcuts facilitate the use of prescribed fire for preparing sites for both natural and planted regeneration which will decrease the wildfire hazard (Haig et al. 1941, Graham et al. 1983). Regeneration of late-seral western hemlock, grand fir, and western redcedar is often prolific in the moist forests; however, clearcuts tend to favor the early-seral species over the late-seral species, particularly if the preferred species regenerate promptly after harvest (Haig et al. 1941, Graham et al. 1983, Jain et al. 2004). Moreover, some suggest that clearcuts are the preferred method for managing rust-resistant western white pine (Fins et al. 2001).

Seed-tree methods are most applicable in the cold and moist forests but also have been used successfully in the dry forests on settings in which shelter is not a prerequisite for successful regeneration (Ryker and Losensky 1983). Very often this occurs on PVTs where ponderosa pine readily regenerates such as those occurring in the Black Hills and some sites in Arizona and New Mexico (Pearson 1950, Shepperd and Battaglia 2002). Seed-tree methods can be used in the moist forests to regenerate western white pine, Douglas-fir, and western larch (Haig et al. 1941). In the cold forests, the seed-tree method can be used to regenerate western larch and Douglas-fir and is very applicable in situations where lodgepole pine does not express cone serotiny (Lotan 1973).

Shelterwood regeneration methods are most applicable on settings in which the preferred species, usually an early-seral species, benefits from the presence of shade. This can occur on Douglas-fir and ponderosa pine PVTs in the dry forests where ponderosa pine regeneration benefits from some shade (Pearson 1950, Ryker and Losensky 1983, Shepperd and Battaglia 2002) (fig. 5). In the moist forests, western white pine readily regenerates with the shelterwood method and, in many settings, it prefers partial shade for the first few years of its life (Haig et al. 1941) (fig. 10). Ponderosa pine is often regenerated using one or two stage shelterwoods (Pearson 1950). The preparatory cut favors seed producing pine developing their wind firmness and crown expansion, and the final seed cut provides growing space for the seedlings to be established (Boldt and Van Deusen 1974). By providing these openings, ponderosa pine has the greatest opportunity to become established and outcompete its late- and mid-seral associates such as Douglas-fir, grand fir, and white fir (fig. 5). However, in many settings Douglas-fir would also be the preferred species especially on the drier grand fir or white fir PVTs.

A consistent drawback of using seed-tree and shelterwood regeneration methods is the possibility of perpetuating dwarf mistletoe (*Arceuthobium* spp.). Ponderosa pine, Douglas-fir, western larch, and lodgepole pine, depending on the location and PVT, are all susceptible to infection from mistletoe. Trees without mistletoe can be selected for retention but if the disease is prevalent in the overstory, the clearcut method usually provides more satisfactory control of the disease (van der Kamp and Hawksworth 1985).

Trees in shelterwood and seed-tree systems can be grouped or spaced based on species composition or other designated criteria. The seed-tree and shelterwood component used in these systems can be short- (removed early in the life of the regenerated stand, 30 yr or less) or long-lived (left on the site through the life of the regenerated stand). However, for use in most production situations, prompt removal of seed and shelter trees, once regeneration is established, is preferred. The longer the overstory remains, the more likely tolerant species will develop and compete with the preferred intolerant species.

Uneven-Aged systems

From a timber management perspective, uneven-aged systems are most likely applicable only on limited sites in which a frequent and continual flow of wood products would be desirable. Uneven-aged systems, both in groups and individual trees, have been used successfully in the ponderosa pine PVTs (Shepperd and Battaglia 2002). However, because these systems perpetuate late-seral species or those favored with closed canopy conditions, uneven-aged systems in most situations would not be preferred for production forestry. However, uneven-aged systems do not have applicability on small scales such as for non-industrial private landowners (Graham and Smith 1983, Graham et al. 1999a)

SITE PREPARATION

The most important component of site preparation is to prepare sites to meet sound and well thought-out objectives. A prescription provides the plan on the kind, composition, and amount of regeneration desired. This plan includes describing seedbed and/or planting site requirements along with the amount, and species (kind) of competing vegetation inherent to the site and its expected response to fire, mechanical, or chemical disturbance. Potential vegetation, habitat types or similar vegetation classifications usually offer excellent descriptions of ground-level vegetation and the seral stage of forest development it in which it commonly occurs (Daubenmire and Daubenmire 1968, Pfister et al.1977, Cooper et al. 1991). In addition, these classifications provide insight into species that may be absent preharvest and their expected response to disturbance.

Ideally, silvicultural systems should be designed to minimize competing vegetation without using expensive control measures. However, disposal of the slash left after yarding also affects soil compaction and soil organic content (Harvey et al. 1987, Page-Dumroese et al. 1997). Broadcast burning is commonly used to prepare sites throughout the Inland Northwest but slash is also burned after machine piling (fig. 11). Whatever method is used, the objectives of site preparation commonly include reducing fire hazard, providing planting access, and controlling competing vegetation (Baumgartner 1982 Lotan 1986).

In cold, dry, and moist forests, the amount of moisture available to young trees during the summer months is

Figure 11—A helicopter igniting a prescribed fire in a clearcut near Sandpoint Idaho. The fire was ignited in the evening ensuring that moisture contents in the lower duff were above 100% and the fine fuel moisture contents were conducive for producing a low severity fire.

almost always the single most important determinant of whether a planted seedling will survive and the rate at which this seedling will grow (Cleary and Greaves 1976). Of course not all water in a soil profile will be available to regenerated trees. Some will percolate out of the soil profile, some will evaporate, and much will be used by comp e t i n g vegetation. Effective site preparation can dramatically increase plantation survival and development. Powers and Reynolds (1999), for example, showed that by completely removing competing vegetation, ponderosa pine volume growth was 400 percent greater 10 years later when compared to tree growth on areas with competing vegetation.

Figure 12—A Salmon blade can be used to effectively prepare sites subject to pine grass competition yet still conserve the nutrient-rich surface soil layers.

Mechanical Preparation

Depending on soils and steepness of slope, timely and proper site preparation most often can be accomplished by using machinery. This usually assures excellent site preparation even with sprouting and herbicide resistant species. For example, *Ceanothus* spp. is often effectively controlled mechanically since this method does not heat scarify seeds stored in the forest floor. Depending on equipment and soil conditions, most machines (except cable machines) can safely and effectively operate on slopes with gradients less than 30 to 40 percent (Miller 1986a). Machine methods include rakes pulled or pushed by tractors, special dozer blades, and cable scarifiers to name a few (Lowman 1986). Very often the site preparation is accomplished simultaneously with reducing the wildfire hazard. In general, machines capable of separating slash of different sizes, often called "grapple machines", displace less soil than rakes attached to the front of tractors; thus the use of grapple machines can help conserve and protect soil layers (Graham et al. 1994a).

Competition from pine grass and other sod-forming grasses present different germination and planting problems than shrub competition. A mechanical option that has shown success for both planting and seed germination is a tractor-mounted rake that exposes mineral soil and prepares planting sites yet does not displace the soil. The machine uses a plow shear blade that rolls the sod, exposes the grass roots, and decreases its survivability, and exposes mineral soil (MTDC 1988) (fig. 12).

In contrast to machinery in the form of tractors, excavators, and other machines, hand tools at the time of planting

are frequently used (Lowman 1986). Scalping or removing competing vegetation using hoes, shovels, hodads, or other hand-tools have been shown to be effective in grass communities. Scalps should be at least two feet in diameter and preferably larger (Miller 1986a). Compared to machinery, hand scalping offers more latitude for locating favorable planting sites. That is, locating sites with deep organic rich soil, away from aggressive competing vegetation, or behind logs that can provide shelter and protection. Site preparation (scalping) should be differentiated from clearing debris prior to opening a planting hole. Clearing is requisite to ensure that organic material (sticks, litter, etc) that may interfere with root to soil contact does not fall into the hole during planting. This can often be accomplished in situations in which soil is covered by litter, which can be cleared, exposing soil often covered with rich humus and fermentation layers. No matter which method of the site preparation used, it is critical that the soil is protected and maintained.

The use of machinery to prepare sites for regeneration is always a compromise between creating soil conditions for regeneration while maintaining and preserving soil productivity (fig. 12). The greatest limitations of mechanical site preparation are slope angle, soil compaction and displacement. As stated earlier, most early-seral species easily germinate and develop on the mineral soil that can readily be exposed by mechanical methods (Haig et al. 1941). A favored micro-site for natural regeneration or for artificial regeneration is one that prepares a weed-free planting/germination spot yet is in proximity to or conserves the nutrient- and water-holding surface organic layers (Graham et al. 1989, Graham et al. 1994a, Graham et al. 1995).

Fire

Fire can reduce fine fuels, prepare germination surfaces, reduce competing vegetation, preserve surface organic layers, and maintain appropriate amounts of coarse woody debris (fig. 11). However, unless fuel and weather conditions are appropriate, fire can create conditions adverse for regeneration and impair soil productivity (Debano 1991, Hungerford et al. 1991). The amount of forest floor consumed by a fire is dependent on its moisture content, particularly in the lower humus and fermentation layers. If the moisture content of these layers exceeds 100 percent when a fire occurs, the majority of litter and fine fuels (≤ 3 inches) do not burn and thus, are generally conserved (Ryan 1982). Under these moisture conditions, nutrients (such as P, N, K) can condense in the humus and fermentation layers and, therefore, are not lost from the site (Harvey et al. 1989). The temperatures at the mineral soil/organic layer interface usually do not exceed 300° C, the temperature at which N is volatilized (Hungerford et al. 1991). At this temperature, water-repellent layers are also less likely to

Figure 13—Shrubs can respond vigorously to prescribed fire.

occur even in coarse-textured soils. Burning when the lower humus layers are moist facilitates consumption of fine fuels, maintenance of CWD levels, and often results in exposure of micro-sites for planting and/or seed germination.

Some ground-level vegetation responds vigorously to heat such as *Ceanothus* spp. with its seed buried in the forest floor. Also, many ground-level species resprout aggressively in response to fire (fig. 13). Therefore, the amount, kind, and severity of fire used to prepare sites needs to be applied with an understanding of the expected response of competing vegetation for a given forest, PVT, and biophysical setting (Baumgartner et al. 1986, 1989).

Chemical Preparation

Chemicals are a very viable technique for site preparation. In particular, herbicides can target specific species or life forms and protect the surface soil layers that can be harmed by both mechanical and fire site preparation techniques. The latitude of site and weather conditions for applying herbicides may be less operationally restrictive than either fire or mechanical methods and, depending on the circumstance, the results may be more cost effective than using either of the other two methods (Baumgartner et al. 1986).

For the optimum growth of plantations, control of competing vegetation is essential. In the dry forests particularly (depending on the PVT), if ground-level vegetation is present before the regeneration harvest is applied, it will likely compete with future seedlings. Therefore, approximately

two years prior to the harvest, an herbicide treatment an be applied to target the shrubby vegetation. Growing in the understory of a high forest canopy, shrubs tend to develop in sun-flecks, be single stemmed, spindly, and weak, thus making them highly susceptible to control by herbicide. When the regeneration harvest is applied, the ground-level vegetation will be absent providing ample planting sites. In contrast, if the chemical treatment is applied after the harvest treatment, ground-level vegetation will most likely be the risk of greater injury to the plantation, delaying the site preparation benefits.

Herbicides used for shrub control in forests include 2,4-D, glyphosate, imazapyr, picloram and triclopyr. To control grasses and forbs, atrizine, 2,4-D, sulfometuron, and hexazinone are suggested (Coop 2004). However, specific time of application and effectiveness of herbicide to affect targeted vegetation varies. Specific details on application and target species are available through the Pacific Northwest 2004 Weed Management Handbook (Coop 2004).

An area mechanically prepared or burned, may provide an ideal setting for the germination, establishment, and development of tree seedlings, but these same conditions are an ideal habitat for weeds (fig. 13). Weeds will quickly develop and compete with the planted seedlings for water, nutrients, occasionally light, and under some circumstances they may be allelopathic, which can further retard seedling development (Ferguson 1991). Pre-emergent herbicides can be applied to the surface of the planting spot such as hexazanone, sulfometuron, metsulfuron, and atrazine products to control competing vegetation as it develops. It is very important to use the right chemical and the right amount to insure only the weed species and not the planted seedlings are affected. For example, sulfometuron and atrazine are poor choices to use when planting ponderosa pine and western larch, respectively (see Baumgartner et al. 1986 and Coop 2004 for discussions on herbicides and their appropriate efficient, and effective use).

REGENERATION

A requirement for the successful application of a silvicultural system is the timeliness of regeneration, its amount and composition. Environments conducive to seedling establishment can be directly influenced by the amount and composition of over-story retained (seed tree, shelterwood selection) and the intensity and extent of site preparation (mechanical, fire, chemical).

Natural Regeneration

The early-seral and/or preferred species for production forestry, e.g., ponderosa pine, lodgepole pine, western larch, Douglas-fir, and western white pine, readily regenerate naturally (Haig et al. 1941, Pearson 1950). Depending on the forest type and the PVT, natural regeneration may be a viable alternative in many settings using a variety of silvicultural systems. However, less control of the timing, amount, density, and consistency of plantation establishment is possible with natural regeneration compared to artificial regeneration.

The cheapest and most site-adapted regeneration can be achieved through natural regeneration. On ponderosa pine and Douglas-fir PVTs, ponderosa pine and Douglas-fir can be naturally regenerated if appropriate site preparation is accomplished (Shearer and Schmidt 1991, Shepperd and Battaglia. 2002). However, many factors such as seed crop frequency and size, animal predation on the seed, weather damage to seed, and the timing and proper seedbed preparation can make the accomplishment of successful regeneration easier said than done (Haig et al. 1941, Pearson 1950). For example, if the site preparation is not well timed with the production of seed, adequate germination substrate and establishment sites may not be available when seed is produced by the desired species. Weather favoring the regeneration might not occur even if the site preparation and seed crops were well coordinated. Western larch is a case in point. A weather event such as a frost injuring flowers or unexpected cold weather hampering germination can spoil the best-laid plans (Graham et al. 1995a).

Species vary widely in seed production and dissemination (Haig et al. 1941). Western redcedar and western hemlock produce larger and more frequent seed crops than most of their associates. For example, the interval between good seed crops in western larch is highly variable and is often greater than 10 years. The other tree species usually produce good seed crops at less than 5 year intervals. For all tree species, wind plays a major role in seed dissemination. Only lodgepole pine exhibits cone serotiny and the degree of serotiny present is variable within the cold forests (Lotan 1973). Mineral soil and burned-over surfaces tend to supply good soil-to-seed contact, maintain moisture levels conducive to seed germination, plus supply water to the roots as they develop. In the Northern Rocky Mountains, temperature tends to be one of the most critical factors for germination. Minimum soil temperature of 51° F is needed and temperatures between 71° and 81° F are preferred (Haig et al. 1941). Organic seedbeds tend to lose soil moisture faster than roots can develop thereby restricting seedling establishment. Douglas-fir, ponderosa pine, western white pine, and lodgepole pine have intermediate germination rates while western larch and grand fir have low germination rates. In addition, western hemlock and western redcedar usually have high seed germination rates and occasionally reproduce by sprouting. Because these species regenerate easily, they can interfere with the regeneration and development of preferred early-seral species.

In moist forests, it is critical to understand the role blister rust plays in stand development especially when using natural regeneration. Shelterwoods can be used to naturally regenerate western white pine and a large proportion of these seedlings would be susceptible to blister rust (Graham et al.1994b). However, Hoff et al. (1976) reported that over 19 percent of natural regeneration in stands suffering high losses from blister rust could be resistant to the disease (figs. 3, 10). Therefore, when western white pine regeneration is abundant (thousands of trees per acre), a number of the seedlings is likely resistant to white pine blister rust. Nevertheless, distinguishing rust resistant from nonresistant seedlings becomes problematic when the stands are cleaned (precommercial thinning to alter species composition or improve stand condition). The resistance level will not approach that of trees produced in improvement programs but there is an excellent chance that some of these naturally regenerated trees will survive and grow well enough to produce commercial products and provide genetic diversity in western white pine (Graham et al. 1994b Fins et al. 2001) (See section on enhancing the survivability of white pine through pruning).

Table 1—The genetic differentiation among populations of tree species. Adaptation of species is based on the environmental interval by which populations must be separated before there is a reasonable assurance that the populations are genetically different (Rehfeldt 1994)

| Species | Environmental Interval | | Adaptation |
	Elevation Range (ft)	Frost Free Days	
Douglas-fir	650	18	Specialist
Lodgepole pine	720	20	Specialist
Engelmann spruce	1215	33	Intermediate
Ponderosa pine	1380	38	Intermediate
Western larch	1480	40	Intermediate
Western redcedar	1970	54	Generalist
Western white pine	none	~90	Generalist

Artificial Regeneration

Because of the uncertainty of natural regeneration, artificial regeneration often provides more assurance and options for timely stand establishment and species composition, micro-site selection, tree density, and horizontal tree distribution. In addition, artificial regeneration offers opportunities to plant improved stock. Currently (2005), improved planting stock is available for western white pine, lodgepole pine, western larch, Douglas-fir, and ponderosa pine. The improvement developed in breeding programs includes improved tree growth, increased disease resistance, increased cold hardiness, and improved tree form compared to trees naturally regenerated.

However, care needs to be exercised to ensure that trees planted are ecologically adapted to the sites. For example, the environmental interval in elevation in which ponderosa pine populations show habitat specificity is approximately 1380 feet or 38 frost-free days (Table 1). In contrast, no habitat specificity in elevation has been found for western white pine and the habitat specificity interval in frost-free days is 90. The narrowest habitat specificity for any Rocky Mountain conifer occurs with Douglas-fir which has an environmental interval of 650 feet in elevation or 18 frost-free days (Table 1) (Rehfeldt 1994). Therefore, Douglas-fir is considered a specialist and western white pine a generalist in their species' adaptability to sites. Beginning in the early 1900s and in earnest during the 1930s during the Civilian Conservation Corp era, a major ecological mistake was planting off-site (seedlings not adapted to their environment) ponderosa pine seedlings throughout the West. Today, these off-site plantings are often dying from insects and disease and producing malformed trees. Unfortunately, a maladapted forest is being propagated, thus showing why it is critical that seedlings be ecologically matched to the site on which they are planted (Rehfeldt 1994).

Probably no other species is more suited to artificial regeneration than western white pine because of the good nursery and planting practices that have been developed over the last 100 years. With the introduction of blister rust from Europe in the early 1900s millions of white pine were killed. When all control efforts (e.g., killing the alternate host Ribes spp., fungicide application) failed, the future of western white pine management in the western United States appeared bleak (Ketcham et al. 1968). By 1950, the Office of Blister Rust Control, Northern Region of the USDA Forest Service, USDA Forest Service Northern Rocky Mountain Forest and Range Experiment Station, and the USDA Forest Service, Pacific Southwest Forest and Range Experiment Station began a program to develop rust-resistant western white pine. By 1985, seed orchards were producing a second-generation of western white pine that were 65+ percent resistant to the disease (a portion of the trees do get infected but survive) (Bingham 1983). The goal of the white pine tree improvement program was to increase its' resistance to blister rust and to accomplish this by using multiple genes, thus minimizing potential disease mutations (Fins et al. 2001). With this multi-gene approach the rust may infect and even kill some trees, but many trees, even if they become infected, continue to survive and grow to a saw timber rotation of 60 to 80 years (Graham et al. 1994b) (figs 2, 3, 9, 10).

In general, there are two types of seedlings that are planted, bare-root and container grown, and both have their place in production forestry. Bare-root seedlings are usually lifted from the nursery beds in the early spring for planting in the spring. Depending upon the silvicultural method and site preparation, a different size and age of seedlings can be specified. In addition, a key characteristic of a proper root-to-shoot ratio can be specified. Generally, seedlings less than three years old can readily be planted. Large-sized seedlings often offer a higher success of establishment compared to smaller seedlings because of their ability to rndure competing vegetation, damage from animals, or harshness of site. Seedlings with large diameters may be specified for areas prone to vegetation, woody debris or snow potentially pushing over small seed- lings (Schubert and Adams 1971, Baumgartner and Boyd 1976, Cleary et al. 1978).

Great strides have occurred in recent years in producing container-grown seedlings that meet a wide range of specifications. This can be accomplished by controlled growing conditions and by different sized and treated containers. In addition to a variety of seedling specifications, seedlings can be produced to plant during different planting cycles determined by the site and management objectives. As with most bare-root seedlings, container seedlings are most often planted in the spring but they can also be grown for planting in the fall (Landis et al. 1990, Landis et al. 1992).

Under special circumstances, seedlings can be planted in the summer if they are properly conditioned. Such situations exist when high elevation areas are not available to plant during the spring or fall because of snow. In the greenhouse, seedlings can be artificially moved through a growth cycle from bud burst through shoot elongation and bud set in a matter of weeks. By doing so, dormant seedlings can be planted during the summer (Landis et al. 1990, Landis et al. 1992).

Even though seedling production from seed collection through planting has been investigated and refined for 100 years, the successful completion of the entire regeneration process is often problematic. Seedlings well prepared in the nursery/greenhouse need to be handled with utmost care while in storage and on the planting site to ensure a dormant seedling is planted (Schubert and Adams 1971, Baumgartner and Boyd 1976, Cleary et al. 1978).

We suggest that choosing desirable micro-site positions that offer protection, have organic matter rich soil, and are free of competing vegetation is preferable to planting on a rigid grid. In most production operations and to minimize future tending operations, 200 to 250 trees per acre would suffice. A preferred micro-site for planting trees includes: places with adequate soil moisture, soil temperatures exceeding 40° F, uniform root-to-soil contact, and no soil impediments that would distort roots (e.g., produce J-rooted seedlings). In high organic soils, container-grown stock appears to do better than bare-root stock because root-to-soil contact can be more readily achieved (Schubert and Adams 1971, Baumgartner and Boyd 1976, Cleary et al. 1978).

Animal Damage

A variety of animals (insects, rodents, omnivores, ungulates, and livestock) may damage tree seedlings by eating, browsing, trampling, and breaking limbs. Animals including, but not limited to, porcupines (*Erethizon dorsatum*), pocket gophers (*Thomomys* spp.), cattle, sheep, hares (*Lepus* spp. and *Sylvilagus* spp.), black bear (*Ursus ameri-canus*), deer (*Odocoileus* spp.), and elk (*Cervus* spp.) can damage seedlings of most western tree species. The potential for damage should be thoroughly evaluated prior to implementing the silvicultural system (Kingery and Graham 1991, Knapp and Brodie 1992).

A variety of preventive and remedial techniques have been tested with mixed results. These have included providing an alternative food source or planting unpalatable tree species (Black and Lawrence 1992), modifying habitat to disfavor specific browsing animals, physically or chemically protecting tree seedlings, frightening browsers away, and trapping or killing browsing threats. Unfortunately, one method does not solve all browsing problems. Many recommend large planting stock because it typically is less vulnerable to animal damage (Loucks et al. 1990, Cafferata 1992, Graham et al. 1992, Marsh and Steele 1992). Nolte (2003a) suggested using a five-step process to reduce the effects of animal damage: 1) assess the severity and potential damage if no action is taken, 2) evaluate the feasibility of alleviating the problem, 3) develop a strategy prior to browse damage prevention measures, 4) implement a program, and 5) monitor the consequences. The preferred approach will depend on the results from site-specific monitoring and the most effective treatment may require integrating several methods within the silvicultural system.

Physical protection of seedlings with polypropylene mesh tubes is an option and appears to be successful in some cases (Black and Lawrence 1992). Fencing areas to keep livestock out can be effective, but expense limits its use (Nolte 2003b). Other forms of physical deterrents might be possible. Graham et al. (1992) noted that seedling damage from livestock fell below 10 percent when coarse woody debris (> 3.0 inches in diameter) was greater than 30 tons per acre. In some cases, minimizing disturbance avoids creating habitat that may increase pocket gopher populations (Marsh and Steele 1992). For example, the grasses that exist on a site can be killed using hexazanone (most commonly Velpar®), and this, in turn, will dissuade gopher use. Pocket gopher predation on planted seedlings is highest the first summer that the trees are planted and the first two winters (Ferguson 1999). Studies have shown that controlling pocket gopher populations with strychnine baiting poses relatively little risk to non-target species (Arjo

2003) but the effects of removal may be short-lived since replacement animals usually occupy the vacant habitat, thus necessitating the repeated application of treatments for maximum efficacy.

FOREST TENDING

The silvicultural system does not end with the regeneration treatment (i.e., clearcut, seed-tree, etc.). After a stand is regenerated or entered, stand tending is generally warranted to ensure the desired stand structures and compositions are developed and maintained (Fisher 1988). Tending activities (i.e., thinning, cleaning, weeding, liberation (overstory removal), sanitation, and fertilization) can occur at a variety of time intervals and intensities depending on forest type, PVT, species present, and past stand development. Release of species after periods of crowding or suppression is directly related to the length and vigor of the crown (McCaughey and Ferguson 1988, Ferguson 1994). Generally, shade intolerant species respond well to release after suppression and intolerant species respond poorly. Lodgepole pine, which often regenerates prolifically, is prone to stagnation early in its development, making later release cuttings less effective (Johnstone and Cole 1988). Therefore, stand tending is an integral part of both even-aged and uneven-aged silvicultural systems. Treatments can occur within all canopy levels and many intermediate treatments can produce forest products (Graham et al. 1999b).

In contrast to not acquiring enough regeneration, the issue in many forests is excessive regeneration that makes weeding and cleaning plantations (natural stands) essential for satisfactory development. For example, in the ponderosa pine forests of the Black Hills in South Dakota, ponderosa pine regeneration is often so prolific it creates a fire hazard and compromises future stand development options (Shepperd and Battaglia 2002). Similarly, in the cold forests, over-abundant lodgepole pine regeneration is often the norm, again making tending operations imperative if the stands are going to develop productively (Johnstone and Cole 1988) (fig. 4). Within the moist forests, natural regeneration is often plentiful making cleaning and weeding operations a necessity (Haig et al. 1941, Deitschman and Pfister 1973 Graham 1988) (fig. 9).

Weedings
Weedings occur during the sapling stage of stand development to remove competitive vegetation, such as specific trees or shrubs, and other vegetation that may compete with crop trees (Smith et al. 1997, Helms 1988). Weedings tend to be applied before or simultaneously with cleanings (treatments aimed at redistributing stand growth to selected stems). Most often weedings are essential in mixed-species stands and those prone to robust development of mid– and late–seral trees or when grass or shrub development interferes with stand development (Deitschman and Pfister 1973, Miller 1986b). In dry forests, this often occurs where grand fir and/or white fir, Douglas-fir, ninebark, or *Ceanothus* spp. tend to aggressively compete with ponderosa pine. Similarly, in the moist forests, grand fir, western hemlock, and alder are frequently removed to favor western white pine and western larch. Weedings can be accomplished most often mechanically or chemically and, in rare situations, fire can be used to weed a plantation of unwanted competing vegetation (Saveland and Neuenschwander 1988).

Chemical
Frequently, within a year or two after plantation establishment, even on settings where the competing vegetation was removed during site preparation, weeds tend to return and interfere with seedling development (Petersen 1986). Weeding young stands with herbicides is a viable alternative on many settings. However, specific time of application and effectiveness of the herbicide to affect targeted vegetation varies (specific details on application and target species are available through the Pacific Northwest 2004 Weed Management Handbook (Coop 2004). The actual timing of when weeds interfere with tree growth depends on forest type, PVT (weed species present and their ability to colonize or survive), type and success of the site preparation applied (Noste and Bushey 1987, Baumgartner et al. 1986). Herbicides that can be applied over the top of established seedlings and have been successful in controlling weeds include several hexazanone products (e.g., Velpar®, Pronone®). These herbicides are effective in removing weeds without damaging most conifers except western larch. Sulfometuron (Oust®) also removes weeds readily but is not preferred for use with ponderosa pine because of potential tree damage. Granular herbicides can be applied with a "weedometer" that distributes herbicides within a 3 to 5 foot radius of seedlings. Glyphosate (Roundup®, Accord®) can be directionally applied to weeds between trees and shields (e.g., PVC-plastic) can be used to apply herbicides within close proximity of seedlings.

Within 4 to 6 years on some PVTs, tall shrubs (e.g., maple, alder, willow) not controlled by a pre-harvest herbicide, readily sprout and often aggressively compete with planted trees (Lotan 1986). Imazapyr (a compound in Arsenal®, Chopper® and Onestep®) can be aerially (helicopter) or hand (backpack sprayer) applied to control this high shrub competition. Glyphosate, applied as a directed spray, can be used to control tall shrub competition as well as hexazanone, applied in the form of Pronone®. In northeastern Oregon, Oester et al. (1995), found that hexazanone, applied as a spot or broadcast spray, increased both survival and growth of planted ponderosa pine. It has been found to be more effective (more toxic) at controlling weeds when it is applied in conjunction with N fertilizers compared to applying the herbicide alone. When applied in this fashion, Pronone® has been found to be toxic to conifers even though the dose was believed to be safe. Presumably, the addition of N makes both the conifers and weeds grow later in the growing season thus making them both vulnerable to the herbicide. The most effective combination of N fertilizer and Pronone® will probably use smaller herbicide dosages, such as only ½ to ¾ of the amount that would be used when applied by itself. The combination of fertilization and weed control should enable stands to develop more quickily than would occur after the application of a single treatment.

Most conifers have a high tolerance for hexazanone and imazapyr, while most grasses and woody (dicot) species are very susceptible. Western larch, however, is very susceptible to damage from both of these herbicides. In most settings, a directed application of gyphosate using a backpack sprayer will control unwanted vegetation in western larch stands. The exact weeding approach and chemicals used will depend on the forest, PVT, biophysical setting, and nature of the competing vegetation (e.g., life form, species, size, distribution) (Coop 2004).

Precommercial Thinning (Cleaning)

Precommercial thinnings are applied during the sapling stage of stand development where specific trees are kept and others are removed so that growth of selected stems is favored (Smith et al. 1997).

In general, all of the early-seral species (ponderosa pine, lodgepole pine, western white pine western larch, and Douglas-fir) respond positively to precommercial thinning (Schmidt 1988). Of course, the magnitude of the response is predicated on the PVT and the biophysical setting. However, with judicial control of planting densities, the need for thinning to redistribute growth to selected trees should be minimized. In stands with prolific natural regeneration (such as may occur with western larch, western white pine, lodgepole pine, and on some sites, Douglas-fir and ponderosa pine), precommercial thinning is necessary to distribute the site's growth potential to a manageable number of trees that will result in future tree sizes consistent with predicted markets for wood products (Schmidt 1988).

Moist Forests

Within the moist forest, the most important period in the life of either a plantation or a natural stand is between 10 and 30 years. Prior to this time, stand densities have minimal impact on tree development. During this 10- to 30-year period, species composition and future stand dynamics are largely determined. Past this age, stand improvement can be accomplished only at high expense and at a heavy sacrifice to growing stock (Davis 1942). Western white pine over 30 years old will respond to release, but the required wide tree spacings will reduce stand yields (Deitschman 1966). Four hundred trees per acre at age 30 appear to be a good goal. These densities provide for good diameter growth, good volume production, and future thinning opportunities. The timing of cleaning a western white pine stand is a compromise impacted by waiting as long as possible to allow blister rust to be fully expressed, maintaining canopy closure to discourage *Ribes* spp. and competing conifer regeneration, and to treat stands early as possible so as to not create an unmanageable fire hazard (abundance of fine fuels) (Graham 1988).

Western larch also readily responds to precommercial thinnings at 10- to 15 –years of age (Schmidt and Seidel 1988). Though expensive, thinning of extremely dense stands, containing 1,000 to 25,000 stems per acre, will respond well to thinning. During these treatments. mistletoe can also be removed from the stand. Western larch benefits greatly from early thinning because it relieves overstocking and allows larch to capitalize on its rapid juvenile growth. Schmidt and Seidel (1988) suggest that stocking levels for western larch range between 45 and 75 percent of normal stocking or in the range of 400 trees per acre or less. Thinning dense stands transfers growth to fewer numbers of rapidly growing trees, thus maintaining good vigor and crown development, increasing resistance to wind, snow, and insects, and permitting more uniform diameter growth. Judicious thinning regimes can result in shorter rotations and increased merchantable yields. Target Douglas-fir densities also fall in the range of 400 trees per acre in precommercial thinnings in the moist forests (Lotan et al. 1988). It appears that the greatest benefit from thinning in mixed stands of western white pine and associates is to improve stand and tree quality. Cleanings do not increase overall volume production, but do increase future value of stands by concentrating growth on fewer, selected better quality trees.

Western White Pine Pruning—Most lethal blister rust infections occur in the lower crown when trees are quite young (≈15 years). Pruning the lower branches of white

Figure 14—A precommercial thinning (cleaning) in a sapling-sized ponderosa pine stand. Note the large amounts of fuel produced, which is a common occurrence, and needs to be decreased to protect the stand from severe wild-fire.

pines to a height of 8 to 10 feet, but not reducing the live-crown ratio to less than 50 percent, appears to offer the tree some protection from blister rust infection while not sub-stantially reducing tree growth rates. In addition, removal of any branches with cankers greater than 6 inches from the bole greatly increases the chances of the tree surviving to produce a commercial product. Schwandt et al. (1994) showed that by cleaning western white pine stands (10 to 18 years old) to a spacing of approximately 10 feet by 10 feet and pruning the lower branches, the value (1992 prices) per acre (22 years later) of the white pine doubled in the treated stands ($2000 per acre) compared to that of untreated stands ($1000 per acre).

Cold Forests

Natural stands of lodgepole pine, which commonly regen-erate following wildfire, are frequently dense (Johnstone 1985, Johnstone and Cole 1988). Likewise, stands that regenerate following harvest and site preparation (scarifica-tion and/or prescribed fire) often establish in dense clumps. Even when lodgepole pine is planted or cleaned at an early age, ingress of seedlings may result in denser stand condi-tions than desired. Lodgepole pine does not self-thin well on any PVT; thus without treatment dense stands tend to remain dense. In these situations, tree growth is suppressed and stands are subject to heavy mortality from snow and wind. Consequently, stand yields will be well below the capacity of the site.

Determining thinning densities for all species and, in particular lodgepole pine, the optimum management density is a tradeoff between tree size and stand volume objectives. Young lodgepole pine responds more readily to density reductions compared to old trees (Murphy et al. 1999). Merchantable cubic volume production per unit area is maximized at relatively high ($\approx$1000 trees per acre) initial stand densities. A single precommercial thin ($\approx$400 trees per acre) at age 20 on many sites would produce commer-cial yields by age 40 compared to never producing a com-mercial product by age 120 years without the treatment (Cole and Edminster 1985). However, for most management considerations, cutting cycles of 30 years seem feasible and offer commercial yields at several points during the rotation ($\approx$ 120 years).

Dry Forests

Within the dry forests, the upper level management zone for Douglas-fir approaches $\approx$2000 trees per acre of 3 inch diameter trees. However, a more realistic precommercial thinning density would approximate 450 trees per acre and, of course, these estimates would be predicated on the future management options and product needs. A target of 140 to 220 ft^2 of basal area and 60 to 100 trees per acre would be the range of tree densities that would be preferred for most Douglas-fir settings (Lotan et al. 1988).

The upper management zone (tree density) for ponderosa pine is, for the most part, roughly based on threshold levels of risk for bark beetle attacks. The lower level of stocking for ponderosa pine is largely determined on the stand density in which regeneration is likely to occur (fig. 14). The highest stand densities for precommercial thinning would be in the range of 700 trees per acre and the minimum values would be in the range of 200 trees per acre. Target stand densities should not exceed 150 ft^2 of basal area and minimums in the range of 50 ft^2 would suffice in most situations (Edminster 1988). As with other species, these values would be based on the PVT, biophysical setting, management objectives, and the markets available for products. Significant declines in volume production will be realized with low residual stand densities. If rapid development of merchantable–sized material is a goal, than the lower residual stand densities are desirable. On lower productivity sites, more than one precommercial thinning may be required to maintain the desired stand structures. Low initial stand densities, either through planting or cleaning, may greatly influence thinning opportunities.

Thinnings

Beyond the sapling stage, thinnings redistribute growth potential to fewer trees leaving stands with the desired structure and composition. Even though thinning from below is the most common method, there are other methods that have applicability depending on the forest, PVT, and management objectives and desires of the landowner. Low (thinning from below), crown (thinning from above), selection (diameter-limit thinning), free thinning, and mechanical thinning all have application in the moist, cold, and dry forests of the Inland Northwest (Nyland 2002, Smith et al. 1997).

Low thinning is when trees are removed from the lower canopy, leaving large trees to occupy the site. This method mimics mortality caused by inter-tree competition or surface fires and concentrates site growth potential on dominant trees. Low thinnings primarily remove intermediate and suppressed trees, but heavy thinnings can also remove many in the codominant crown class. Low thinnings not only remove understory canopies but can also alter species compositions. Usually, different tree species have characteristic development rates that result in individual species dominating specific canopy layers. For example, in dry forests, ponderosa pine primarily occupies the dominant canopy layers, whereas shade-tolerant grand fir, white fir, or Douglas-fir occupy the intermediate and suppressed layers. A low thinning in these stands therefore favors the development of the dominant and codominant ponderosa pine. Depending on the desired stand structure, low thinnings can remove few to many trees. Also, thinnings need not create regular spacings but rather can vary both the number and degree of clumping of residual trees.

Crown thinning, or thinning from above, reduces crowding within the main canopy. Dominant and codominant trees are removed to favor residual trees in these same classes. This method is used to remove selected trees in the dominant and codominant crown classes that are competing with more desirable trees (Nyland 2002). Selection thinning removes dominant trees to favor smaller trees. This method is often applied by removing trees greater than a certain diameter. Diameter-limit cuts that continually remove the largest trees may well be dysgenetic and can be a disguise for high grading (removing trees of high economic value without concern for future stand development). By maximizing removal of the current value from a stand, future options may be limited and the only recourse for the future may be to regenerate. Stand structures and species compositions created by using selection thinning are limited and, in general, favor shade-tolerant species or trees occupying the intermediate and suppressed crown classes. Often the stands created by selection thinnings are prone to epidemics of insects and diseases. Compared to the other thinning methods, selection thinning is less useful in these forests because of the limited stand structures and compositions it creates.

Free thinning, sometimes called crop-tree thinning, primarily releases selected trees. This method favors specific trees, whereas the remainder of the stand goes untreated. Depending on what is presented in various portions of a stand (tree spacing, species, vertical structure, etc.), the thinning criteria can be highly flexible and produces stands with large amounts of diversity. It can be used in any of the crown classes for releasing specific trees. This method has the most flexibility for creating various stand structures and compositions.

Mechanical thinning removes trees based on specified spatial arrangements (Nyland 2002). This method is often applied in plantations where every other row or every other tree in a row is removed. Such a rigid thinning prescription

Figure 15—Helicopters can be used to apply nitrogen fertilizer (urea pellets).

Fertilization

As stated earlier, nitrogen (N) is the most limiting nutrient in the Inland Northwest and the greatest growth response comes from the addition of N (fig. 15). The combination of stand density control, along with the application of N, appears to be the best approach for managing young stands and accelerating their growth and crown development (Graham and Tonn 1979, Weetman et al. 1985, Moore 1988, Moore et al. 1991)

Within the dry forests, ponderosa pine shows a strong linear response up to approximately 400 pounds of N per acre. Plantations with weed control can show twice the fertilization response as unweeded plantations (Powers et al. 1988). Powers (1988) found that volume growth was nearly four times greater with weeding than no treatment but the combination of fertilization and weeding produced volume growth nine times greater than untreated stands. Similarly, Douglas-fir can be rather responsive to fertilization and response varies by stand density, soil parent material and pre treatment N. Two-hundred pounds per acre appears to be a good treatment and the response appears to last about 6 years but most likely depends on stand density (Moore 1988).

Within the cold forests, lodgepole pine grows on some rather infertile sites making it respond dramatically to improved nutrition, especially following precommercial thinning (Weetman 1988). Some evidence suggests that thinning, along with fertilization, increases lodgepole pine's resistance to attack by mountain pine beetle. Also fertilizing in the spring prior to bud burst seems to provide the best response. Hamilton and Christie (1971) showed that mean annual increments of 172 to 214 ft^3 per acre were achievable by fertilizing prior to crown closure.

There is a shift of nutrients from soil to tree, once the canopy is closed. As the tree's demands on soil rapidly decline following canopy closure, the nutrient cycles within the tree and through the tree-litter system are then fully charged (Weetman 1988). The cycle within the tree is based on the recovery and reuse of nutrients prior to the death of old tissues, including those of the leaf before abscission, and can be up to 85 percent efficient. However, the slow release of N from litter can lead to late-rotation ($\approx$ 60-80 years) N deficiency. In Oregon, fertilization of a 40-year-old closed-canopy lodgepole stand with 600 pounds of N per acre produced an 8-year volume response of 79 percent over a control stand and 370 pounds of N per acre produced a 3-year volume response of 87 percent over a control (Cochran 1979).

is easy to apply, but the stands created often lack diversity in either structure or composition. This method also resembles strip thinning, where a strip of trees is removed. Mechanical thinning may be well suited for timber production on uniform sites but has limited value for producing conditions that meet other resource values.

Use of herbicides following any form of thinning has rarely, if ever, occurred in an Inland Northwest forest. Nevertheless, there are some situations where past heavy thinning and/or patchy stocking have created stands with substantial biomass in competing vegetation. In these situations some form of herbicide application might be appropriate to maintain the desired forest structure. The repertoire of herbicides that might be considered at this point would be very similar to those applicable for use in stand weeding.

Within the moist forests, grand fir is very responsive to fertilization. The other species appear to be well adapted to the nutrition regime of the moist forests. This lack of fertilization response could possibly be related to the prevalence of the nutrient-rich volcanic soils. It also appears that western white pine has wide amplitude of N demand (Graham and Tonn 1979).

Most conifers favorably respond to the application of N at the time of planting, especially in concert with competitive vegetation control and proper site preparation. One option is to apply nutrients in the nursery which will provide robust root growth and enhance establishment when the seedlings are planted. Another opportune time to apply fertilizer is when a planting is about 5 years of age. Both of these fertilizer applications tend to further plantation establishment and increase juvenile tree growth.

STAND MANAGEMENT PLANNING

In the Inland Northwest, stand density studies, in particular thinning and precommercial thinning (cleaning and weeding), have been conducted for nearly 100 years. The concept of yield tables and normal stocking was produced from this research (Haig 1932). In some settings, the information in these yield tables are as valid today as the day they were produced (1930s). The concept of site index and the site index curves produced during that time are also still very applicable (in 2005).

However, today there are more precise and robust tools available for stand management planning. In particular, the Forest Vegetation Simulator (FVS), with variants available for areas across the United States, can be calibrated to a given site and species mix (Dixon 2002). FVS contains three major components: regeneration establishment, small tree development, and large tree development (Wykoff et al. 1982, Ferguson et al. 1986). These components can be related to the physical setting based on location, slope, aspect, elevation, PVT (e.g., habitat type, plant association), site index, and stand density index. The small-tree component can be calibrated to a specific site by inputting the periodic height increment of seedlings and saplings and the large-tree component can be calibrated by inputting the periodic diameter increment of large trees (Dixon 2002).

All three components work in concert to project stands into the future by incorporating various management activities including harvesting, site preparation, planting, thinning, pruning, and fertilization to name a few. The influence these and other stand treatments have on stand development can be projected into the future and displayed using a variety of stand metrics. Some of these include: stand diameter,

height and species distributions, total and merchantable volume distributions by species and diameter, volume accretion and mortality by diameter and species, total and merchantable removals by diameter and species, amount and characteristics of regeneration by species and individual tree characteristics. Several extensions are available to display attributes such as those related to wildfire and fuel treatments, root diseases, blister rust, bark beetles (e.g., Douglas-fir beetle (*Dendroctonus pseudotsugae*), mountain pine beetle (*Dendroctonus ponderosae*)), and defoliators such as the spruce budworm (*Choristoneura occidentalis*) and tussock moth (*Orgyia pseudotsugata*). The FVS output can be customized for desired time intervals, readily linked to economic analysis, and pictorially displayed using the Stand Visualization System. And, most importantly, FVS can be linked to geographic information systems making the management tool both spatially explicit and providing information at resolutions customized for each owner and application (Dixon 2002).

SUMMARY

Silvicultural systems describe the planned treatments through the life of a stand and are documented in a silvicultural prescription (Smith et al. 1997, Nyland 2002). By doing so, all of the treatments and their expected outcomes from stand establishment through tending activities are integrated and designed specifically for the biophysical environment presented and designed to meet the management objectives for that stand fulfilling the goals of the land-owner. Developing silvicultural systems for specific sites enables silviculturists to recognize the different vegetation complexes and successional pathways inherent to the moist, cold, and dry forests. In other words, one prescription does not fit all stands, especially for the different forests and environments intrinsic to the Inland Northwest.

In general, the early-seral species western white pine, western larch, ponderosa pine, Douglas-fir, and lodgepole pine, are the most resistant to native insects and diseases, the fastest growing, and the most aggressive establishers on the given potential vegetation type (PVT) on which they occur. For production forestry, the most appropriate regeneration method to apply in the cold forests is a properly applied clearcut. Likewise, within the moist forests, clearcutting provides good results but seed-tree and shelterwood regeneration methods are also applicable depending on the desired species mix and the biophysical setting (potential vegetation type, slope, aspect, current vegetation). Within the dry forests and especially on the grand fir and/or white fir potential vegetation types, clearcutting and seed-tree regeneration methods are very appropriate for the production of ponderosa pine and Douglas-fir. However, on the drier PVTs (e.g., dry Douglas-fir and ponderosa pine), a shelterwood system offers protection for the seedlings during the establishment period and may provide better results than the total or majority canopy removal of clearcutting and seed-tree methods. Two-stage shelterwoods (preparatory cut followed by a seed-cut) are suitable on ponderosa pine PVTs. Also, under most circumstances, selection systems are most appropriate for use on ponderosa pine PVTs for the production of wood crops.

The foundation of all forestry is the soil resource. The soil and its management in all phases of the silvicultural system need to be recognized. In many portions of the Inland Northwest, the residual soils are covered with volcanic ash and/or loess deposits enriching them and, more often than not, contain the majority of the site's productive potential. Frequently the biological and nutrient capital of a forest soil tends is near the surface of the mineral soil or integrated into surface organic layers. The humus, fermentation, and buried rotten wood layers in forest soils especially need to be recognized for their contribution to the nutrition of a site. In some settings, a major contributor to the organic matter on a site is coarse woody debris and it should be recognized and managed appropriately.

Because of the importance of soil and especially the nutrient rich (e.g., N) surface layers, we hope that the role these layers play in maintaining forest productivity will be more widely appreciated and suggest that these soil layers should only be scarified and/or scalped for a purpose. The contributions of ground-level vegetation to maintaining forest productivity in many settings should also be recognized. In particular, many shrubs and forbs fix N and ground-level vegetation can conserve both nutrients and soil in the face of catastrophic disturbances such as wildfire. Prescribed fire is an excellent tool for preparing sites for both natural and artificial regeneration, managing competing vegetation, and reducing the wildfire hazard. However, prescribed fire needs to be integrated into the silvicultural system and used judicially to produce desired conditions.

Each conifer species is ecologically adapted to a site and it is paramount that seedlings be adapted to the site on which they are planted. The ramifications of planting maladapted seedlings may not become apparent until the stand is developing disease and/or insect epidemics or the trees are malformed. Because the forest sites are so variable on a fine scale, all planting and tending activities should take advantage of the small differences inherent to a site and multi-species, multi-spacing plantings, cleanings, weedings, and thinnings should be considered and used where appropriate.

The benefits of using appropriate herbicides are often substantial when managing forests in the Inland Northwest. However, herbicides can be costly and environmentally difficult to use. Research continues on herbicide alternatives. For example, some research addresses herbicides that have not yet been tried in the Inland Northwest, some focuses on herbicide doses, some on formulation, and some on fertilizer-herbicide combinations. No doubt, herbicide use will continue to be a viable alternative for managing many Inland Northwest forests for wood production.

To facilitate stand and forest management planning, a calibrated, spatially explicit version of the Forest Vegetation Simulator (FVS) is an effective tool. FVS can be created and adapted to particular settings and provide realistic views of stand and forest management alternatives and their impacts on forest development over time. Various extensions of FVS are available for evaluating and displaying insect, disease, and wildfire impacts to a stand. Most importantly, FVS is a very appropriate way of integrating all aspects of stand establishment and tending into a silvicultural system and its use fosters documentation of silvicultural prescriptions.

LITERATURE CITED

Alexander, R.R.; Shearer, R.C.; Shepperd, W.D. 1990. Silvics of subalpine fir. In: Burns, R.M.; Honkala, B.H., tech. coords. Silvics of North America. Volume 1: Conifers. Agric. Handb. 654. Washington, DC: U.S. Department of Agriculture. 60-70.

Arjo, W.M. 2003. Is it a pocket gopher or mole? Western Forester 48(4): 12-13.

Atkins, D.; Byler, J.; Livingston, L. [et al.]. 1999. Health of Idaho's Forests. Report No. 99-4. Missoula, MT: U.S. Department of Agriculture, Forest Service, Northern Region.

Baumgartner, D.M.; Boyd, R.J. 1976. Proceedings: Tree planting in the Inland Northwest. Pullman, WA: Cooperative Extension, Washington State University. 311 p.

Baumgartner, D.M. 1982. Proceedings: Site preparation and fuel management on steep terrain. Pullman, WA: Cooperative Extension, Washington State University. 178 p.

Baumgartner, D.M.; Boyd, R.J.; Breuer, D.W.; Miller, D.L. 1986. Proceedings: Weed control for forest productivity in the Interior West. Pullman, WA: Cooperative Extension, Washington State University. 148 p.

Baumgartner, D.M.; Breuer, D.W.; Zamora, B. 1989. Proceedings: Prescribed fire in the intermountain region, forest site preparation and range improvement. Pullman, WA: Cooperative Extension, Washington State University. 171 p.

Bingham, R.T. 1983. Blister rust resistant western white pine for the Inland Empire: the story of the first 25 years of the research and development program. Gen. Tech. Rep. INT-146. Ogden, UT: U.S. Department of Agriculture, Forest Service, Intermountain Forest and Range Experiment Station. 45 p.

Black, Hugh C.; Lawrence, William H. 1992. Animal damage management in Pacific Northwest Forests. In: Black, H.C., tech. ed. Silvicultural approaches to animal damage management in Pacific Northwest forests. Gen. Tech. Rep. PNW-GTR-287. Portland, OR: U.S. Department of Agriculture, Forest Service, Pacific Northwest Research Station. Chapter 2.

Boldt, C.E.; Van Deusen, J.L. 1974. Silviculture of ponderosa pine in the Black Hills: the status of our knowledge. Res. Pap. RM-124. Fort Collins, CO: U.S. Department of Agriculture, Forest Service, Rocky Mountain Forest and Range Experiment Station. 45 p.

Boyd, R.J. 1982. Chemical site preparation for herbaceous plant communities. In: Baumgartner, D.M. Proceedings: Site preparation and fuel management on steep terrain. Pullman, WA: Cooperative Extension, Washington State University. 49-53.

Brown, J.K.; See, T.E. 1981. Downed woody fuel and biomass in the northern Rocky Mountains. Gen. Tech. Rep. INT-117. Ogden, UT: U.S. Department of Agriculture, Forest Service, Intermountain Research Station. 48 P.

Brown, J.K. 1983. The "unnatural fuel buildup" issue. In: Lotan, J.E.; Kilgore, B.M.; Fischer, W.C. [et al.], coords. Proceedings, symposium, and workshop on wilderness fire. Gen. Tech. Rep. INT-128. Ogden, UT: U.S. Department of Agriculture, Forest Service, Intermountain Forest and Range Experiment Station. 127-128.

Brown, J.K.; Reinhardt, E.D.; Kramer, K.A. 2003. Coarse woody debris: managing benefits and fire hazard in the recovering forest. Gen. Tech. Rep. RMRS-GTR-105. Ogden, UT: U.S. Department of Agriculture, Forest Service, Rocky Mountain Research Station. 16 p.

Burns, R.M. 1983. Silviculture systems for the major forest types of the United States. Agric. Handb. No. 445. Washington, DC: U.S. Department of Agriculture, Forest Service. 191 p.

Cafferata, S.L. 1992. Mountain beaver. In: Black, H.C., tech. ed. Silvicultural approaches to animal damage management in Pacific Northwest forests. Gen. Tech. Rep. PNW-GTR-287. Portland, OR: U.S. Department of Agriculture, Forest Service, Pacific Northwest Research Station. Chapter 11.

Cleary, B.; Greaves, R. 1976. Determining planting stock needs. In: Baumgartner, D.M.; Boyd, R.J., eds. Proceedings: Tree planting in the Inland Northwest. Pullman, WA: Cooperative Extension, Washington State University. 60-81.

Cleary, B.D.; Greaves, R.D.; Hermann, R.K. 1978. Regenerating Oregon's forests. Corvallis, OR: Oregon State University Extension Service. 287 p.

Cochran, P.H. 1979. Response of thinned lodgepole pine after fertilization. Res. Note. PNW-335. Portland, OR: U.S. Department of Agriculture, Forest Service, Pacific Northwest Forest and Range Experiment Station. 6 p.

Cole, D.M.; Edminster, C.B. 1985. Growth and yield of lodgepole pine. In: Baumgartner, D.M. [et al.], eds. Lodgepole pine the species and its management. May 8-10, 1984 , Spokane, WA. Pullman, WA: Cooperative Extension, Washington State University. 263-290.

Coop, L.B. 2004. Pacific Northwest weed management handbook. Corvallis, OR: Integrated Plant Protection Center, Botany and Plant Pathology Department, Oregon State University. Available at http://pnwpest.org/pnw/weeds?20W_FORS01.dat.

Cooper, S.V.; Neiman, K.E.; Roberts, D.W. 1991. Forest habitat types of northern Idaho: a second approximation. Revised. Gen. Tech. Rep. INT-236. Ogden, UT: U.S. Department of Agriculture, Forest Service, Intermountain Research Station. 143 p.

Daubenmire, R.; Daubenmire, J.B. 1968. Forest vegetation of eastern Washington and northern Idaho. Tech. Bull. 60. Pullman, WA: Washington Agricultural Experiment Station. 104 p.

Davis, K.P. 1942. Economic management of western white pine forests. Tech. Bulle. 830. Washington, DC: U.S. Department of Agriculture. 77 p.

DeBano, L. 1991. Effects of fire on soil properties. In: Harvey, A.E.; Neuenschwander, L.F., comps. Proceedings: Management and productivity of western-montane forest soils. Gen. Tech. Rep. INT-280. Ogden, Utah: U.S. Department of Agriculture, Forest Service, Intermountain Research Station. 151-156.

Deitschman, G.H. 1966. Diameter growth of western white pine following precommercial thinning. Res. Note. INT-47. Ogden, UT: U.S. Department of Agriculture, Forest Service, Intermountain Forest and Range Experiment Station. 4 p.

Deitschman, G.H.; Pfister, R.D. 1973. Growth of released and unreleased young stands in the western white pine type. Res. Pap. INT-132. Ogden, UT: U.S. Department of Agriculture, Forest Service, Intermountain Forest and Range Experiment Station. 14 p.

Dixon, G.E. 2002. Essential FVS: a user's guide to the Forest Vegetation Simulator. Internal Report. Fort Collins, CO: U.S. Department of Agriculture, Forest Service, Forest Management Service Center. 189 p.

Edgren, J.W.; Stein, W.I. 1974. Artificial regeneration. In: Cramer, O.P., ed. Environmental effects of forest residues management in the Pacific Northwest, a state-of-knowledge compendium. Gen. Tech. Rep. PNW-24. Portland, OR: U.S. Department of Agriculture, Forest Service, Pacific Northwest Forest and Range Experiment Station. M1-M32.

Edminster, C. 1988. Stand density and socking level in even-aged ponderosa pine stands. In: Baumgartner, D.M.; Lotan, J.E., eds. Ponderosa pine the species and its management. Pullman, WA: Cooperative Extension, Washington State University. 253-260.

Ferguson, D.E.; Stage, A.R.; Boyd, R.J. 1986. Predicting regeneration in the grand fir-cedar-hemlock ecosystem of the northern Rocky Mountains. Forest Science Monograph. 26. Society of American Foresters. 41 p.

Ferguson, D.E. 1991. Allelopathic potential of western coneflower (*Rudbeckia occidentalis*). Canadian Journal of Botany 69: 2806-2808.

Ferguson, D.E. 1994. Advance regeneration in the Inland West: consideration for individual tree and forest health. Journal of Sustainable Forestry 2: 411-422.

Ferguson, D.E. 1999. Effects of pocket gophers, bracken fern, and western coneflower on planted conifers in northern Idaho–an update and two more species. New Forests 18: 199-217.

Fins, L.; Byler J.; Ferguson, D. [et al.]. 2001. Return of the giants: restoring white pine ecosystems by breeding and aggressive planting of blister rust-resistant white pines. Moscow, ID: University of Idaho. 20 p.

Fisher, R.F. 1988. Enhancing forest growth: the role of cultural practices. In: Schmidt, W., ed. Future forests of the mountain west: a stand culture symposium. Gen. Tech. Rep. INT-243. Ogden, UT: U.S. Department of Agriculture, Forest Service, Intermountain Research Station. 23-26.

Foiles, M.W.; Graham, R.T.; Olson, D.F. Jr. 1990. Silvics of grand fir. In: Burns, R.M.; Honkala, B.H., tech. coords. Silvics of North America, 1: Conifers. Agric. Handb. 654. Washington, D.C.: U.S. Department of Agriculture. 52-59.

Franklin, J.F.; Dyrness, C.T. 1973. Natural vegetation of Oregon and Washington. Corvallis, OR: Oregon State University Press. 417 p.

Graham, R.T.; Tonn, J.R. 1979. Response of grand fir, western hemlock, western white pine, western larch, and Douglas-fir to nitrogen fertilizer in northern Idaho. Res. Note. INT-270. Ogden, UT: U.S. Department of Agriculture, Forest Service, Intermountain Forest and Range Experiment Station. 8 p.

Graham, R.T.; Wellner, C.A.; Ward, R. 1983. Mixed conifers, western white pine, and western redcedar. In: Burns, R.M., ed. Silvicultural systems for the major forest types of the United States. Agric. Handb. 445. Washington, DC: U.S. Department of Agriculture, Forest Service. 67-69.

Graham, R.T.; Smith, R.A. 1983. Techniques for implementing the individual tree selection method in the grand fir-cedar-hemlock ecosystems of northern Idaho. Res. Note. INT-332. Ogden, UT: U.S. Department of Agriculture, Forest Service, Intermountain Forest and Range Experiment Station. 4 p.

Graham, R.T. 1988. Influence of stand density on western white pine, redcedar, hemlock, and grand fir in the Rocky Mountains. In: Schmidt, W., ed. Future forests of the mountain west: a stand culture symposium. Gen. Tech. Rep. INT-243. Ogden, UT: U.S. Department of Agriculture, Forest Service, Intermountain Research Station. 175-184.

Graham, R.T.; Harvey, Alan E.; Jurgensen, M.F. 1989. Effect of site preparation on survival and growth of Douglas-fir (*Pseudotsuga menziesii* Mirb. Franco.) seedlings. New Forests 3: 89-98.

Graham, R.T. 1990. Silvics of western white pine. In: Burns, R.M.; Honkala, B.H., tech. coords. Silvics of North America. Volume 1. Conifers. Agric. Handb. 654. Washington, DC: U.S. Department of Agriculture. 385-394.

Graham, R.T.; Kingery, J.L.; Volland, L.A. 1992. Livestock and forest management interactions. In: Black, H.C., ed. Silvicultural approaches to animal damage management in Pacific Northwest forests. Portland, OR: U.S. Department of Agriculture, Forest Service, Pacific Northwest Research Station. 351-364.

Graham, R.T.; Harvey, A.E.; Jurgensen, M.F. [et al.]. 1994a. Managing coarse woody debris in forests of the Rocky Mountains. Res. Pap. INT-RP-477. Ogden, UT: U.S. Department of Agriculture, Forest Service, Intermountain Research Station. 13 p.

Graham, R.T.; Tonn, J.R.; Jain, T.B. 1994b. Managing western white pine plantations for multiple resource objectives. In: Baumgartner, D.M.; Lotan, J.E.; Tonn, J.R., eds. Proceedings: Interior cedar-hemlock-white pine forests: ecology and management. Pullman, WA: Department of Natural Resource Sciences, Washington State University. 357-362.

Graham, R.T.; Tonn, J.R.; Jain, T.B. 1995a. Cone and seed production of western larch in response to girdling and nitrogen fertilization—an update. In: Schmidt, W.C.; McDonald, K.J., comps. Proceedings: Ecology and management of Larix forests: a look ahead. Gen. Tech. Rep. GTR-INT-319. Ogden, UT: U.S. Department of Agriculture, Forest Service, Intermountain Research Station. 204-208.

Graham, R.T.; Harvey, A.E.; Jurgensen, M.F. [et al.]. 1995b. Response of western larch to site preparation. In: Schmidt, W.C.; McDonald, K.J., comps. Proceedings: Ecology and management of Larix forests: a look ahead. Gen. Tech. Rep. GTR-INT-319. Ogden, UT: U.S. Department of Agriculture, Forest Service, Intermountain Research Station. 185-191.

Graham, R.T.; Jain, T.B.; Tonn, J.R. 1999a. Uneven-aged silviculture in cedar-hemlock-grand fir ecosystems of the Northern Rocky Mountains. In: Emmingham, W.H., comp. Proceedings of the IUFRO interdisciplinary uneven-aged management. Corvallis, OR: Oregon State University. 70-87.

Graham, R.T.; Harvey, A.E.; Jain, T.B.; Tonn, J.R. 1999b. The effects of thinning and similar stand treatments on fire behavior in western forests. Gen. Tech. Rep. PNW-GTR-463. Portland, OR: U.S. Department of Agriculture, Forest Service, Pacific Northwest Research Station. 27 p.

Haig, I.T. 1932. Second-growth yield, stand, and volume tables for western white pine type. Tech. Bulle. 323. Washington, DC : U.S. Department of Agriculture. 68 p.

Haig, I.T.; Davis, K.P.; Weidman, R.H. 1941. Natural regeneration in the western white pine type. Tech. Bulle. 767. Washington, DC: U.S. Department of Agriculture. 99 p.

Hamilton, G.J.; Christie, J.M. 1971. Forest management tables (metric). Booklet. No. 34. London, UK: Forestry Commission. 201 p.

Hann, W.J; Jones, J.L.; Karl, M.G. [et al.]. 1997. Landscape dynamics of the Basin. In: Quigley, T.M.; Arbelbide, S.J., tech. eds. An assessment of ecosystem components in the Interior Columbia Basin and portions of the Klamath and Great Basins.. Gen. Tech. Rep. PNW-GTR-405. Portland, OR: U.S. Department of Agriculture, Forest Service, Pacific Northwest Research Station. Chap. 3. Vol. II

Harvey, A.E.; Jurgensen, M.F.; Larsen, M.J. 1981. Organic reserves: importance to ectomycorrhizae in forest soils in western Montana. Forest Science 27: 442-445.

Harvey, A.E.; Jurgensen, M.F.; Larsen, M.J.; Graham, R.T. 1987. Decaying organic materials and soil quality in the Inland Northwest: a management opportunity. Gen. Tech. Rep. INT-225. Ogden, UT: U.S. Department of Agriculture, Forest Service, Intermountain Research Station. 15 p.

Harvey, A.E.; Jurgensen, M.F.; Graham, R.T. 1989a. Fire-soil interactions governing site productivity in the northern Rocky Mountains. In: Baumgartner, D.; Breur, D.W.; Zamora, B.A. [et al.], comps. Prescribed fire in the intermountain region, forest site preparation and range improvement. Pullman, WA: Cooperative Extension, Washington State University. 9-18.

Harvey, A.E.; Meurisse, R.T.; Geist, J.M. [et al.]. 1989b. Managing productivity processes in the Inland Northwest-mixed conifers and pines. In: Perry, D.A.; Meurisse, R.; Thomas, B. [et al.], eds. Maintaining long-term forest productivity of Pacific Northwest forest ecosystems. Portland, OR: Timber Press. 164-184.

Harvey, A.E. 1994. Integrated roles for insects, diseases, and decomposers in fire dominated forests of the Inland Western United States: past, present, and future forest health. Journal of Sustainable Forestry 2: 211-220.

Helms, J.A. 1998. The dictionary of forestry. Bethesda, MD: Society of American Foresters. 210. p.

Hermann, R.K.; Lavender D.P. 1990. Silvics of Douglas-fir. In: Burns, R.M.; Honkala, B.H., tech. coords. Silvics of forest trees of the United States. Agric. Handb. 654. Washington, DC: U.S. Department of Agriculture, Forest Service. 385-394.

Hessburg, P.F; Mitchell, R.G.; Filip, G.M. 1994. Historical and current roles of insects and pathogens in eastern Oregon and Washington forested landscapes. In: Hessburg, P.F., tech. ed. Eastside forest ecosystem health assessment, Volume III, assessment. Portland, OR: U.S. Department of Agriculture, Forest Service, Pacific Northwest Research Station. 72 p.

Hoff, R.J.; McDonald, G.I.; Bingham, R.T. 1976. Mass selection for blister rust resistance: a method for natural regeneration of western white pine. Res. Note. INT-202. Ogden, UT: U.S. Department of Agriculture, Forest Service, Intermountain Forest and Range Experiment Station. 11 p.

Hungerford, R.D.; Harrington, M.G.; Frandsen, W.H. [et al.]. 1991. Influence of fire on factors that affect site productivity. In: Harvey, A.E.; Neuenschwander, L.F., comps. Proceedings: Management and productivity of western-montane forest soils. Gen. Tech. Rep. INT-280. Ogden, UT: U.S. Department of Agriculture, Forest Service, Intermountain Research Station. 32-50.

Jain, T.B.; Graham, R.T.; Morgan, P. 2004. Western white pine growth relative to forest openings. Canadian Journal of Forest Research 34: 2187-2197.

Jain, T.B.; Graham, R.T. 2005. Restoring dry and moist forests of the Inland Northwestern U.S. In: Stanturf, J.A. ; Madsen, P., eds. Restoration of boreal and temperate forests. Boca Raton, FL: CRC Press. 463-480.

Johnstone, W.D. 1985. Thinning lodgepole pine. In: Baumgartner, D.M.; Krebill, R.G.; Arnott, J.T.; Weetman, G.F., eds. Lodgepole pine: the species and its management. Pullman, WA: Cooperative Extension, Washington State University. 253-262.

Johnstone, W.D.; Cole, D.M. 1988. Thinning lodgepole pine: a research review. In: Schmidt, W., ed. Future forests of the mountain west: a stand culture symposium. Missoula, MT. Gen. Tech. Rep. INT-243. Ogden, UT: U.S. Department of Agriculture, Forest Service, Intermountain Research Station. 160-164.

Jurgensen, M.F.; Arno, S.F.; Harvey, A.E. [et al.]. 1979. Symbiotic and nonsymbiotic fixation in northern Rocky Mountain ecosystems. In: Gordon, J.C.; Wheeler, C.T.; Perry, D.A. Symbiotic nitrogen fixation in the management of temperate forests. Corvallis, OR: Forest Research Laboratory, Oregon State University. 294-308.

Jurgensen, M.F.; Harvey, A.E.; Graham, R.T. [et al.] 1997. Impacts of timber harvesting on soil organic matter, nitrogen, productivity, and health of Inland Northwest forests. Forest Science 43(2): 234-251.

Ketcham, D.A.; Wellner, C.A.; Evans, S.S., Jr. 1968. Western white pine management programs realigned on Northern Rocky Mountain National Forests. Journal of Forestry 66(4): 329-332.

Kingery, J.L.; Graham, R.T. 1991. The effect of cattle grazing on ponderosa pine regeneration. Forestry Chronicle 67(3): 245-248 .

Knapp, W.H.; Brodie, J.D. 1992. The process of managing animal damage. In: Black, H.C., tech. ed. Silvicultural approaches to animal damage management in Pacific Northwest forests. Gen. Tech. Rep. PNW-GTR-287. Portland, OR: U.S. Department of Agriculture, Forest Service, Pacific Northwest Research Station. Chap.18.

Landis, T.D.; Tinus, R.W.; McDonald, S.E.; Barnett, J.P. 1990. Containers and growing media, the container tree nursery manual. Vol. 2 Agric. Handb. 674. Washington, DC: U.S. Department of Agriculture, Forest Service. 88 p.

Landis, T.D.; Tinus, R.W.; McDonald, S.E.; Barnett, J.P. 1992. Atmospheric environment, the container tree nursery manual. Vol. 3 Agric. Handb. 674. Washington, DC: U.S. Department of Agriculture, Forest Service. 145 p.

Larsen, M.J.; Harvey, A.E.; Jurgensen, M.F. 1980. Residue decay processes and associated environmental functions in northern Rocky Mountain forests. In: Proceedings: Environmental consequences of timber harvesting in Rocky Mountain coniferous forests. Gen. Tech. Rep. Ogden, UT: U.S. Department of Agriculture, Forest Service. 157-174.

Lillybridge, T.R.; Kovalchik, B.L.; Williams, C.K.; Smith, B.G. 1995. Field guide for forested plant associations of the Wenatchee National Forest. Gen. Tech. Rep. PNW-GTR-359. Portland, OR: U.S. Department of Agriculture, Forest Service, Pacific Northwest Research Station. 335 p.

Lotan, J.E. 1973. The role of cone serotiny in lodgepole pine forests. In: Baumgartner, D.M., ed. Proceedings: Management of lodgepole pine ecosystems. Pullman, WA: Cooperative Extension, Washington State University. 471-495.

Lotan, J.E. 1986. Silvicultural management of competing vegetation. In: Baumgartner, D.M.; Boyd, R.J.; Breuer, D.W.; Miller, D.L., eds. Proceedings: Weed control for forest productivity in the Interior West. Pullman, WA: Cooperative Extension, Washington State University. 9-16.

Lotan, J.E.; Carlson, C.E.; Chew, J.D. 1988. Stand density and growth of interior Douglas-fir. In: Schmidt, W., ed. Proceedings: Future forests of the mountain west: a stand culture. Gen. Tech. Rep. INT-243. Ogden, UT: U.S. Department of Agriculture, Forest Service, Intermountain Research Station. 185-191.

Loucks, Donna M.; Black, Hugh C.; Roush, Mary Lynn; Radosevich, Steven R. 1990. Assessment and management of animal damage in Pacific northwest forests: an annotated bibliography. Gen. Tech. Rep. PNW-GTR-262. Portland, OR: U.S. Department of Agriculture, Forest Service, Pacific Northwest Research Station. 371 p.

Lowman, B. 1986. New equipment for spot site preparation. In: Baumgartner, D.M.; Boyd, R.J.; Breuer, D.W.; Miller, D.L., eds. Proceedings: Weed control for forest productivity in the Interior West. Pullman, WA: Cooperative Extension, Washington State University. 74-78.

Lull, H.W. 1959. Soil compaction on forest and range lands. Misc. Pub. 768. Washington, DC: U.S. Department of Agriculture. 33 p.

Marsh, R.E.; Steele, R.W. 1992. Pocket Gophers. In: Black, Hugh C. Tech. Ed. Silvicultural approaches to animal damage management in Pacific Northwest forests. Gen. Tech. Rep. PNW-GTR-287. Portland, OR: U.S. Department of Agriculture, Forest Service, Pacific Northwest Research Station. Chap. 10.

McCaughey, W.W.; Ferguson, D.E. 1988. Response of advance regeneration to release in the Inland Mountain West: a summary. In: Schmidt, W., ed. Future forests of the mountain west: a stand culture symposium. Gen. Tech. Pap. INT-243. Ogden, UT: U.S. Department of Agriculture, Forest Service, Intermountain Research Station. 255-266.

Mika, P.G.; Moore, J.A. 1990. Foliar potassium explains Douglas-fir response to fertilization in the Inland Northwest. Water, and Air, and Soil Pollution 54: 477-491.

Miller, D.L. 1986a. Manual and mechanical methods of vegetation control–what works and what doesn't. In: Baumgartner, D.M.; Boyd, R.J.; Breuer, D.W.; Miller, D.L., eds. Proceedings: Weed control for forest productivity in the Interior West. Pullman, WA: Cooperative Extension, Washington State University. 55-60.

Miller, D.L. 1986b. Conifer release in the inland north west–effects. In: Baumgartner, D.M.; Boyd, R.J.; Breuer, D.W.; Miller, D.L., eds. Proceedings: Weed control for forest productivity in the Interior West. Pullman, WA: Cooperative Extension, Washington State University. 17-24.

Minore, D. 1972. Germination and early growth of coastal tree species on organic seedbeds. Portland, OR: U.S. Department of Agriculture, Forest Service, Pacific Northwest Forest and Range Experiment Station. 18 p.

Moore, J.A. 1988. Response of Douglas-fir, grand fir, and western white pine to forest fertilization. In: Schmidt, W., ed. Future forests of the mountain west: a stand culture symposium. Gen. Tech. Rep. INT-243. Ogden, UT: U.S. Department of Agriculture, Forest Service, Intermountain Research Station. 226-230.

Moore, J.A.; Mika, P.G.; Vanderploeg, J.L. 1991. Nitrogen fertilization fertilizer response of Rocky Mountain Douglas-fir by geographic area across the Inland Northwest. Western Journal of Applied Forestry 64: 94-98.

Moore, J.A.; Mika, P.G.; Schwandt, J.W.; Shaw, T.M. 1994. Nutrition and forest health. In: Baumgartner, D.M.; Lotan, J.E.; Tonn, J.R., eds. Proceedings: Interior cedar-hemlock-white pine forests: ecology and management. Pullman, WA: Department of Natural Resource Sciences, Washington State University. 173-176.

Missoula Technology and Development Center [MTDC]. 1988. The Salmon Blade. Missoula, MT: U.S. Department of Agriculture, Forest Service, Missoula Technology and Development Center.

Murphy, T.E. L.; Adams, D.L.; Ferguson, D.E. 1999. Response of advanced lodgepole pine regeneration to overstory removal in eastern Idaho. Forest Ecology and Management 120: 235-244.

Neuenschwander, L.F.; Byler, J.W.; Harvey, A.E. [et al.]. 1999. White pine in the American west: a vanishing species - Can we save it? Gen. Tech. Rep. RMRS-GTR-35. Ogden, Utah: U.S. Department of Agriculture Forest Service, Rocky Mountain Research Station. 20 p.

Nolte, D.L. 2003a. Developing approaches to reduce wildlife damage to forest resources. Western Forester 48(4): 1-3.

Nolte, D.L. 2003b. Managing ungulates to protect trees. Western Forester 48(4): 14.

Noste, N.V.; Bushey, C.L. 1987. Fire response of shrubs of dry forest habitat types of Montana and Idaho. Gen. Tech. Rep. INT-239. Ogden, UT: U.S. Department of Agriculture, Forest Service, Intermountain Research Station. 22 p.

Nyland, R.D. 2002. Silviculture: concepts and applications: 2nd edition. New York, NY: McGraw-Hill. 633 p.

Oester, P.T.; Clements, S.; Larson, P.; Emmingham, W. 1995. Performance of ponderosa pine seedlings under four herbicide regimes in northeast Oregon. New Forests 10(2): 123-131.

Oliver, W.W.; Ryker, R.A. 1990. Silvics of ponderosa pine. In: Burns, R.M.; Honkala, B.H., tech. coords. Silvics of North America, Volume 1, Conifers. Agric. Handb. 654. Washington, DC: U.S. Department of Agriculture. 413-424.

Packee, E.C. 1990. Silvics of western hemlock. In: Burns, R.M.; Honkala, B.H., tech. coords. Silvics of North America. Agric. Handb. 654. Washington, DC: U.S. Department of Agriculture, Forest Service. 613-622.

Page-Dumroese, D.S.; Jurgensen, M.F.; Harvey, A.E. [et al.]. 1997. Soil changes and tree seedling response associated with the site preparation in northern Idaho. Western Journal of Applied Forestry 12(3): 81-88.

Pannkuk, C.D.; Robichaud, P.R. 2003. Effectiveness of needle cast reducing erosion after forest fires. Water Resource Research 39(12): 1333, doi:10.1029/2003 WR002318.

Pearson, G.A. 1950. Management of ponderosa pine in the southwest as developed by research and experimental practice. Monograph 6. Washington, DC: U.S. Department of Agriculture, Forest Service. 218 p.

Petersen, T.D. 1986. Ecological principles for managing forest weeds. In: Baumgartner, D.M.; Boyd, R.J.; Breuer, D.W.; Miller, D.L., eds. Proceedings: Weed control for forest productivity in the Interior West. Pullman, WA: Cooperative Extension, Washington State University. 3-7.

Pfister, R.D.; Kovalchik, B.L.; Arno, S.F.; Presby, R.C. **1977.** Forest habitat types of Montana. Gen. Tech. Rep. INT-34. Ogden, UT: U.S. Department of Agriculture, Forest Service, Intermountain Forest and Range Experiment Station. 174 p.

Powers, R.F.; Webster, S.R.; Cochran, P.H. **1988.** Estimating the response of ponderosa pine forests to fertilization. In: Schmidt, W., ed. Proceedings: Future forests of the mountain west: a stand culture symposium. Gen. Tech. Rep. INT-243. Ogden, UT: U.S. Department of Agriculture, Forest Service, Intermountain Research Station. 219-225.

Powers, R.F.; Reynolds, P.E. **1999.** Ten year responses of ponderosa pine plantations to repeated vegetation and nutrient control along an environmental gradient. Canadian Journal of Forest Research 29: 1027-1038.

Quigley, T.M.; Haynes, R.W.; Graham, R.T. **1996.** Integrated scientific assessment for ecosystem management in the interior Columbia Basin. Gen. Tech. Rep. PNW-GTR-382. Portland, OR: U.S. Department of Agriculture, Forest Service, Pacific Northwest Research Station. 303 p.

Rehfeldt, G.E. **1994.** Microevolution of forest trees in cedar-hemlock forests. In: Baumgartner, D.M.; Lotan, J.E.; Tonn, J.R., comps. Proceedings: Interior cedar-hemlock-white pine forests: ecology and management. Pullman, WA: Department of Natural Resources, Washington State University. 92-100.

Reinhardt, E.D.; Brown, J.K.; Fischer, W.C.; Graham, R.T. **1991.** Woody fuel and duff consumption by pre-scribed fire in northern Idaho mixed conifer logging slash. Res. Pap. INT-443. Ogden, UT: U.S. Department of Agriculture, Forest Service, Intermountain Research Station. 22 p.

Robichaud, P.R.; Byers, J.L.; Neary, D.G. **2000.** Evaluating the effectiveness of postfire rehabilitation treatments. Gen. Tech. Rep. RMRS-GTR-63. Fort Collins, CO: U.S. Department of Agriculture, Forest Service, Rocky Mountain Research Station. 85 p.

Rose, S.L.; Perry, D.A.; Pilz, D.; Schoeneberger, M.M. **1983.** Allelopathic effects of litter on growth and colonization of mycorrhizal fungi. Journal of Chemical Ecology 9: 1153-1162.

Rothacher, J.; Lopushinsky, W. **1974.** Soil stability and water yield and quality. In: Cramer, O.P., ed. Environmental effects of forest residues management in the Pacific Northwest, a state-of-knowledge compendium. Gen. Tech. Rep. PNW-24. Portland, OR: U.S. Department of Agriculture, Forest Service, Pacific Northwest Forest and Range Experiment Station. D1-D23.

Ryan, K.C. **1982.** Burning for site preparation on steep-slope helicopter-logged clearcuts in northwestern Montana. In: Baumgartner, D.M., ed. Proceedings: Site preparation and fuel management on steep terrain. Pullman, WA: Cooperative Extension, Washington State University. 25-33.

Ryker, R.A.; Losensky, J. **1983.** Ponderosa pine and Rocky Mountain Douglas-fir. In: Burns, R.M., ed. Silviculture systems for the major forest types of the United States. Agric. Handb. No. 445. Washington, DC: U.S. Department of Agriculture, Forest Service. 53-55.

Saveland, J.M.; Neuenschwander, L.F. **1988.** Changing stand density and composition with prescribed fire. In: Schmidt, W., ed. Future forests of the mountain west: a stand culture symposium. Gen. Tech. Rep. INT-243. Ogden, UT: U.S. Department of Agriculture, Forest Service, Intermountain Research Station. 330-331.

Schlich, W. **1906.** Manual of forestry, volume II. Silviculture. Bradbury, Agnew & Co, London. 393. p.

Schmidt, W.C.; Alexander, R.R. **1985.** Strategies for managing lodgepole pine. In: Baumgartner, D.M.; Krebill, R.G.; Arnott, J.T.; Weetman, G.F., eds. Proceedings: Lodgepole pine: the species and its management. Pullman, WA: Cooperative Extension, Washington State University. 201-210.

Schmidt, W. **1988.** Future forests of the mountain west: a stand culture symposium. Gen. Tech. Rep. INT-243. Ogden, UT: U.S. Department of Agriculture, Forest Service, Intermountain Research Station. 402 p.

Schmidt, W.C.; Seidel, K. **1988.** Western larch and space: thinning to optimize growth. In: Schmidt, W., ed. Future forests of the mountain west: a stand culture symposium. Gen. Tech. Rep. INT-243. Ogden, UT: U.S. Department of Agriculture, Forest Service, Intermountain Research Station. 165-174.

Schmidt, W.C.; Shearer, R.C. 1990. Silvics of western larch. In: Burns, R.M.; Honkala, B.H., tech. coords. Silvics of North America. Agric. Handb. 654. Washington, DC: U.S. Department of Agriculture, Forest Service. 160-172.

Schubert, G.H.; Adams, R.S. 1971. Reforestation practices for conifers in California. Sacramento, CA: State of California, The Resources Agency, Department of Conservation, Division of Forestry. 359 p.

Schwandt, J.W.; Marsden, M.A.; McDonald, G.I. 1994. Pruning and thinning effects on white pine survival and volume in northern Idaho. In: Baumgartner, D.M.; Lotan, J.E., eds. Proceedings: Interior Douglas-fir: the species and its management. Pullman, WA: Cooperative Extension, Washington State University. Pullman, WA: Department of Natural Resource Sciences, Washington State University. 167-172.

Shearer, R.C.; Schmidt, J.A. 1991. Natural and planted regeneration of interior Douglas-fir in western Montana. In: Baumgartner, D.M.; Lotan, J.E., eds. Proceedings: Interior Douglas-fir: the species and its management. Pullman, WA: Cooperative Extension, Washington State University. 217-226.

Shepperd, W.D.; Battaglia, M.A. 2002. Ecology, silviculture, and management of Black Hills ponderosa pine. Gen. Tech. Rep. RMRS-GTR-97. Fort Collins, CO: U.S. Department of Agriculture, Forest Service, Rocky Mountain Research Station. 112 p.

Smith, D.M.; Larson, B.C.; Kelty, M.J.; Ashton, P.M.S. 1997. The practice of silviculture: applied forest ecology. New York, NY: John Wiley & Sons, Inc. 537 p.

Smith, H.Y.; Arno, S.F. 1999. Eighty-eight years of change in a managed ponderosa pine forest. Gen. Tech. Rep. RMRS-GTR-23. Ogden, UT: U.S. Department of Agriculture, Forest Service, Rocky Mountain Research Station. 55 p.

van der Kamp, Bart J.; Hawksworth, F.G. 1985. Damage and control of the major diseases of lodgepole pine. In: Baumgartner, D.M.; Krebill, R.G.; Arnott, J.T.; Weetman, G.F., eds. Proceedings: Lodgepole pine: the species and its management. Pullman, WA: Cooperative Extension, Washington State University. 125-131.

Weetman, G.F.; Yang, R.C.; Beella, I.E. 1985. Nutrition and fertilization of lodgepole pine. In: Baumgartner, D.M.; Krebill, R.G.; Arnott, J.T.; Weetman, G.F., eds. Proceedings: Lodgepole pine: the species and its management. Pullman, WA: Cooperative Extension, Washington State University. 223-232.

Weetman, Gordon F. 1988. Nutrition and fertilization of lodgepole pine. In: Schmidt, W., ed. Future forests of the mountain west: a stand culture symposium. Gen. Tech. Rep. INT-243. Ogden, UT: U.S. Department of Agriculture, Forest Service, Intermountain Research Station. 231-239.

Wykoff, W.R.; Crookston, N.L.; Stage, A.R. 1982. User's guide to the stand prognosis model. Gen. Tech. Rep. INT-133. Ogden, UT: U.S. Department of Agriculture, Forest Service, Intermountain Forest and Range Experiment Station. 112 p.

Yarie, John. 1980. The role of understory vegetation in the nutrient cycle of forested ecosystems in mountain hemlock biogeoclimatic zone. Ecology 61(6): 1498-1514.

SILVICULTURAL TOPICS

LINKAGE BETWEEN RIPARIAN BUFFER FEATURES AND REGENERATION, BENTHIC COMMUNITIES, AND WATER TEMPERATURE IN HEADWATER STREAMS, WESTERN OREGON

Michael Newton[1] and Elizabeth C. Cole[1]

ABSTRACT

Riparian forests can be managed using a range of harvesting and regeneration methods to achieve multiple environmental and economic objectives. In this study, seven low-elevation second- or third-order streams were subjected to either patch clearcutting with no buffers or one-sided narrow buffers divided by uncut reaches. Of these streams, four were sites of intensive regeneration experiments, and the other three evaluated only the effect of harvest pattern on water temperature. Regeneration was successfully installed along four streams with intensive planting experiments in which three clearcuts on each spanned the stream for distances of 90 or 180 m. Regeneration cutting in these drainages included clearcutting to the water's edge in openings amounting to 25% of 1,500-m reaches. Planting tests evaluated three species: Douglas-fir (*Pseudotsuga menziesii* (Mirb.) Franco var. *menziesii*), western hemlock (*Tsuga heterophylla* (Raf.) Sarg.), and western redcedar (*Thuja plicata* Donn). Douglas-fir was represented by two different stock types, bareroot plug+1 and 1+1 transplants on two sites and bareroot 1+1 and 2+0 seedlings on the other two sites. All regeneration efforts are on a path that will eventually result in conifer-dominated riparian zones, with degree of success influenced by choice of stock type, overtopping cover, animal damage and frost. Damage from deer (*Odocoilius hemionus columbianus* Rich.), elk (*Cervus elaphus canadensis* L.), beavers (*Castor canadensis* Kuhl.) and/or mountain beavers (*Aplodontia rufa* Raf.) occurred on all four stream systems. There were no patterns of beaver or mountain beaver damage among the stock types; browsing on hemlock was minor. Growth status of the plantations at age four was a function of overtopping vegetation where there is low risk of frost damage; freezing temperatures were limiting to seedling growth along one stream. All three of the primary tree regeneration species studied exhibited decreased growth with overtopping. As has been found on upland sites elsewhere, size of seedlings had a strong influence on their competitive ability in riparian zones.

Aquatic insect communities displayed approximately a doubling of abundance with either unbuffered clearcuts or those buffered on just the south side. Minor shifts occurred in insect community composition; none decreased and certain genera increased markedly, with a net increase in abundance of food organisms that could be utilized by salmonids. Stream temperature increased in response to silvicultural clearing when all cover was removed. Warming and cooling trends on the four streams with regeneration experiments were not definitive, but were within the range reported by Zwieniecki and Newton (1999). In the three clearcuts along streams having narrow buffer screens on the south side only, no evidence of warming was observed in uncut areas 300 m downstream of cut areas compared with pre-harvest temperature patterns.

KEYWORDS: Stream temperature, reforestation, aquatic macroinvertebrates, riparian management, buffer design.

INTRODUCTION

Some states have adopted regulatory best management practices (BMPs) while other states use voluntary BMPs to address the interface between streams and forests to protect water quality and maintain aquatic habitat. These state BMPs must be sensitive to forest landowner needs to ensure that the practices will benefit fishery resources, meet other environmental objectives, and maintain landowner support and interest in forest management (Hairston-Strang and

---

[1] Michael Newton is professor emeritus, and Elizabeth C. Cole is senior research assistant, Oregon State University Department of Forest Science. Corvallis, OR 97331.

Adams 1997). Reports of potentially harmful elevations of stream temperatures in some studies have raised concerns about harvesting practices (Brown and Krygier 1970, Caldwell et al. 1991), leading to eventual adoption of pre-scriptive BMPs. Although current riparian regulations in Oregon allow for some harvesting within riparian areas, such management is expensive and may not eventually be appropriate for regeneration of desired species or for pro-viding economic benefits to justify it. Berg (1995) explored the notion that active management of riparian forests can be both economically and ecologically beneficial. His analysis relies on partial cutting of riparian stands and model pro-jections of growth. In this report, we explore several physi-cal and biological interactions associated with clearcut harvesting adjacent to streams with a goal of providing long-term renewal of desirable species while protecting streams.

Removal of riparian forest cover immediately over streams can increase solar radiation and stream temperature in the short term (Brown and Krygier 1970, Tait et al. 1994). Even if vegetation removal is such that there are no direct effects on fish, fish may be impacted by indirect effects on aquatic invertebrates. Fish feed intensively on aquatic inver-tebrates as both nymphs and adults. Immature benthic (bottom-dwelling) insects live primarily on in-stream sub-strates but actively and passively enter the water flow and drift downstream, becoming highly vulnerable to predation by fish. Temperature and solar radiation loads may affect insects by altering food sources, life cycles, and habitat (Newbold et al. 1980, Murphy and Hall 1981, Tait et al. 1994), with potential changes being either negative or posi-tive, depending on organisms used for a response index. Changes in stream temperature directly impact numbers, fecundity, body size emergence phenology, metabolic rate and diurnal patterns of insects (Merritt and Cummins 1984). Temperature changes indirectly affect aquatic insects through oxygen saturation levels, respiration rates, food availability and nutritive value, and competition from other insects (Sweeney 1984; Walsh 1996). Photosynthetically-active radiation levels affect the amount of primary produc-tion in the stream, and thus, influence the kind and amount of food for benthic (bottom-dwelling) insects. Changes in some species may occur independently of others, so relative abundance of species as well as total species present are both important indicators of change. High levels of primary productivity can be achieved with high levels of diffuse radiation, whereas most energy leading to increased stream-water temperature is attributed to direct radiation (Brown 1969). In short, there are several elements of riparian habi-tat management where there can be legitimate debate about whether a particular procedure enhances one element of the

stream environment or degrades another, and whether prac-tices with consistent improvement in over-all fish habitat are achievable.

Whether any given level of protection is needed depends on status of resources to be protected. Of particular interest for many forest settings is the interaction of water tempera-ture and food supply for fish (Sullivan et al. 2000). States evaluate stream water quality conditions using standards that include temperature. Whether the desired temperature criteria can be met with buffer design depends on whether any given stream is in a desirable range of temperatures to start with, and whether forest management approaches affect water quality just locally versus downstream. The studies we undertook were designed to provide coarse-res-olution answers to questions about managing for favorable temperature and food supply while also setting up future conifer-dominated stands for recruitment of large wood and other values.

We begin with several assumptions. First, that findings of Warren (1971) and Sullivan et al. (2000) relating to interaction of food supply and tolerance of elevated temper-atures are valid, and that short-term exposures of well-fed fish to temperatures above 17.8°C (64°F) will not materially harm most salmonids. Second, that future structural fea-tures of streams will be enhanced by long-term develop-ment of durable conifers suitable for either tree-fall or placement in streams within the riparian management areas. Finally, that abundance and diversity of benthic macroin-vertebrates are indicators of potential food supply for fish in the presence of adequate pool and riffle habitat and moderate temperatures (Wilzbach et al. 1988).

This report summarizes data from a series of experi-ments that integrates silvicultural manipulation of riparian forests with three key elements of riparian habitat: future riparian stand establishment, water temperature, and aquatic macroinvertebrate abundance. These experiments evaluate a series of reforestation techniques based on upland experi-ence to facilitate rapid establishment of conifers and green-up of riparian systems following commercial harvest. They were based on two approaches to clearcut harvesting: clear-cutting to the water's edge on both sides versus clearcut-ting with one-sided buffers. Harvests with no buffers were combined with trials of several coniferous stock types with and without weed control with the general approach out-lined by Newton et al. (1993). The object of the one-sided buffer was to manipulate streamside shade to gain protec-tion from direct radiation while allowing maximum regen-eration opportunity. The regeneration studies rely on repeated measurements of several planted coniferous tree species and competing hardwood and shrub cover, measurement of water temperatures along streams passing through the various treatments (including data from Zwieniecki and Newton 1999), and samplings of bottom-dwelling macroinvertebrates to assess impacts on potential abundance of aquatic insects well utilized by salmonids.

Our specific objectives were to: 1) evaluate the regeneration success and growth of combinations of planting stock species and size combined with and without overstory removal and shrub control in streamside environments, 2) determine how alternative approaches to removing tree cover near streams influence abundance and diversity of benthic insect communities, and 3) develop a coarse-resolution estimate of whether openings to facilitate forest rehabilitation affect downstream water temperature. Robison and Beschta (1990) and others have reported that most large wood contributing to stream structure originates within 15 m from the banks. The first objective specifically addresses the problem of establishing conifers near streams on low-elevation sites in the Douglas-fir (*Pseudotsuga menziesii* (Mirb.) Franco var. *menziesii*) Region where most low-elevation streams are bounded largely by hardwoods. The persistence of these species as functional large wood in streams tends to be short compared to that of large conifers. While there are reports that upslope or upstream sources may provide much large wood for these streams (Reeves et al. 2003), a local source is presumably a better guarantee that a local supply of wood will be present when needed. Thus, in the event incentives develop for establishing large conifers, there is a need to understand the environments and management approaches in which such trees may develop. The other objectives address impacts of buffer design on aspects of the stream system that might relate to fish.

METHODS

Layout

The studies occurred in two primary phases, both of which utilized fish-bearing headwaters streams passing through low-elevation, intensively managed forest ownerships. Precipitation for all creeks is between 1200 and 2000 mm/year, of which roughly 85 percent occurs between October and April. In Phase I, four second- or third-order fish-bearing streams (Ames, Bark, Buttermilk, Mosby Creeks, fig. 1) were scheduled for clearcut harvests, with coniferous reforestation according to hardwood conversion rules (Oregon Forest Practices Act) that allowed clearcutting to the streambank according to a written plan. These were the streams on which all reforestation experiments were conducted.

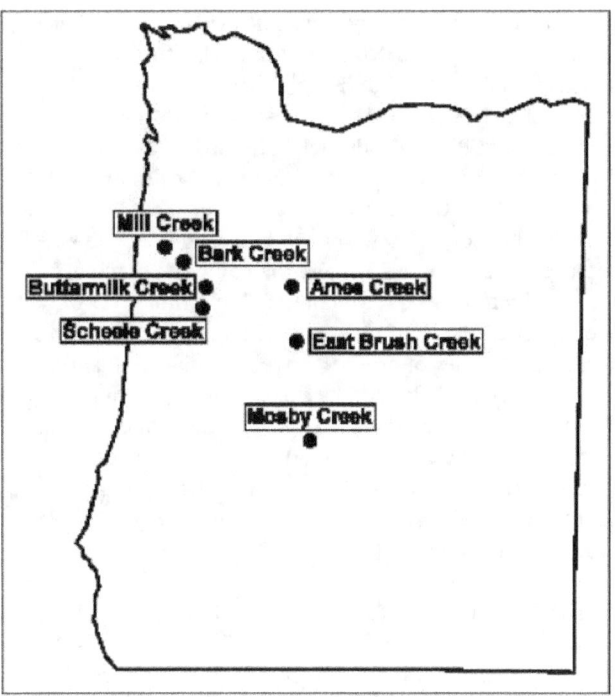

Figure 1—Map of stream locations in western Oregon.

Each Phase I stream was laid out to provide a basis for both reforestation and study of effects of small clearcuts with no buffers on water temperature. In each, a 1500-m reach was identified for study. Two creeks (Bark and Buttermilk) are in the central part of the Oregon Coast Range, and are bedded in sedimentary rock. Buttermilk Creek drains a basin of 702 ha at a gradient of three percent, and Bark Creek drains 1560 ha with a gradient of less than two percent in the study reach. The other two (Ames and Mosby) drain lower slopes of the Oregon Cascade Mountains, and are bedded in basalt bedrock and boulders. Ames Creek drains a basin area of 1441 ha and has a gradient in the study reach of three percent. Mosby Creek drains 26,022 ha with a gradient of five percent in the study reach.

Buttermilk and Bark Creeks flow between terraces largely of deposits of medium-textured material from sedimentary rocks of the Tyee formation, a readily weathered siltstone in this area. These soils are extremely productive for either conifers or red alder (*Alnus rubra* Bong.). Except in poorly drained depressions and gravel piles, all soils are of good to excellent productivity, capable of growing a Douglas-fir tree 38 m to 40 m tall in 50 years (King 1966). Stands removed in the harvests were dominated by red alder, with understories of salmonberry (*Rubus spectabilis* Pursh.). Ames Creek soils are a mixture of alluvial gravelly loam terraces with scattered wet depressions, and residual well drained Jory silty clay loam soils; site quality is heterogeneous, and estimated 50-year Douglas-fir site index ranges from 33 m to 37 m (King 1996). The previous stands were primarily hardwoods, mixtures of bigleaf maple (*Acer macrophyllum* Pursh.) and black cottonwood (*Populus trichocarpa* T. & G.) with some willows (*Salix* [Tourn.] L.) and Douglas-fir. Of the four Phase I streams, Mosby Creek differed markedly from the others in having been subjected to placer mining, probably more than 50 years previously. The soil there was largely comprised of a thin layer of organic litter on top of piles of gravel and boulders, with occasional patches of original gravelly loam soil. Planting was exceedingly difficult. The stand removed in preparation for this study consisted primarily of immature red alder with intermixed conifers of assorted sizes and understories of mixed shrubs, depending on degree of suppression. Estimated 50-year site index for Douglas-fir at Mosby Creek ranges from 30 m to 35 m (King 1996).

The 1500-m study reach for each of the four Phase I streams was divided in half so that one 750-m sub-reach had 25% of its length clearcut-harvested in one 180-m reach and the other sub-reach had two 90-m openings (fig. 2). The remainder of each 1500-m reach was uncut or remained buffered according to pre-1994 Oregon Forest Practice Rules (22 m or more both sides), and there was at least 200 m of uncut stand or standard buffer between any two clearcuts. Logging of all units was completed in late 1992. Phase I included all reforestation experiments, for which all clearcuts were made with no buffers.

Phase II streams evaluated only the influence of a one-sided buffer design on water temperature and stream productivity. Each had a single clearcut installation, in late 1993, with a buffer represented by a "sun-sided" vegetative screen on each of three similar-sized streams (East Brush, Mill, and Scheele Creeks, figs. 1 and 3). East Brush Creek drains about 1100 ha of basaltic foothills of the Cascade Mountains. In the Coast Range, Scheele Creek drains 1743 ha of deeply weathered Siletz River basaltic rock, and is bounded by Jory soil with negligible terrace areas. Mill Creek drains about 440 ha of sedimentary rocks and deep soils. In each, cutting was done on both sides of the stream so that a 760-m to 800-m reach was exposed, but a vegetated screen 12-m wide remained between any point in the stream and the path of direct solar radiation through the summer. The screen consisted of whatever trees and shrubs were present in the uncut condition so long as they were within 12 m of the streambank. Where streams were east-west in orientation, no buffer was left on the north side, but the sun shining on open water between 9:00 AM and 6:00 PM PDT was intercepted to a major degree by a screen of

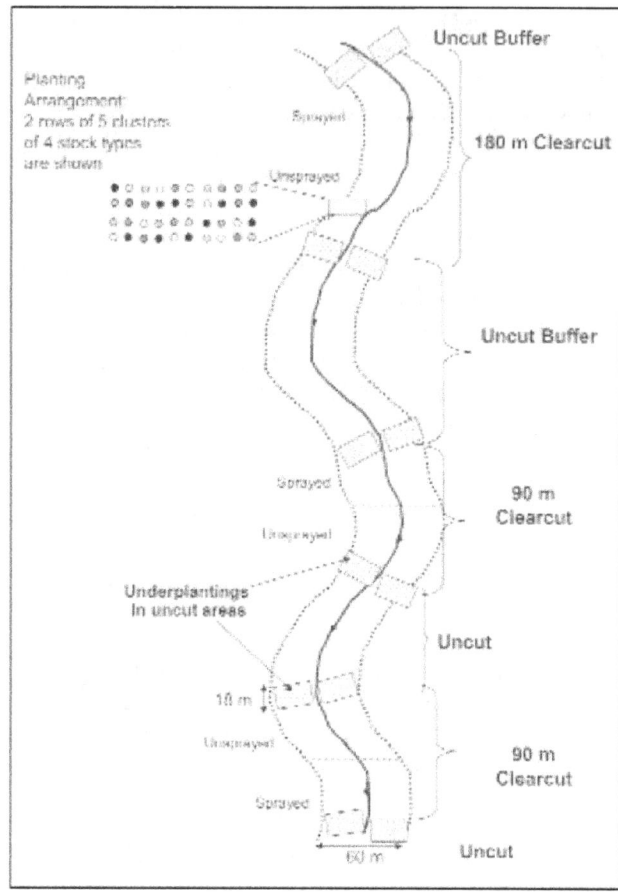

Figure 2—Schematic of unit layout for reforestation (Phase I) studies.

cover. The protection was provided in meandering streams by leaving all cover in a 150-degree fan-shaped range of directions between true azimuths of 120 and 270 degrees for a distance of 12 m from the bank as shown in figure 3 (adapted from Newton 1993).

All cutting units were laid out specifically for the study. The methods used in these experiments were within the bounds of Oregon Forest Practice Rules, with the exception that buffer removal to the water's edge and one-sided buffers required specific written plans and research protocols. Logging operations were conducted with equipment and approaches according to cable or ground-based systems normal for each owner with special priority for avoidance of damage to streambanks.

Reforestation

In each clearcut established for Phase I, planting was done with four stock types, including large and small Douglas-fir, and plug+1 western redcedar (*Tsuja plicata* Donn) and western hemlock (*Tsuga heterophylla* (Raf.)

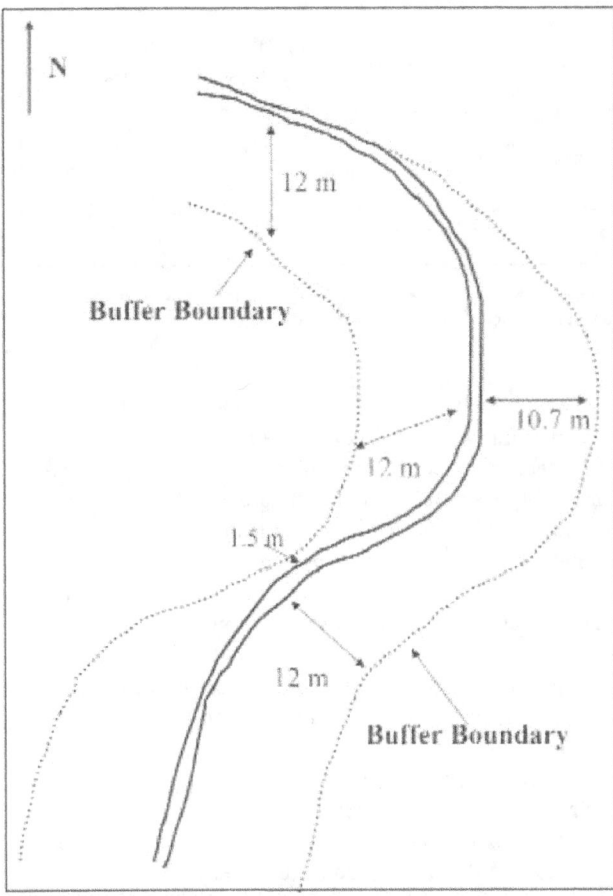

Figure 3—Schematic of fan-projection method of implementing one-sided buffer boundaries for fish-bearing streams. Buffer design places 12 m of cover between stream and water between 9:00 am and 6:00 pm PDT (azimuth of 120 to 270).

Sarg.). The seedlings were planted in clusters of four seedlings, one of each species or stock type, in five rows of clusters 6 m apart parallel to the stream, beginning about three m from the bank, overall approximating a 3 x 3-m spacing in a 30-m strip on each side of the stream (fig. 2). The rows extended 18 m into the uncut timber upstream and downstream from each clearcut. Half of each planting was treated with a broadcast site preparation application of glyphosate herbicide so as to leave a 3-m wide untreated zone along the stream at Bark and Buttermilk Creeks. Spot-treated release applications of glyphosate were applied at Ames and Mosby Creeks. For each cutting unit, spraying left a 3-m buffer along both banks of the stream. Spraying extended 20 m into understories of the uncut stands at the sprayed end of the unit where seedlings were to be planted. A total of some 12,000 seedlings were planted. For each seedling, annual measurements during the first four years recorded seedling diameter 15 cm aboveground, diameter at breast height (137 cm, dbh) if seedlings were of sufficient

size, and current and previous-year's height (for confirmation). If data did not match previous year's data, the site was revisited and measurements confirmed.

At each seedling, visual estimates were made of competing cover of herbaceous plants, shrubs, and ferns within a 1-m radius for years one and two, and of overtopping (Howard and Newton 1984) by shrubs and residual trees for all years; residual trees were present primarily in underplanted stands at the ends of each unit. Condition of seedlings, including animal damage from beavers (*Castor canadensis* Kuhl.), mountain beaver (*Aplodontia rufa* Raf.), and deer (*Odocoilius hemionus columbianus* Rich.)/elk (*Cervus elaphus canadensis* L.) and mortality, were recorded separately.

Stock quality problems were encountered for the Buttermilk and Bark Creek plantations, both of which had ideal conditions for seedling survival and vigor; the same lot of seedlings planted on good sites elsewhere also performed poorly. Survival was lower than expected (65%) at Buttermilk Creek, but we determined that would be acceptable. Survival at Bark Creek was less than 50%, and we replanted there and removed the original survivors. Thus, for Bark Creek, we have only three years of measurement. Freezing damage and severe elk browsing occurred at Mosby Creek. Survival was below 40% after two years, and the landowner elected to replant vacant spots with a mixture of valley ponderosa pine (*Pinus ponderosa* Dougl. ex Laws) 2+0 seedlings, grand fir (*Abies grandis* (Dougl.) Lindl.) plug+1 transplants, western white pine (*Pinus monticola* Dougl.) 1+0 containerized seedlings and western redcedar plug+1 transplants with 5-cm Vexar® tubes installed before planting. This plantation (replants only) was two years old at last measurement, and the residual seedlings of the original planting reflected four growing seasons under severe elk pressure. They are summarized separately.

For the seedling data, two types of analyses were performed. The first set of analyses examined the relationship between 1) seedlings planted in the clearcut areas and those planted under the residual stands, 2) seedlings in weeded and unweeded areas in the clearcuts, 3) browsed and unbrowsed seedlings in the clearcuts, and 4) browsed and unbrowsed seedlings in the weeded and unweeded areas in the clearcuts. All stock types were analyzed separately, and only those seedlings that were alive at the time of the last measurement were included in the analyses. For these analyses, we used PROC MIXED in SAS® and the analysis of covariance for comparison of regression lines as outlined in Littell et al. (1996). The dependent variable was stem volume index (an easily measured estimator of total stem volume), calculated as height*basal diameter^2*π/12 and the independent variable was year of measurement (zero to three or four). For the second set of analyses, equations for each species and site were developed relating stem volume index in year three (Bark Creek) or four (other sites) to different cover variables. For all species and sites, the best equation was ln(volume index) = β_0+ β_1 ln(initial volume) + β_2 overtopping + β_3 overstory cover. For Bark Creek cover, overtopping and overstory cover were from year three, and for all other sites, from year four.

Benthic Sampling

The sampling design for insects was described by Walsh (1996) and was first developed on the Phase I streams, then extended to Phase II streams. Among the four Phase I streams, Bark Creek was not sampled, because the bottom was covered with fine sediments and organic detritus on which few insects were observed, and the invertebrate biomass was dominated by snails. Initial insect sampling was done on Phase I streams in the first season following harvest (1993), and was repeated in the second year to determine whether populations were still responding. Phase II streams were sampled in July and September, 1995, two years after harvest, and at this time Phase I streams were re-sampled so the two groups of streams could be compared. For both Phases we placed four sampling stations on each stream, with one station upstream at least 20 m from cutting units, one 20+m below the cutting unit, and two within the cutting unit representing the upstream half and downstream half of the cutting unit. All samples were taken in riffles to minimize variance so as to increase sensitivity to harvest effects. In each designated sampling area, all stretches of riffle at least 4.5-m long were noted, and one was randomly chosen for sampling. Fish also consume insects washed down into pools, eddies, backwaters, and the downstream edge of riffles; our sampling system did not capture these drift organisms, and they are not reflected in our findings.

For each sampling station, a 4.5-m length of stream was divided into 45 sample spots in a 3 x 15 grid pattern, each being 1/3 of the channel width wide by 30 cm long (fig. 4). Six of the sections were then sampled each date following a systematic non-aligned design so that two samples were randomly chosen from the 15 sections on each of left, middle, and right part of the stream on each sampling date. These six subsamples were pooled for analysis. Sections of the grid that were sampled in July were not resampled in September.

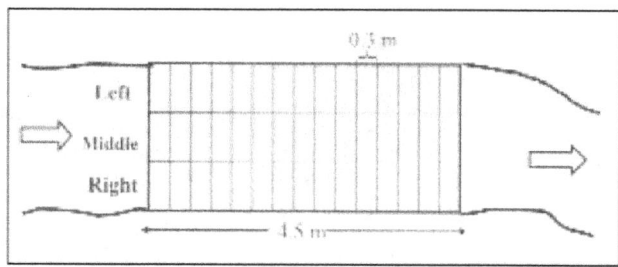

Figure 4—Schematic design of sample location grid used to randomize collections at each benthic sampling station.

A 30-cm X 30-cm Surber sample (sample collected from a net into a jar) was collected on the stream bottom within each sampled section with the following specifications. Every rock in the sample square to a depth of 8 cm was cleaned while in the water upstream from the collection net. Variability between subsamples was examined by Walsh (1996) and provided the basis for pooling and subsampling for eventual estimation of populations with 50% of the original combined sample material. July samples were sub-sampled again in the lab, to reduce identification time. Identification of insects smaller than 1.1 mm was extremely time-consuming and inexact, hence samples of record were restricted to insects larger than 1.1 mm after the first year. This resulted in small sample sizes, and seasonal comparisons were not attempted. Insects were identified down to the family and genus level where possible. It was extremely difficult to differentiate between genera in some families (e.g., Plecoptera, Perlidae), and a few of the insects were damaged from handling. Genera were assigned to functional feeding groups as per Merritt and Cummins (1994).

Data were analyzed for Phase I in 1993 and 1994 by Walsh (1996) in substantial detail to show immediate responses to clearcutting. Those analyses included only the three streams with reforestation experiments on them. Briefly, influence of substrate composition, stream velocity, temperature and estimated radiation load (evaluated by estimating vegetative cover with a densiometer) were evaluated for their effects on both abundance and diversity of genera, using regressions based on log-transformed insect counts. Residuals from regression were subjected to repeated measures analyses of variance for tests of differences between streams, stations within streams, and interactions.

In 1995, additional samples (third year) were run in Phase I streams and compared to second-year samples in Phase II streams. In view of the increased sample sizes when analyzing 1995 samplings of Phase I and II installations together, a separate analysis was used with the primary objective of comparing effects of treatment on large insect populations. Sample data were first transformed to approximate normality in order to run parametric statistics. Analyses of variance (ANOVAs) were performed for total abundance, relative abundance, functional feeding groups, and generic richness for all experimental streams together combining Phase I and II experiments. Means were compared between treatment streams, cut and uncut reaches, and stations. Relative abundance was calculated as the percent of each order in each sample collected. Tukey's Honest Significant Difference test (HSD) was used to compare multiple means. Spearman's rank correlations were done for each of the insect variables with stream temperature and discharge.

Stream Temperature

Stream temperatures were recorded for two years immediately following harvest treatments (Phase I) and one year before and one year after for Phase II installations. Four to six thermistors (two-channel Omnidata Datapod Digital Recorders) were placed in each Phase I stream to record water and air temperature, including one or two thermistors above the entire study reach, below the study, in one clearcut, and at one or more other locations in covered sections between clearcuts. The thermistors recorded diurnal temperature fluctuations through the June-September season. Reflecting the importance of temperature extremes, our findings are presented in terms of the influence of treatment on the means of the maximum temperatures occurring in the seven consecutive days with the highest seven-day-mean temperature in each year of record, the standard regulatory criterion. We bring in data from Zwieniecki and Newton (1999) reflecting temperature patterns before and after harvest in sixteen headwaters streams that include the three Phase II installations with sun-sided cover screens. On the other 13 streams they described, clearcut harvesting had been done in which a portion were buffered according to conventional harvest buffer rules (15-21-m buffers on both sides), and half were done with hardwood conversion rules (6-m no-touch buffers, with up to 180 m of stream length per unit having all trees removed).

RESULTS

Reforestation

Each stream had unique features and events that force a presentation of data separately for each. Bark and Buttermilk Creeks, our Coast Range sites, had heavy mortality immediately after planting of all stock types. Because of the replanting at Bark Creek, we only have three years of data for those seedlings. In both Bark and Buttermilk Creek studies, it will also be noted that the "large" and "small"

Douglas-fir seedlings were of similar size, but one was 1+1 and the other was plug+1 in nursery regimes, so differences between stock types were minor initially. Ames Creek and Mosby Creek differed from the Coast Range streams in having been prepared too late for site-preparation herbicides, necessitating the use of directed spot herbicide treatments instead. Ames Creek had significant herbicide injury to a number of seedlings. Unrelated to this, Mosby Creek plantings were devastated by frost, elk and rocky substrate resulting from prior mining activity; hence there is great uncertainty in evaluating their future growth.

Bark Creek: Although the large and small Douglas-fir stock types were similar in size when planted, analyses indicate that there was a difference in the volume trajectory ($p = 0.0495$). Examination of the means for year three (table 1) indicate that the small Douglas-fir continued to be smaller than the large Douglas-fir when underplanted in unweeded areas. The volume growth from year two to three (not shown) was three times greater for the large Douglas-fir than the small Douglas-fir in these areas. Results for the two stock types elsewhere along Bark Creek were similar (table 1). Both stock types of Douglas-fir and redcedar were larger ($p < 0.0022$) in clearcut areas than in underplanted areas.

Within the clearcut areas, the large Douglas-fir and western hemlock did not show an increase in growth due to weeding ($p = 0.5041$ and 0.1395, respectively). Spraying did not consistently result in the low levels of cover that are usually needed for major increases in growth (table 2). Redcedar ($p = 0.0024$) and the small Douglas-fir ($p = 0.0137$) did have greater growth in the weeded areas. Year three stem volume for all species was negatively correlated with both overstory cover and overtopping with similar patterns to those shown for Ames Creek in figures 5 to 8.

Buttermilk Creek: Although initial size of the Douglas-fir stock types did not differ, by the end of the fourth year, there were differences ($p < 0.0001$) among the two stock types especially where weeded (table 1). It is not known if these differences are attributable to greater vigor at the time of planting, differences in root mass, or both. However, by the end of the fourth growing season, the large Douglas-fir (1+1) were over 35% larger in volume than the small Douglas-fir (plug+1) in both the weeded and unweeded clearcut areas. All species had greater volume in clearcut areas than in underplanted areas ($p < 0.0724$). All stock types were affected by competition ($p < 0.0619$). In the clearcut areas, stem volume of weeded redcedar, hemlock, and small and large Douglas-fir averaged 62, 79, 20, and 32% larger than the unweeded seedlings after four years.

Table 1—Height, basal diameter at 15 cm, and stem volume index for year 3 (Bark Creek) and year 4 (Buttermilk, Ames and Mosby Creeks)

		Bark Creek			Buttermilk Creek			Ames Creek			Mosby Creek		
		Height (cm)	Diameter (mm)	Volume (cm³)	Height (cm)	Diameter (mm)	Volume (cm³)	Height (cm)	Diameter (mm)	Volume (cm³)	Height (cm)	Diameter (mm)	Volume (cm³)
Overstory <=15%													
Unweeded	Large Douglas-fir	130	16.0	115	205	26.2	477	191	22.9	360	137	21.3	198
	Small Douglas-fir	126	15.3	101	167	21.5	298	120	14.8	103	90	14.2	68
	Redcedar	69	9.9	24	147	19.4	234	130	15.7	120	75	11.5	38
	Hemlock	106	10.1	42	176	16.3	182	117	11.0	60	100	11.8	60
Weeded	Large Douglas-fir	120	18.2	129	216	28.8	628	185	24.5	390	126	21.4	188
	Small Douglas-fir	125	18.2	124	179	23.2	356	120	16.5	132	90	15.0	68
	Redcedar	72	11.6	30	164	23.7	378	130	17.8	167	80	13.8	61
	Hemlock	107	11.3	46	205	20.2	326	138	13.8	105	112	13.9	81
Overstory >15%													
Unweeded	Large Douglas-fir	111	12.6	59	168	21.3	293	133	15.3	98	121	24.1	131
	Small Douglas-fir	98	11.4	36	177	20.0	253	85	9.0	25	87	10.7	32
	Redcedar	60	8.1	12	138	17.8	197	99	9.6	31	62	7.3	11
	Hemlock	100	9.0	28	159	14.9	171	71	6.8	11	86	8.8	20
Weeded	Large Douglas-fir	117	14.9	84	204	25.1	409	136	15.6	106	103	13.6	60
	Small Douglas-fir	123	14.8	82	150	18.1	158	93	10.6	41	77	10.4	35
	Redcedar	74	9.9	23	121	14.7	98	108	12.4	60	76	8.4	21
	Hemlock	130	11.4	54	158	13.2	117	100	9.8	34	96	10.3	34

Table 4—Percent overtopping and overstory cover in year 3 (Bark Creek) and year 3 (other creeks) and percent total cover in years 1 and 2 for all creeks in Phase 1

—Percent—

		Bark Creek				Buttermilk Creek				Ames Creek				Mosby Creek			
		Over-topping yr 3	Over-story cover yr 3	Total cover yr 1	Total cover yr 2	Over-topping yr 4	Over-story cover yr 4	Total cover yr 1	Total cover yr 2	Over-topping yr 4	Over-story cover yr 4	Over-story cover yr 1	Total cover yr 2	Total topping yr 4	Over-story cover yr 4	Total cover yr 1	Total cover yr 2
Overstory <=15%																	
Unweeded	Large Douglas-fir	21	10	75	90	12	9	76	75	33	11	45	73	19	11	41	61
	Small Douglas-fir	22	11	77	89	16	12	73	75	43	11	40	74	20	9	38	58
	Redcedar	39	12	79	94	24	15	77	76	42	12	46	73	23	10	41	61
	Hemlock	33	10	75	92	23	9	74	77	42	12	42	71	25	8	38	6
Weeded	Large Douglas-fir	3	10	63	76	17	5	51	70	30	12	34	62	10	11	35	55
	Small Douglas-fir	5	10	63	75	20	6	46	68	39	12	32	60	9	9	33	53
	Redcedar	10	12	64	77	25	7	53	70	36	13	33	61	13	15	32	55
	Hemlock	7	10	65	80	23	5	50	67	38	12	35	61	17	13	35	56
Overstory >15%																	
Unweeded	Large Douglas-fir	34	55	70	88	13	48	76	67	36	52	33	66	8	56	20	37
	Small Douglas-fir	47	53	74	89	22	36	82	75	48	43	35	76	17	47	30	35
	Redcedar	58	57	81	98	23	48	75	76	41	51	35	71	14	58	30	29
	Hemlock	45	46	78	95	23	48	72	66	62	42	40	71	4	54	15	31
Weeded	Large Douglas-fir	13	51	54	65	17	28	33	63	14	57	23	53	9	71	31	36
	Small Douglas-fir	11	51	59	65	27	26	36	67	15	59	24	47	7	59	26	30
	Redcedar	11	57	60	71	28	41	48	66	26	57	33	53	4	72	30	32
	Hemlock	11	54	63	74	32	32	37	60	17	54	25	55	24	44	22	39

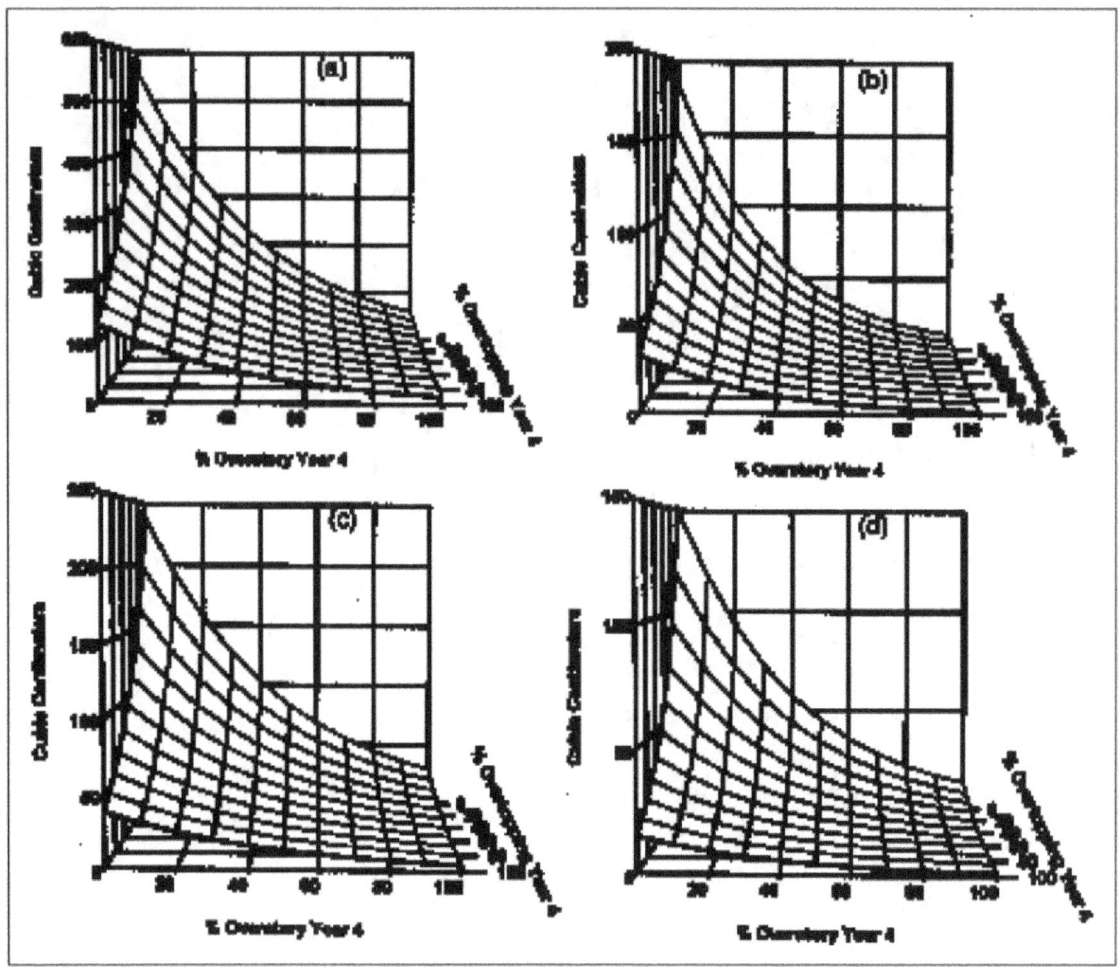

Figure 5—Stem volume index of (a) unbrowsed large Douglas-fir, (b) unbrowsed small Douglas-fir, (c) unbrowsed western redcedar, and (d) unbrowsed western hemlock at age 4 as a function of overtopping by hardwoods and shrubs, Ames Creek. Note: Scale for z axes is different for each species.

Ames Creek: Differences between stock types (1+1 and 2+0 bare-root) of Douglas-fir were still apparent after four years (table 1). The relative difference between the types has been decreasing, but absolute differences are increasing. Initially, the large 1+1 seedlings were seven times larger in volume than the small 2+0 seedlings. At age four, large seedlings were only three times larger, but had more absolute growth for the first four years.

This installation was established too late to complete broadcast site preparation sprays in the appropriate season, and careful spot treatments during active conifer growth were all that could be done. In the process some seedlings were damaged despite care. There were no differences in growth between weeded and unweeded areas for large Douglas-fir seedlings (p = 0.2034), but the other stock types had greater growth in the weeded clearcut areas (p < 0.0322).

Redcedar and hemlock seedlings averaged 39 and 75% larger in volume, respectively, in weeded clearcut areas than in the unweeded clearcut areas. Regression equations indicated that for all stock types, level of competition affected growth (fig. 5).

Mosby Creek: A variety of sources of damage have severely compromised the initial plantation at Mosby Creek. In addition to the rockiness that was atypical of riparian soils, the mining had relocated some water channels that eventually flooded or buried some of the plantings. Thus, success was limited by physical circumstances. Nevertheless, the site remains fundamentally productive, as measured by its initial condition when selected. In addition to the physical limitations of this site, problems with spring and fall freezing damage occurred in both sprayed and unsprayed portions of the study.

Table 3—Height, diameter[a], and stem volume for new plantings, age 2, at Mosby Creek

		Overstory<=15%			Overstory>15%		
		Height (cm)	Diameter[a] (mm)	Volume (cm³)	Height (cm)	Diameter[a] (mm)	Volume (cm³)
Unweeded	Grand Fir	43	7.3	7.1	39	6.4	5.3
	Redcedar	57	7.7	9.6	66	7.5	10.6
	Ponderosa Pine	38	9.2	10.4	29	7.8	5.3
	White Pine	19	5.0	1.5	16	4.5	0.9
Weeded	Grand Fir	49	9.1	12.1	46	7.6	8.2
	Redcedar	55	8.2	10.9	58	6.8	8.3
	Ponderosa Pine	38	10.1	12.7	29	7.7	5.2
	White Pine	21	5.9	2.1	17	5.0	1.3

[a] Diameter refers to diameter at 15 cm above ground for grand fir, redcedar, and ponderosa pine. Diameter is root collar diameter for white pine.

The large Douglas-fir stock type (1+1) continued to be the largest seedlings on the units (table 1). In clearcut areas, the large Douglas-fir averaged almost three times greater volume than the small Douglas-fir. Both stock types of Douglas-fir and redcedar had less growth in underplanted areas ($p < 0.0001$). Hemlock averaged over twice the size in clearcut areas than in underplanted areas, but differences were not significant ($p = 0.7869$) in part due to low survival (14 %) in underplanted areas.

Although differences in average seedling size for Douglas-fir and redcedar in the weeded and unweeded areas were relatively small ($p > 0.0984$), competition reduced seedling growth similar to that shown for Ames Creek in figure 5, but with smaller volumes in general. Hemlock seedlings were larger in the weeded areas ($p = 0.0065$).

For the "new" plantings, at the end of two years, the grand fir and ponderosa pine were growing best (table 3). Although redcedars were the largest initially, they were exhibiting poor growth, as with the first planting. Although relative growth between the two pines was similar, the white pines were still very small, and survival was poor.

All Sites: Animal damage had a major impact on all plantations. Mountain beaver clipping occurred on three of the sites (table 4), and beaver clipping occurred on two of the sites. At least 50% of the seedlings that had been damaged by beavers were dead. Although the overall percentage of damage by beavers was low, the local impacts were severe. As would be expected, the damage by beavers was concentrated within 15 m of streams, but damage was seen more than 30 m from the stream.

Hemlock was infrequently browsed on all sites. For the other stock types, browsing impacts were related to location of the seedling (weeded or unweeded areas, clearcut or underplanted areas), whether or not the browsing was done by deer or elk, whether browsing reduced shrub cover adjacent to the seedling, and inherent productivity of the site. Browsed Douglas-fir were reduced in stem volume at age four by 23-45 percent at the various sites. Redcedar volume reduction from browsing was greater, ranging from 50-60 percent relative to unbrowsed seedlings. As overtopping increased, the absolute impact of browsing decreased; the unbrowsed seedlings growing under high degrees of overtopping do not grow as well as those with low amounts of overtopping. The lesser impact is associated with loss of potential, over all, as long as overtopping remains.

Insect Abundance

Phase I analyses for the first and second years of response to harvest showed that stream substrate explained more variation in absolute abundance, diversity and functional feeding groups than any other stream variable ($p < 0.001$). The order in which substrate had a positive effect on total abundance was cobble>bedrock>boulder=sand=silt>gravel. Walsh (1996) provides details of this analysis by genera showing which genera were favored by each substrate medium. Of the remaining environmental variables, stream velocity explained the most variance, as would be expected from the comparatively high velocities of riffles compared with other substrates. Collector-filterers were positively associated with velocity. Mayfly (Ephemeroptera) and caddisfly (Trichoptera) genera were positively correlated with stream velocity and also negatively correlated with exposed bedrock; those which were negatively associated with velocity were positively correlated with fine-textured substrates. Radiation load, as estimated by densiometer, did

Table 4—Animal damage and mortality after 3 years (Bark Creek) or 2 years (other creeks)

		Beaver live and dead (no.)	Beaver damaged dead	Mountain beaver live and dead (no.)	Mountain beaver damaged dead	Browsing live and dead (no.)	Browsing live	Mortality and not found (no.)	Total (no.)
					—————Percent———				
Bark Creek	Large Douglas-fir	8 (50)	87	5.7 (36)	42	42 (264)	64	46 (291)	629
	Small Douglas-fir	9 (56)	61	6.9 (43)	26	44 (273)	62	43 (264)	620
	Redcedar	6 (38)	50	3.3 (21)	24	63 (397)	85	32 (201)	630
	Hemlock	3 (19)	63	3 (19)	63	4 (25)	6	49 (305)	620
Buttermilk Creek	Large Douglas-fir	9.2 (77)	86	3.8 (32)	34	27 (225)	39	51 (423)	835
	Small Douglas-fir	9.3 (77)	77	2.9 (24)	29	25 (208)	48	63 (526)	830
	Redcedar	16 (130)	43	1.8 (15)	27	3.2 (27)	5.6	55 (457)	835
	Hemlock	13 (111)	58	4.0 (33)	70	3.0 (25)	4.7	49 (406)	835
Ames Creek	Large Douglas-fir	—	—	—	—	22 (374)	27	23 (166)	721
	Small Douglas-fir	—	—	—	—	25 (178)	34	30 (217)	714
	Redcedar	—	—	—	—	27 (193)	31	15 (108)	716
	Hemlock	—	—	—	—	0.8 (6)	1	38 (269)	708
Mosby Creek	Large Douglas-fir	—	—	8 (74)	47	25 (220)	43	62 (555)	890
	Small Douglas-fir	—	—	5 (45)	51	14 (128)	32	69 (612)	890
	Redcedar	—	—	5 (44)	32	14 (128)	48	75 (667)	890
	Hemlock	—	—	3 (25)	36	3 (24)	15	87 (777)	890

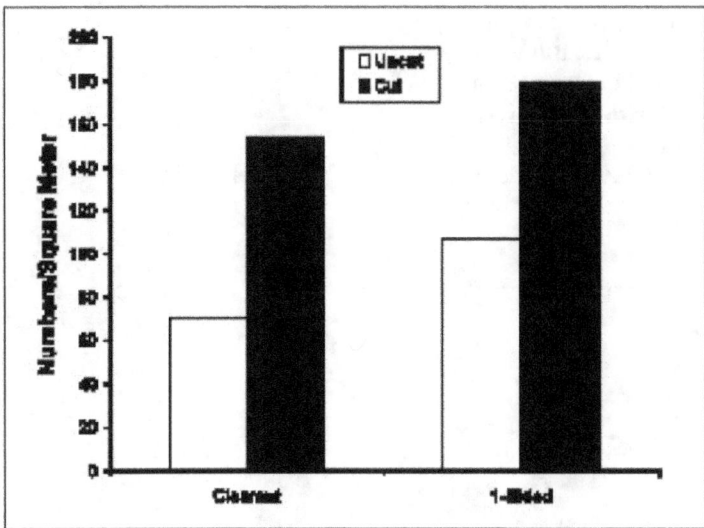

Figure 6—Total abundance of insects in each treatment type for Phase I and II studies.

not significantly explain the variance of any mayfly or caddisfly groups or functional feeding group, nor did stream temperature.

Absolute abundance of most genera increased between the first and second years following harvest ($p < 0.01$) and most genera responded positively to harvest, with the strongest response being in the second year. Only one genus, *Drumella*, displayed more abundance outside the cutting unit than within it, in general, and was more abundant both upstream and downstream from a clearing than within the clearcut. All others showing a significant response were in greater numbers within the harvest unit than above or below it ($p < 0.05$). *Cyningmula* and *Rhithrogena* were more abundant downstream from the harvest units than above the unit ($p < 0.05$).

The analyses of abundance in cut versus uncut units of Phase II data all reflected second-year responses, and they are compared here with third-year responses in Phase I experimental streams; both sets of data compare same year cut versus uncut while total abundance following clearcutting versus one-sided buffered cuts are based on two versus three years since cutting. Mean total abundance (per square meter) of benthic insects in the two uncut reaches up and downstream from each clearcut unit was half (82.6) the mean abundance in the cut reaches (165.4, $p = 0.002$, fig. 6) in both Phases I and II. Overall abundance between the clearcut and one-sided streams did not differ ($p = 0.18$). Upstream stations had lower abundance than the two stations within cuts ($p = 0.004$) (table 5, fig. 7), and there was

a general increase in insect abundance in a downstream direction, as streams increased in size. Initial conditions in streams were not identical, but numbers were comparable. Within the uncut reaches, there appeared to be fewer insects in streams scheduled for zero-buffer treatment than there were in one-sided streams, but the difference is not significant ($p = 0.132$). Abundance was similar between the two treatment types (one-sided buffers and clearcuts) in cut reaches ($p = 0.737$).

Different orders of insects displayed varying responses to harvest, but three orders were more abundant in cut than in uncut reaches. Diptera (true flies) displayed the greatest differences in mean abundance between the cut plots (17.2) and uncut plots (6.5, $p = 0.009$). Trichoptera displayed a large difference between cut (mean = 67.0) and uncut (mean = 40.7) reaches ($p = 0.025$), and Ephemeroptera also differed (22 versus 13, $p = 0.09$).

Some, but not all, effect of clearing on caddisflies and mayflies showed up a short distance downstream, where numbers were greater than upstream densities. We were unable to separate the effect of stream position from that of increased light when combining up-and downstream data for these orders with data from the clearings, but both were generally less abundant in the upstream uncut plots than in the cut plots ($p = 0.017$ and 0.09, respectively) (fig. 7). Plecoptera (stoneflies) and Coleoptera (beetles) did not differ in overall abundance between cut and uncut reaches, hence post-harvest species ratios were somewhat altered although no order decreased with harvest.

Table 5—Total abundance, insects of all genera >1.1 mm long per composite sample taken from six low-elevation western Oregon streams. Ames, Buttermilk, and Mosby Creeks were harvested both sides with no buffers in 90 or 180 m patches; Brush, Mill, and Scheele were clearcut both sides with 12 m screen south of stream for buffer on 805 m reaches

Stream	Upstream uncut	Within cuts		Downstream uncut
		Upstream	Downstream	
Ames (CC)	114	392	258	163
Buttermilk (CC)	27	115	71	2
Mosby (CC)	100	194	312	142
Percent of all insects/reach, all streams	13	37	33	17
Brush (OS)	136	140	129	131
Mill (OS)	134	163	371	137
Scheele (OS)	132	185	283	101
Percent of all insects/reach, all streams	20	24	38	18

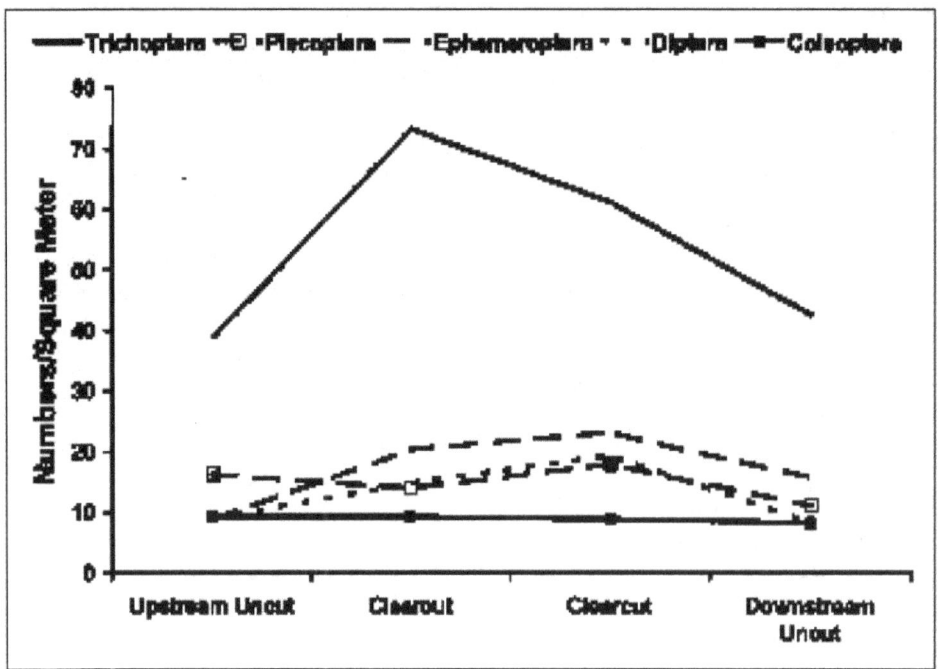

Figure 7—Total abundance of each taxonomic order for the four stations in the one-sided buffer (Phase II study).

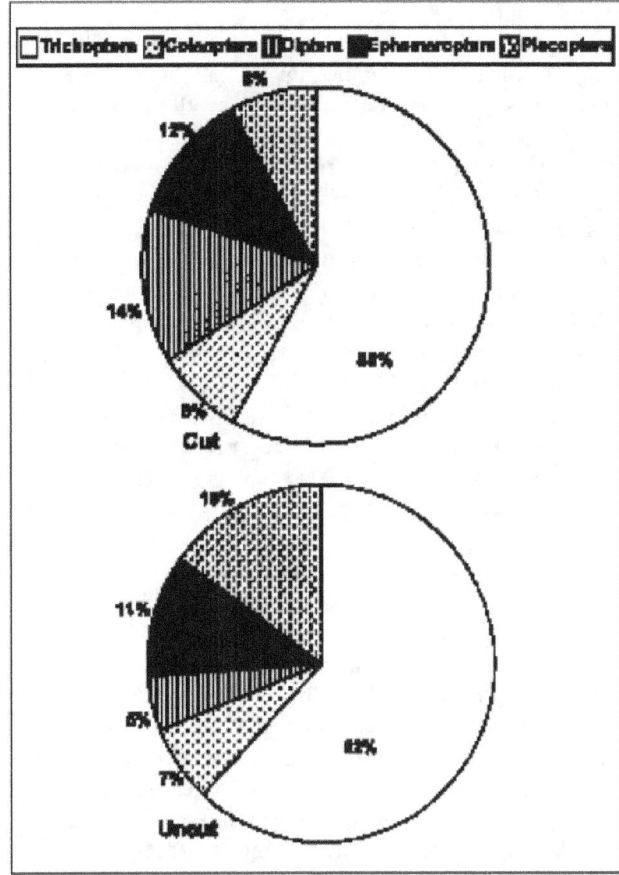

Figure 8—Relative abundance of insect taxonomic orders in cut and uncut reaches for Phase I and II studies.

Within cut reaches only, there appears to be 50% more Ephemeroptera and 60% fewer Coleoptera in one-sided streams than in clearcut reaches, but results were not significant ($p > 0.10$). Only five individuals of Odonata (Gomphidae, dragonflies) were collected, thus they were left out of analyses by taxonomic orders, but included in the functional feeding group analysis.

Total abundance was mildly and positively correlated with both stream discharge ($r = 0.36$, $p = 0.013$) and the seven-day maximum mean temperature ($r = 0.31$, $p = 0.032$). Plecoptera and Ephemeroptera abundance were more strongly correlated with discharge, with fewer insects when discharge was low ($r = 0.49$, $p = 0.0004$ and $r = 0.51$, $p = 0.0002$, respectively). At the genus level, *Baetidae Baetis* and *Ephemerellidae Eurylophella* in Ephemeroptera were positively correlated to discharge. No individual genera could be identified in Plecoptera.

Abundances for some insects were positively related to temperatures of streamwater. Trichoptera abundance was

positively correlated with the seven-day maximum mean temperature ($r = 0.53$, $p = 0.0001$), which may explain much of the correlation for total abundance. Only two of the four genera (with adequate numbers) within Trichoptera were significantly correlated, and here the correlation was positive: *Glossosomatidae Glossosoma* ($r= 0.39$, $p = 0.006$) and *Limnephilidae Neophylax* ($r= 0.41$, $p = 0.004$). The mayflies in *Ephemerellidae Euryophella/Ephemerella* had a positive correlation ($r = 0.49$, $p = 0.0004$). No other taxonomic orders were generally correlated with temperature.

The relative taxonomic composition did not differ substantially between cut and uncut reaches of different streams (fig. 8). Only Diptera increased in relative abundance in cut stands ($p = 0.03$), and Plecoptera decreased slightly ($p = 0.07$). Relative abundance of insects between clearcut and one-sided streams differed for two insect orders. Coleoptera were more abundant in the clearcut streams ($p = 0.052$), both in the uncut (100% more) and cut (200% more) reaches than in the streams with one-sided buffers. The interaction was not significant ($p = 0.42$). Ephemeroptera were more abundant in the one-sided streams ($p = 0.09$), with 50% more in uncut reaches and 100% more in cut reaches, reflecting both random differences between streams independent of treatment, and also effect of treatment.

The insect genera were divided into five functional feeding groups (FFG): collector-filterers, collector-gatherers, scrapers, shredders, and predators. Some genera or families contain diverse species that belong in more than one type of FFG, thus separate categories of collector-gatherers/scrapers and collector-gatherers/shredders were included. Few genera in this sample fell into the collector-gatherer/shredder category, so those were not analyzed statistically.

Collector-filterers, collector-gathers, and predators responded similarly to harvest design (clearcut vs. one-sided buffer), and types of harvest were pooled for analysis. All functional feeding groups were more abundant in cut reaches than uncut reaches in both clearcut and one-sided streams ($p = 0.009$, 0.017, and 0.030, respectively). The relative abundance of insect groups did not change markedly after harvest (fig. 9). Although predators increased by almost 50%, their percentage of all insects decreased due to the overall increase in benthic insect of all kinds in cut reaches. Shredders displayed an interaction effect, with more specimens from uncut portions of one-sided streams and more in the cut portion of clearcut streams ($p = 0.037$). At least one of the clearcut streams (Buttermilk) had large amounts of wood only in the cut portions, which may have trapped significant detritus and attracted more shredders.

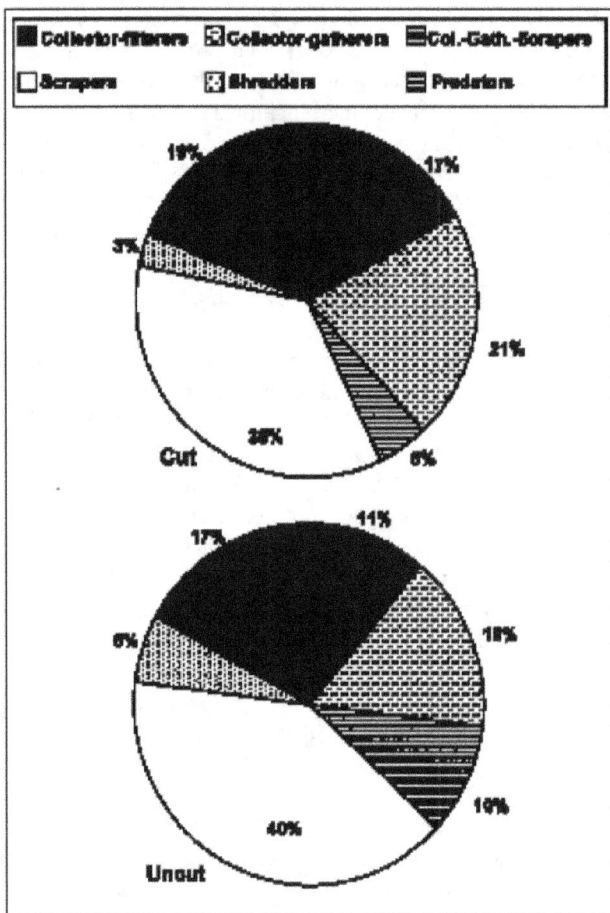

Figure 9—Relative abundance of functional feeding groups in cut and uncut reaches for Phase I and II studies.

Abundance of some FFGs varied by treatment type. Within the uncut plots there were more shredders and predators in streams with one-sided buffers, and more collector-gatherers and collector-gatherer/scrapers in the clearcut streams. Despite these apparent differences, within-cut comparisons showed only the shredders differed between treatments, with twice as many insects in the clearcuts than in the one-sided cuts. There were no differences in overall abundance between streams of the two treatment types.

The number of genera represented in each stream system did not differ by treatment types ($p = 0.743$), or between cut versus uncut ($p = 0.122$). The mean number of genera found in the uncut portions of both sets of treatment was about the same (9.3 for clearcut, 9.5 for one-side), and the means in cut reaches were also similar (10.9 for clearcut, 11.4 for one-side). East Brush Creek (one-side) had low generic richness (2-4) at all stations in September, although the number of individuals in the samples was normal.

Stream Temperature

Temperature of water was evaluated at the warmest part of each summer, based on the moving maxima of water temperatures for seven consecutive days with the warmest mean temperatures. Temperature profiles in the four unbuffered (Phase I) experimental streams were not consistent, either in their patterns of warming or in uniformity from year to year. None appeared to warm significantly more than would be expected for a 750-m-long reach less than 8 km from the source, but lack of pre-harvest basin-wide trends were not recorded for reference. Dent (1995) indicated that there were some measurable impacts on stream temperature, but she had not compensated for the expected rate of warming in covered reaches of comparable position in the basins, a procedure regarded as necessary for estimation of net warming (Newton and Zwieniecki 1996, Zwieniecki and Newton 1999).

Streams showed variation in the amount of temperature change between clearcuts, both among streams and among years of observations, as reported by Dent (1995). The first two years of data following harvest reflected contrasts in summer temperature, with 1993 being cool and wet, and 1994 being extremely hot and dry. In 1993, the first year following harvest, water exiting the study reach ranged from 0.2°C in Bark Creek to 1.2°C in Buttermilk (main stem) warmer than water at the upper end of each study reach, based on seven-day moving mean maxima. Nearly all the net rise occurred in harvested units, as shown by Dent (1995). In 1994 during the period of least discharge, Bark Creek gained 0.6°C over all, representing gains in clearcut units and losses between cut units, while Buttermilk Creek gained about 1.6°C over all, with no consistent pattern between cut and uncut units even though the previous year had shown maximum warming to occur in harvest units. No stream gained more than 1.6°C in the length of a study reach (Dent 1995), a rise typical of the natural downstream warming trends of several headwaters streams reported by Newton and Zwieniecki (1996). Unfortunately, without baseline measurements, we are unable to determine if the observed trends represent a change from pre-harvest conditions.

The uppermost cut unit on Buttermilk Creek was actually on a major tributary rather than on the main stem. The main stem was largely slack water behind beaver dams above the confluence, hence unsuitable for study, but there was a large temperature rise at the confluence reflecting the warm water from the shallow beaver impoundments. This accounted for much of the total increase in the study reach. Phase II streams were described in the report by Zwieniecki and Newton (1999) which did have both pre- and post-harvest data. Their report showed that all three of the Phase II streams (sun-side buffered) were at or below pre-harvest rates of warming with downstream flow soon after water re-entered uncut stands.

DISCUSSION

The reforestation experiments demonstrate the difficulty in establishing conifers in the presence of overtopping shrubs and animals that damage seedlings. Problems with low temperature can likely be reduced or eliminated by choice of frost-hardy species, but their suitability for long-term growth in streamside environments remains untested. Herbivory will remain a serious problem regardless of species planted as long as beavers have unrestricted access to streamside regeneration.

Robison and Beschta (1990) have identified sites within 15 m of the streambank as the potential sources for most local tree-fall recruitment of large wood. Losses of regeneration attributable to beavers were most frequent in this zone, and led to elimination of most regeneration in large portions of both Bark and Buttermilk Creek experiments. Beavers were not selective among species. In these streams, beavers were not restricted in their locations by dams or other obvious residence areas, and they appeared to travel over the length of experiments and occasionally forage more than 30 m from the streams. The long-term effects of this are important, because the possibility of recruitment of conifers by natural regeneration in these areas is low owing to re-development of competing cover. Even if conifers did occasionally regenerate naturally, new seedlings would likely be damaged or killed unless the beaver pressure decreased. Fencing to keep beavers in the stream and away from the plantations worked at one site for a time. However, flooding breached the fences in several places, and cattle grazing in the units resulted in trampling of the fence. Fence failure allowed the beavers to continue foraging on the seedlings, and damage was often lethal.

Damage by deer and elk was generally not lethal, but did reduce growth. Visual examination of these plantations after ten years reveals good plantation development in clearcuts except where mortality from herbivory created large gaps. Regeneration in uncut stands was ultimately unsuccessful. The need to reduce competition for establishment and growth of conifers in riparian areas was noted by Chan et al. (1998) and Emmingham et al. (2000) in their reviews of riparian regeneration studies. They also noted that both shade tolerant and shade intolerant species were limited by overhead competitors, as we demonstrate with illustrations of interactions between canopy cover and shrubs in uncut stands, and with shrubs as overtopping where

unsprayed. We also confirm that use of large, vigorous planting stock increases the likelihood of survival in both browsing and competitive environments, provided overtopping is not extreme and seedlings can be adequately planted. Howard and Newton (1984), Wagner and Radosevich (1991), and Newton et al. (1993) demonstrated a general adaptability of very large conifer seedlings in areas subject to herbivory and shrub competition in the Oregon Coast Range. Some success has also previously been observed after planting wild seedlings averaging 1.5 m tall in untreated salmonberry in shrub-dominated riparian systems near the Oregon coast (Newton, M., unpublished data, 1970, from cooperative experiments with the USDA Forest Service, Siuslaw National Forest, Waldport, OR). At Mosby Creek, the rocky soils made planting large seedlings difficult, and planting large seedlings may not be feasible in such areas.

Differences between sprayed and unsprayed areas were less than expected. Spraying with glyphosate soon after logging is typically unreliable because leaf area of shrubs has been removed to the extent that translocation to roots is sub-marginal. Application of this herbicide at least a month prior to late-summer harvest would likely have nearly eliminated shrub development except in the 3-m buffer required under Oregon Forest Practice rules for hand application. The spot treatments at Ames and Mosby Creeks were of inadequate size to be the equivalent of site preparation and were applied in spring, which led to rapid resprouting of shrubs and some damage to seedlings; treated and untreated areas were almost indistinguishable on those streams. There was also some suppression of shrubs in unsprayed parts of the experiments by herbivory, as noted in Mosby, Buttermilk and Bark Creeks where elk were abundant.

Large openings created by clearcutting demonstrated advantages in riparian management areas beyond those associated with establishment of conifers, and extend Berg's (1995) analysis beyond that associated with thinnings. The increase in benthic macroinvertebrates is consistent, both qualitatively and quantitatively with earlier reports from the Pacific Northwest. Murphy and Hall (1981) noted increased insect abundance in stream riffles within clearcuts with no residual overhead cover compared to riffles in streams dominated by old-growth stands; they observed somewhat decreased abundance in pools. Diversity was greater in clearcuts in their work, but we did not record either increases or decreases at the species level. Murphy et al. (1981) noted roughly the same increase in aquatic insects between uncut and clearcut reaches in summer, but also noted that differences in autumn after leaf-fall were not significant except for an increase beneath a hardwood canopy after leaf-fall. Insect numbers in riffles were consistently greater in clearcuts than in streams under canopies.

They noted no differences in insect response in riffles of high- vs. low-gradient streams although there were more decreases in insect abundance in pools than increases within clearcuts, regardless of gradient. We did not determine whether there was complete compensation by autochthonous sources for decreases in allochthonous inputs of food substrates.

Favorable effects of clearcutting in terms of stream productivity and regeneration must be interpreted in the same context as reported negative consequences. Concern has been expressed with respect to temperature (Sullivan et al. 1990, Brown and Krygier 1970) to the extent that the Environmental Protection Agency recommends a temperature standard of 17.8°C (64° F) maximum for seven-day moving mean of daily maximum temperatures in streams supporting salmonids. This level is exceeded in many streams under natural conditions of forest cover (Ice et al. 2004), suggesting that silvicultural activities potentially leading to a warming trend on such streams are likely to have negative effects on stream biota. In the event clearcutting were to raise temperature to a harmful level, the practice would not be permitted; under Oregon, Washington and California laws, clearcutting to the stream is either prohibited or tolerated only in rehabilitation situations regardless of baseline temperature patterns. The question remains open as to whether this limits future net stream productivity by restricting creation of openings with positive long-term effects.

Our streams did, on occasion, exceed 17.8°C briefly. We have inadequate data to determine whether downstream temperature was consistently raised or not raised as the result of cutting, and data reported by Zwieniecki and Newton (1999) suggest that increases in uncut areas downstream were in a range to be expected high in headwaters basins. In no case did reported temperatures rise enough to threaten mortality or cause a persistent depression of metabolism of fish or macroinvertebrates, according to current literature (Sullivan et al. 2000). Beschta et al. (1987) and Sullivan et al. (2000) have pointed out that fish can tolerate short-term exposure to temperatures several degrees higher than optimum without injury. Their reviews pointed out that the higher temperatures slow feeding rates while metabolism is elevated in the warmer conditions, and that this results in slower weight gain. Brett et al. (1969) describe maximum growth as increasing with temperature up to 15°C so long as food supplies are adequate. His data also indicate that growth of sockeye salmon fingerlings is positive (although not maximum) at temperatures well above 20°C. Data, largely from laboratory studies, has shown that tolerance to elevated temperatures is inversely related to duration or exposure to elevated temperatures (Sullivan et al. 2000). They reported that salmon can spend lengthy periods above 24°C without mortality or loss of vigor on return to cool conditions. The temperature effects reported above were from laboratory studies with temperatures held at constant levels. McMahon et al. (2001) exposed bull trout and brook trout to constant versus temperatures fluctuating plus or minus 3°C with the same mean temperatures. They observed that fish growth was slightly greater when water temperature was constant than when mean water temperature was the same but fluctuating, reflecting that less time is spent within the optimum range. These data indicate that it may be possible for fish populations to tolerate some exposure to temperatures above 17.8°C, but the impacts of fluctuating natural streams, repeated occurrences of such peaks for several days, and duration of exposure under different levels of food supply are unknown.

Inferences from this study pertaining to water temperature from the reforested reaches were limited in their ability to determine specifically where warming took place under variable canopies. Dent (1995) did show that most warming occurred in complete clearings and that some warming but more cooling occurred in shaded reaches. Data gathered in the sun-sided buffered streams were more comprehensive. None of the sun-sided buffers except Scheele Creek resulted in a net rise in temperature within the cutting unit despite the lack of buffer on one side. Scheele Creek showed slight warming in the lower end of the treated reach, but that peak was not observed immediately downstream from the cut unit. The data from Zwieniecki and Newton (1999) from clearcuts 16 to 48 ha in size indicated that average maximum temperatures on 16 streams may or may not rise above baseline maximum temperatures within harvest units. Their highest seven-day moving mean maximum temperature 300 m downstream from the harvest units never exceeded 2°C more than baseline trends, and based on one year of baseline and one year post-harvest data, there were as many streams cooler 300 m downstream from units as there were streams warmer than the baseline trends. These data demonstrated the pitfalls of reliance on single-year observations, of looking only in clearcuts and immediately upstream areas, and of failure to adjust for the expected downstream temperature rise before cutting.

The "sun-sided" buffers accomplished what was predicted for them by Newton's (1993) report regarding silvicultural prescriptions in riparian zones. The sun-screen on the south side intercepted most incoming direct radiation, and also presumably allowed outgoing radiation. Related work on streams in California (Newton and Zwieniecki

1997) has shown that streams flowing with no cover whatever, as in large burns, fluctuate greatly in diurnal temperature. In those streams, warming during the day appeared to be attenuated by streams becoming very cold at night, presumably reducing the stored heat in sediments and rocks so as to reduce heating during the day in the direct sun.

When streams absorb heat, as in a fully exposed clearcut reach on a hot day, peak temperatures tend to decrease when they re-enter a covered reach, but in an uneven pattern. The degree to which cooling may occur downstream from cutting units in the cooler air provided by shade is variable, depending on the individual stream system. It appears that over all, stream temperature is determined by a downstream temperature fluctuation pattern, or "signature" comprised of combinations of discharge, velocity, points of cool-water baseflow and confluences, coupled with patterns of gaps in cover (direct radiation) and air temperature patterns with decreasing altitude. Year-to-year variation in air temperature could be expected to raise or lower the whole trend. Radiation level does not appreciably vary from year to year except through changes in interception of radiation attributable to changes in plant cover. The combination of increased radiation and elevated air temperature on fresh slash adjacent to the stream would lead to energy loading on the stream that would increase with regional air temperature. Of significance is that the "sun-sided" buffers permitted the streams to stay within their signature patterns with no persistent hot spots, as nearly as we can determine, and are favorable to both regeneration and benthic insect productivity.

We have not addressed other impacts of clearcutting to streams. These may include bank damage, loss of existing trees with their woody debris recruitment potential, and loss of sources of leaf-fall and other inputs of organic debris used as food for aquatic invertebrates. We have also not addressed whether increases in insect abundance affect fish productivity and whether clearings affect insect abundance and stream temperature at other times of the year. We close with the caveat that logging needs to be done with care to avoid soil and streambank disturbance. It also is likely advantageous to leave strips of shrubs several meters wide along the banks both for shade and litter, regardless of other features of buffer design.

CONCLUSIONS

1. All three principal species of conifer—Douglas-fir, western hemlock, and western redcedar—displayed potential for good growth in riparian environments. Large seedlings grew better than small seedlings. Seedlings of ponderosa pine and grand fir were frost-hardy, but we have no measure of their long-term suitability for these types of plantings.

2. For satisfactory seedling growth of all species, both residual hardwoods and overtopping shrubs should be kept at a low level, however, a screen of shrubs should be retained along the bank to shade the stream and provide litter inputs.

3. Cover removal to the extent done in these experiments (Phases I and II) did not appear to cause warming of water by 300 m downstream of harvest units. In a companion study, none of the streams gained or lost more than 2°C compared to pre-harvest conditions when measured in uncut units 300 m downstream of cut units, based on the seven-day moving mean maximum for the seven consecutive warmest days. Clearcutting to the streambank facilitated regeneration and increased benthic productivity.

ACKNOWLEDGEMENTS

Sites and financial support for this study were provided by Starker Forests Inc, Corvallis, OR, Cascades Timber Consultants, Sweet Home, OR, Georgia Pacific Co, Toledo, OR, and Weyerhaeuser Co, Tacoma, WA. Financial assistance was provided by Oregon Department of Forestry, Salem, OR. Assistance in collecting and analyzing benthic insect samples and data was provided by Jennifer Walsh of Monmouth OR and Kajsa Wing of Corvallis OR. Assistance in monitoring and analyzing water temperature was provided by Elizabeth Dent and Ruth Willis.

LITERATURE CITED

Berg, R.B. 1995. Riparian silvicultural system design and assessment in the Pacific Northwest Cascade Mountains, USA. Ecological Applications 5: 87-96.

Beschta, R.L.; Bilby, R.E.; Brown; G.W.; Holtby, L.B.; Hofstra, T.D. 1987. Stream temperature and aquatic habitat: fisheries and forestry interactions. In: Salo, E.O.; Cundy, T.W., eds. Streamside management: forestry and fishery interactions Contribution 57. Seattle, WA: University of Washington College of Forest Resources. Chap. 6.

Brett, J.R.; Shelbourne, J.E.; Shoop, C.T. 1969. Growth rate and body composition of fingerling sockeye salmon (*Oncorhynchus nerka*), in relation to temperature and ration size. Journal of the Fisheries Research Board of Canada 26: 2363-2394.

Brown, G.W. 1969. Predicting temperature of small streams. Water Resources Research 5(1): 68-75

Brown, G.W.; Krygier, J.T. 1970. Effects of clearcutting on stream temperature. Water Resources Research 6(4): 1133-1140.

Caldwell, J.E.; Doughty, K.; Sullivan, K. 1991. Evaluation of downstream temperature effects of type 4/5 waters. Olympia, WA: Timber-Fish-Wildlife Water Quality Steering Committee and Washington Department of Natural Resources MS EL-03. 71 p.

Chan, S.S.; Minore, D.; Owston, P.W.; Hibbs, D.W. 1998. Tree regeneration in response to growing conditions in red alder dominated riparian areas. Progress Report. Corvallis, OR: COPE Program, Oregon State University College of Forestry. 7 p.

Dent, E.F. 1995. Influence of small clearcut openings in riparian areas on summer stream temperatures on coastal Oregon and western Cascade streams. COPE Report 8. Corvallis, OR: Oregon State University Forest Research Laboratory, COPE Program (3): 4-8.

Emmingham, W.E.; Chan, S.; Mikowski, D.; Owston, P.; Bishaw, B. 2000. Silvicultural practices for riparian forests in the Oregon Coast Range. Research Contribution 24. Corvallis, OR: Oregon State University Forest Research Laboratory. 34 p.

Hairston-Strang, A.B.; Adams, P.W. 1997. Oregon's streamside rules: achieving public goals on private lands. Journal of Forestry 95(7): 14-18.

Howard, K.M.; Newton, M. 1984. Overtopping by successional coast-range vegetation slows Douglas-fir seedlings. Journal of Forestry 82: 178-180.

Ice, G.G.; Light, J.; Reiter, M. 2004. Use of natural temperature patterns to identify achievable stream temperature criteria for forest streams. Western Journal of Applied Forestry. 19(4): 252-259.

King, J. 1966. Site index curves for Douglas-fir in the Pacific Northwest. Weyerhaeuser Forestry Paper No. 8. Centralia, WA: Weyerhaeuser Company Forestry Research Center. 46 p.

Littell, R.C.; Milliken, G.A.; Stroup, W.W.; Wolfinger, R.D. 1996. SAS® system for mixed models. Cary, NC: SAS Institute Inc. 633 p.

McMahon, T.; Zale, A.; Selong, J. 2001. Growth and survival temperature criteria for bull trout. Annual Report 2000. Corvallis, OR: National Council of Air and Stream Improvement. 31p.

Merritt, R.W.; Cummins, K.W., eds. 1984. An introduction to the aquatic insects of North America. 2nd edition. Dubuque, IA: Kendall/Hunt. 722 p.

Murphy, M.L.; Hall, J.C. 1981. Varied effects of clear-cut logging on predators and their habitat in small streams of the Cascade Mountain, Oregon. Canadian Journal of Fisheries and Aquatic Sciences 38: 137-145

Murphy, M.L.; Hawkins, C.P.; Anderson, N.H. 1981. Effects of canopy modification and accumulated sediment on stream communities. Transactions of the American Fisheries Society 110: 469-478.

Murphy, M.L.; Meehan, W.R. 1991. Stream ecosystems. Influences of forest and rangeland management on salmonid fishes and their habitats. American Fisheries Society 9(Special pub.): 17-46.

Newbold, J.D.; Ermen, D.C.; Roby, K.B. 1980. Effects of logging on macroinvertebrates in streams with and without buffer strips. Canadian Journal of Fisheries and Aquatic Sciences 37(7): 1076-1085.

Newton, M. 1993. Silvicultural alternatives in riparian zones: a management proposal, with technical background, for riparian forest management in the Douglas-fir region. Report. Oregon Forest Industries Council. 78 p.

Newton, M.; Cole, E.C.; White, D.E. 1993. Tall planting stock for enhanced growth and domination of brush in the Douglas-fir region. New Forests 7: 107-121.

Newton, M.; Zwieniecki, M. 1996. Temperature and streamflow regulation by streamside cover. Final Report, Oregon Department of Forestry. Corvallis, OR: Oregon State University, Forest Research Laboratory.

Newton, M.; Zwieniecki, M. 1997. Forest cover and water quality in northern California. Final Report, Roseburg Resources Co. Corvallis, OR: Oregon State University, Forest Research Laboratory.

Reeves, G.H.; Burnett, K.M.; McGarry, E.V. 2003. Sources of large wood in the main stem of a fourth-order watershed in coastal Oregon. Canadian Journal of Forest Research 33: 1363-1370.

Robison, E.G.; Beschta, R.L. 1990. Identifying trees in riparian areas that can provide coarse woody debris to streams. Forest Science 36(3): 790-801.

Sullivan, K.; Tooley, K.; Doughty, J.E.; Caldwell, J.E.; Knudsen, P. 1990. Evaluation of prediction models and characterization of stream temperature regimes in Washington. Timber/Fish/Wildlife Rep. TFW-WQ3-90-006. Olympia, WA: Washington Department of Natural Resources. 224 p.

Sullivan, K.; Martin, D.J.; Cardwell, D.J.; Toll, J.E.; Duke, S. 2000. [Draft] An analysis of the effects of temperature on salmonids of the Pacific Northwest, with implications for selecting temperature criteria. Portland, OR: Sustainable Ecosystems Institute, 0605 SW Taylors Ferry Road.

Sweeney, B.W. 1984. Factors influencing life-history patterns of aquatic insects. In: Resh, V.H.; Rosenberg, D.M., eds. The Ecology of Aquatic Insects. New York, NY: Praeger: 56-100.

Tait, C.K.; Li, J.L.; Lamberti, G.A.; Pearsons, T.N.; Li, H.W. 1994. Relationships between riparian cover and community structure of high desert streams. Journal of the North American Benthological Society 13(1): 45-56.

Wagner, R.G.; Radosevich, S.R. 1991. Interspecific competition and other factors influencing the performance of Douglas-fir saplings in the Oregon Coast Range. Canadian Journal of Forest Research 21: 829-835.

Walsh, J.B.S. 1996. Effects of streamside riparian forest management on *Ephemeroptera* and *Trichoptera* community structure in four western Oregon streams. Corvallis, OR: Oregon State University, Department of Forest Science. MS thesis.189 p.

Warren, C.E. 1971. Biology and water pollution control. Philadelphia, PA: W. B. Asunders Co. 434 p.

Wilzbach, M.A.; Cummins, K.W.; Knapp, R.A. 1988. Toward a functional classification of stream invertebrate drift. Verhandlungen der Internationalen Vereinigung für Theoretische und Angewandte Limnologie 23: 1244-1254.

Zwieniecki, M.; Newton, M. 1999. Influence of streamside cover and stream features on temperature trends in forested streams of western Oregon. Western Journal of Applied Forestry 14(2): 106-113.

SLENDERNESS COEFFICIENT IS LINKED
TO CROWN SHYNESS AND STEM HYDRAULICS
IN LODGEPOLE PINE

Victor J. Lieffers[1] and Uldis Silins[1]

ABSTRACT

This paper outlines several studies on hydraulic limitations, crown size and leaf area development in lodgepole pine (*Pinus contorta* var. *latifolia* Engelm.). A central theme of this work is that the bole slenderness coefficient (height/diameter ratio) is linked to productivity by means of two mechanisms. First, trees with slender boles are less stiff and thus are more likely to move widely in wind. In taller stands, wide movement of trees in windstorm will result in violent collisions with neighboring trees; this results in crown abrasion and narrow crowns with unoccupied space between crowns, i.e., crown shyness. Stout trees, in contrast, have only small oscillations in wind and neighboring trees often have overlapping branches. Second, slender trees develop narrow annual rings with reduce permeability of the wood for transport of water to crowns. Also, the reduced strength of slender trees will results in increased bending of the bole, which is also likely to reduce the permeability of the xylem. Bole slenderness, therefore, likely plays a role in stand productivity, the ability of trees to release following thinning, and in the probability of trees remaining alive after canopy disturbance late in stand development. Managers can manipulate bole slenderness by stand density management.

KEYWORDS: Lodgepole pine, thinning, crown slenderness, height/diameter ratio, xylem permeability.

SUMMARY[2]

Slenderness coefficient, i.e., the height/diameter ratio of a tree, has long been linked to the biomechanical relationships of trees and wind stability (Ruel 1995). Trees with stout stems will resist deflection in wind much more than slender stems (fig. 1). This short paper briefly outlines how the slenderness coefficient of trees may be important to the development and maintenance of crown size, crown leaf area (crown shyness) and the hydraulic supply of that leaf area. Examples are given for lodgepole pine (*Pinus contorta* var. *latifolia* Engelm.).

Crown shyness is the empty space that develops around individual crowns of trees in fully stocked, maturing stands (Putz et al. 1984) (fig. 2). Some researchers believe that the empty space develops as a result of shading of foliage between crowns (Umeki 1995; Cescatti 1997), but in reality there is usually less leaf area in older stands (Ryan et al. 1997) than in young stands, where there is little crown shyness. In contrast, there is increasing evidence that the space between crowns develops as a result of abrasion of the crown during movement of trees during wind (Long and Smith 1992; Smith and Long 2001, Rudnicki et al. 2001). Indeed, the crown of a 15-m tall lodgepole pine tree may collide with neighboring trees more than 40 times per minute when wind speed averages 5 m/s (Rudnicki et al. 2002). Similarly, crowns may oscillate more than 6 m in a wind gust (Rudnicki et al. 2001), and reach velocities of > 7 m/s (Rudnicki et al. 2002). Impacts in these conditions would therefore have sufficient energy to cause serious damage to twigs, and branches (Grier 1988) especially in

---

[1] Victor J. Lieffers is professor and Uldis Silins is associate professor, Department of Renewable Resources, University of Alberta, Edmonton, Alberta, Canada, T6G 2H1. victor.lieffers@ualberta.ca

[2] An extended version of this paper was not submitted for the proceedings.

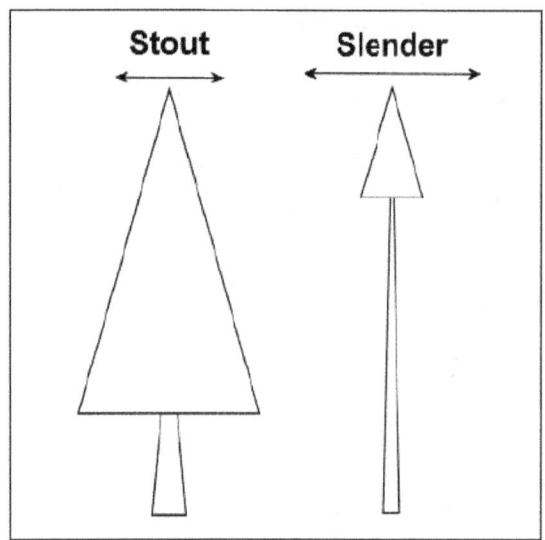

Figure1—Deflection from a gust of wind for trees of the same height with slender and stout boles.

Figure 2—A fully stocked, 16-m tall lodgepole pine stand in the Yukon Territory. The photograph was taken at 1.7 m above the ground with a 55-m lens.

cold weather where twigs are very brittle (Lieffers et al. 2001). As bole stiffness and the ability of the stem to resist deflection is strongly related to bole diameter (Silins et al. 2001), stems with low slenderness coefficient are expected to move less in wind storms than slender stems. As hypothesized, stands with slender stems had much wider movement of crowns than those with stout boles of the same height (Rudnicki et al. 2002). In a second study, crown shyness was estimated in small plots in wild stands of lodgepole pine (Rudnicki et al. 2004). When stems were less than about 12 m tall, there was little crown shyness in fully stocked stands; in these short stands crown closure was apparently driven by relative density. In stands > 12 m high however, there was increasing crown shyness in plots with trees of high slenderness coefficient.

Water relations of trees are also likely to be related to the slenderness coefficient. First, slender trees have narrow annual rings. Sapwood of lodgepole pine with rings < 0.5 mm has reduced permeability to water flow compared to sapwood with wide annual rings (Reid et al. 2004). Reduced permeability to water flow is expected to become a limiting factor in transport of water to foliage in crowns, thereby limiting growth. Secondly, there is increasing evidence that bending deflection of trees by wind damages the permeability of tree stems (Frederickson et al. 1994, Silins et al. unpublished). In a study of juvenile lodgepole pine following thinning, stems were either tethered to reduce sway or

had sails added to increase deflection in wind (Liu et al. 2003). Sapwood permeability after thinning was related to sway treatments; sapwood permeability was ranked control (unthinned) > tethered (thinned) > untethered (thinned) > sail added (thinned).

Since managers can use stand density management to manipulate the bole slenderness coefficient, we hypothesize that a thinning regime where stems are kept at slightly lower relative density than typically develops in self-thinning stands will produce stems with stiffer boles that are more resistant to deflection. Stems that flex less will maintain larger crowns in the second half of the rotation. Stems that resist bending will also suffer less damage to xylem sapwood during strong wind events and maintain their ability to deliver water to crowns. Finally lodgepole pine stems with wider rings (often produced after stand spacing) have higher sapwood permeability.

ACKNOWLEDGEMENTS

We thank NSERC, Weldwood of Canada, Westfraser Timber, Weyerhaeuser Company and the Sustainable Forest Management Network for funding these projects. We thank Mark Rudnicki, Doug Reid, Mike Liu, Heather Fish and Simon Landhäusser for their work.

LITERATURE CITED

Cescatti, A. 1997. Modelling the radiative transfer in discontinuous canopies of asymmetric crowns. I. Model structure and algorithms. Ecological Modelling 101: 263-274.

Fredericksen, T.S.; Hedden, R.L.; William, S.A. 1994. Effect of stem bending on hydraulic conductivity and wood strength of loblolly pine. Canadian Journal of Forest Research 24: 442-446.

Grier, C.C. 1988. Foliage loss due to snow, wind, and winter drying damage: its effects on leaf biomass of some western conifer forests. Canadian Journal of Forest Research 18: 1097-1102.

Lieffers, S.M.; Lieffers, V.J.; Silins, U.; Bach, L. 2001. Effects of cold temperature on breakage of lodgepole pine and white spruce twigs. Canadian Journal of Forest Research 31: 1650-1653.

Liu, X.; Silins, U.; Lieffers, V.J.; Man, R.Z. 2003. Wind, bending and thinning, affect the hydraulic conductivity of conifer stems. Canadian Journal of Forest Research 33: 1295-1203.

Long, J.N.; Smith, F.W. 1992. Volume increment in *Pinus contorta* var. *latifolia*: the influence of stand development and crown dynamics. Forest Ecology and Management 53: 53-62.

Putz, F.E.; Parker, G.G.; Archibald, R.M. 1984. Mechanical abrasion and intercrown spacing. American Midland Naturalist 112: 24-28.

Reid, D.E.B.; Lieffers, V.J.; Silins, U. 2004. Growth and crown efficiency of height repressed lodgepole pine: are suppressed trees more efficient? Trees Structure and Function 18: 390-398.

Ruel, J.C. 1995. Understanding windthrow: silvicultural implications. Forestry Chronicle 71: 434-445.

Ryan, M.G.; Binkley, D.; Fownes, J.H. 1997. Age-related decline in forest productivity: patterns and process. Advances in Ecological Research 27: 213-261.

Rudnicki, M.; Silins, U.; Lieffers, V.J. 2001. Measure of simultaneous tree sways and estimation of crown interactions among a group of trees. Trees-Structure and Function 15: 83-90

Rudnicki, M.; Silins, U.; Lieffers, V.J. 2002. Stand structure governs the crown collisions of lodgepole pine. Canadian Journal of Forest Research 33: 1238-1244.

Rudnicki, M.; Silins, U.; Lieffers, V.J. 2004. Relative density, tree slenderness and tree height determine the crown cover of lodgepole pine. Forest Science 50: 356-363.

Smith, F.W.; Long, J.N. 2001. Age-related decline in forest growth: an emergent property. Forest Ecology and Management 144: 175-181.

Umeki, K. 1995. Modeling the relationship between the asymmetry in crown display and local environment. Ecological Modelling 82: 11-20

WOOD PRODUCTS AND EMERGING TECHNOLOGIES

FOREST MEASUREMENT AND MONITORING USING HIGH-RESOLUTION AIRBORNE LIDAR

Hans-Erik Andersen,[1] Robert J. McGaughey,[2] and Stephen E. Reutebuch[2]

ABSTRACT

Airborne laser scanning has emerged as a highly-accurate, high-resolution forest survey tool, providing the opportunity to develop and implement forest inventory and monitoring programs using a level of detail not previously possible. In this paper, we will present results from several research studies carried out at a study area within Capitol State Forest in the state of Washington, where we investigated the utility of LIDAR for measurement of terrain and forest structure characteristics. Previous studies at this site have shown that LIDAR can be used to accurately measure terrain elevation even under dense forest canopy. The results of another study have indicated that LIDAR can also be used to accurately estimate a number of forest inventory variables, including basal area, stem volume, dominant height, and biomass. The laser-reflection intensity information provided by LIDAR can also be used for species classification. Individual tree crowns can be recognized by using computer vision algorithms applied to a detailed LIDAR-based canopy surface model. This approach can be used to extract measurements of individual trees, including top height and crown base height. Preliminary results have shown that if high-density LIDAR data are collected in different years, measurements of individual-tree height growth can be obtained for an entire forest area, allowing for detailed, spatially explicit analyses of site quality and productivity.

KEYWORDS: Forest measurement, remote sensing, LIDAR, terrain mapping, canopy mapping.

INTRODUCTION

The development of high-resolution, active remote sensing measurement systems has the potential to support the development and application of highly site-specific to forest management. One of the more promising forest remote sensing tools to emerge in recent years is small-footprint airborne laser scanning, or light detection and ranging (LIDAR). LIDAR is an optical remote sensing technology capable of providing direct three-dimensional (3-D) measurements of forest canopy structure. The components of an airborne LIDAR system include a laser scanner, which emits from 7,000 to 100,000 laser pulses each second, coupled with a precise airborne positioning system, which uses differentially corrected GPS (global positioning system) and an inertial measurement unit to accurately determine the position and orientation of the scanner at the moment each pulse is emitted[3]. Because the speed of light is a known constant, the distance corresponding to each laser reflection from the ground can be calculated from the time delay between the emission and reception of the laser pulse. This distance is used along with the position and orientation information to calculate the 3-D coordinates of each reflection. Most airborne LIDAR systems designed for topographic mapping applications use lasers with wavelengths in the near-infrared region of the electromagnetic spectrum. These sensors typically use a system of oscillating or rotating mirrors to generate a scan pattern of measurements in a swath beneath the aircraft (fig. 1). LIDAR

---

[1] Hans-Erik Andersen is a research scientist, Precision Forestry Cooperative, University of Washington, College of Forest Resources, Seattle, WA 98195.

[2] Robert J. McGaughey and Stephen E. Reutebuch are research foresters, USDA Forest Service, Pacific Northwest Research Station, Seattle, WA 98195.

[3] LIDAR systems are typically classified into two types, depending upon the size of the "footprint" for the laser pulse. "Small footprint" systems have ground spot sizes from 0.1 to 1 m, whereas "large-footprint" systems have spot sizes from 5 to 100 m. Given that large footprint, continuous waveform LIDAR systems are neither commercially available nor capable of providing high-resolution data, in this paper we restrict our discussion to the use of small-footprint, discrete-return LIDAR data. The application of large-footprint LIDAR to forestry applications has been discussed in Harding et al. (2001) and Lefsky et al. (2002).

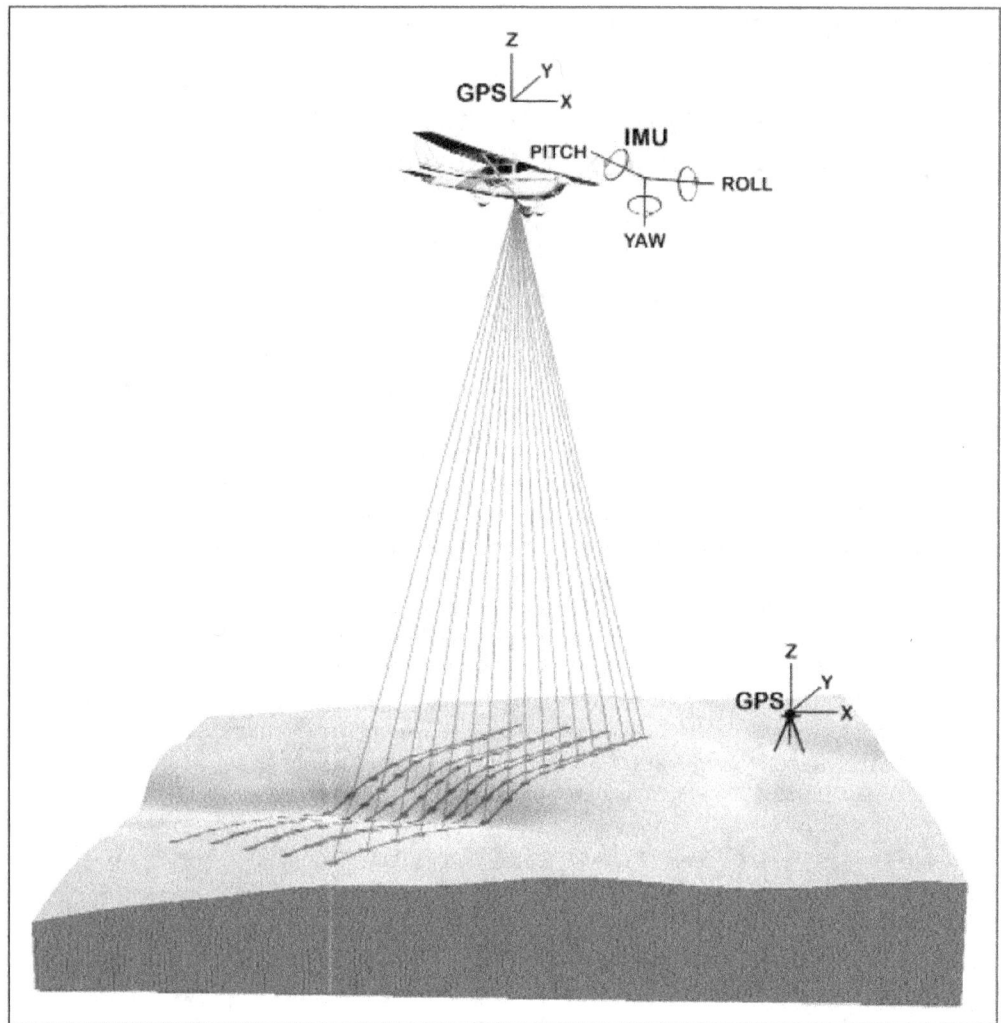

Figure 1—Components of an airborne laser scanning (LIDAR) system.

systems typically collect data at a density between 0.5 and 4 pulses per square meter and with a pulse diameter between 0.4 and 0.7 m, depending upon the specific system and flight parameters for the project. Many LIDAR systems also have the capability to detece several reflections from a single pulse. In a forested area, LIDAR pulses reflect from the canopy foliage, branches, understory vegetation, and the terrain surface. The LIDAR point cloud therefore represents a detailed 3-D measurement of the spatial organization of canopy materials (foliage, branches, stems, shrubs, etc.) down to the ground surface for the scanned area. Quantitative metrics describing the spatial distribution of these LIDAR returns will therefore be related to a wide variety of critical forest structure metrics, including dominant height, basal area, stem volume, and biomass. A highly detailed model of the canopy surface can be generated by using the LIDAR returns from the surface of the canopy.

The application of computer vision (object recognition) algorithms then allows individual tree crowns composing the canopy to be isolated and measured. Furthermore, if LIDAR data are acquired over the same area of forest in different years, detailed measurements of forest change (mortality and forest growth) can be obtained. In this paper, we present the results of a study investigating the use of LIDAR for forest measurement and monitoring in a conifer forest within western Washington state.

STUDY AREA

The study area for this project was a 5.2 km^2 area within Capitol State Forest in western Washington (fig. 2). This forest is composed primarily of coniferous timber species, including Douglas-fir (*Pseudotsuga menziesii*), western hemlock (*Tsuga heterophylla*), and western redcedar (*Thuja*

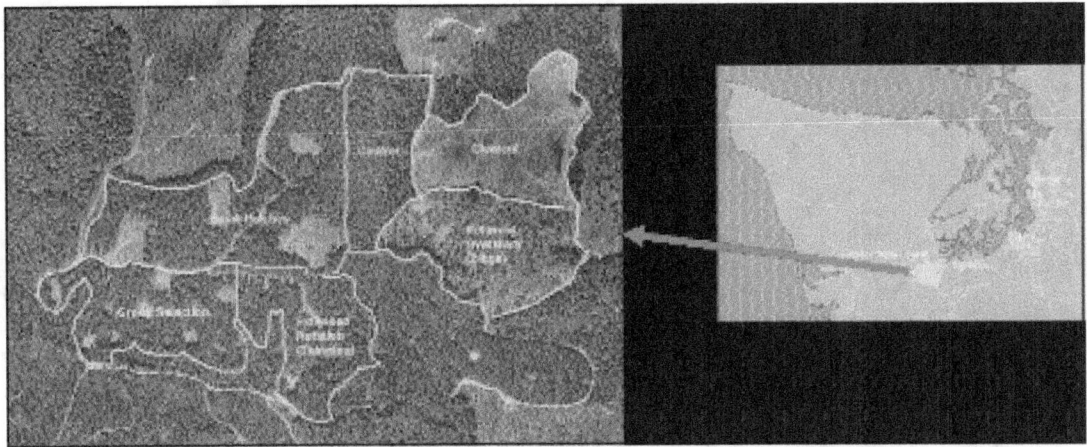

Figure 2—Capitol Forest study site. Image courtesy of Washington State Department of Natural Resources.

plicata), along with various hardwood species, including red alder (*Alnus rubra*) and big-leaf maple (*Acer macrophyllum*). This area is the site of an on-going silvicultural trial investigating the effects of several different harvest treatments designed to create a variety of residual stand densities (clearcut unit: 0 trees per hectare (TPH); heavily-thinned unit[4]: 40 TPH; lightly-thinned unit: 175 TPH; and control unit: 280 TPH).

A total of 99 inventory plots were established within this study area, extending over a range of stand types including young stands (about 35 years) and mature stands (about 70 years) with variable stand densities. Plot sizes ranged from 0.02 to 0.2 ha. A variety of measurements were obtained at each plot, including species and diameter at breast height for all trees greater than 14.2 cm in diameter. Additional measurements of total height and height-to-live-crown were acquired for a representative selection of trees over the range of diameters by using a handheld laser rangefinder. A detailed description of the plot measurement protocol can be found in a previous report (chapter 3, Curtis et al. 2004).

LIDAR DATA

High-density LIDAR data were acquired over the study area in the spring of 1999 and the summer of 2003, a period that represented five growing seasons. The 1999 LIDAR data were acquired with a SAAB[5] TopEye system operated from a helicopter platform in the spring of 1999 (leaf-off conditions). The 2003 LIDAR data were acquired with a Terrapoint ALTMS system operating from a fixed-wing platform in September 2003 (leaf-on conditions). Both data sets were acquired with a nominal density of 4 returns (or reflections) per square meter. The vendor provided raw LIDAR data consisting of XYZ coordinates and return-intensity information for all LIDAR returns in an ASCII text format. In addition, the vendor provided "filtered ground" data representing ground returns isolated via a proprietary filtering algorithm. The filtered ground returns from the 1999 data set were used to generate a 1.52-meter (5 ft) digital terrain model (DTM) over the entire study area, using the Surfer software system (Golden Software, Inc. 1999) with the inverse distance interpolation algorithm and a 4-sector search with a radius of 60 m (fig. 3). The same gridding algorithm was used to generate a 1-m DTM from the filtered ground 2003 LIDAR data (fig. 4).

LIDAR-BASED TERRAIN MEASUREMENT

In a previous study, the accuracy of the 1999 LIDAR-based DTM was assessed via comparison to 347 high-accuracy topographic checkpoints collected using survey-grade equipment (Reutebuch et al. 2003). This study showed that the LIDAR-derived DTM had a mean error of +0.22 m with a standard deviation of 0.24 m. This study showed that the accuracy of the DTM is slightly reduced by the presence of heavy canopy or near-ground vegetation. A similar accuracy assessment of the 2003 LIDAR-based terrain model showed that the DTM had a mean error of +0.31 m with a standard deviation of 0.34 m. The difference between the 1999 and 2003 DTM errors is statistically significant (at $\alpha = 0.05$), and may be attributed to the fact

[4] The heavily-thinned unit is called the 2-aged stand in Curtis et al. 2004.

[5] The use of trade or firm names in this publication is for reader information and does not imply endorsement by the U.S. Department of Agriculture of any product of service.

Figure 3—1999 LIDAR digital terrain mode (UTM coordinate system).

Figure 4—2003 LIDAR digital terrain model.

that the 2003 LIDAR was acquired in leaf-on conditions whereas the 1999 LIDAR was acquired in leaf-off conditions. In leaf-on conditions, it can be expected that fewer LIDAR pulses will penetrate through deciduous t r e e crowns. In addition, there was significant growth of the near-ground vegetation in the treated areas between 1999 and 2003 that could also have an effect on DTM accuracy. However, the difference between the mean error of the leaf-off 1999 DTM and the leaf-on 2003 DTM is remarkably small, indicating that LIDAR is capable of measuring terrain under this predominantly coniferous forest canopy at a very high accuracy in both leaf-on and leaf-off conditions.

LIDAR-BASED FOREST MEASUREMENT

Canopy Surface Measurement

LIDAR canopy surface measurements were extracted by filtering out the highest return within each 1-m grid cell area. These filtered "canopy-level" returns were then gridded into a canopy surface model again using an inverse distance interpolation algorithm and a 3-sector search with a radius of 3 m. The 1999 LIDAR canopy surface model is shown in figure 5, and the 2003 LIDAR canopy model is shown in figure 6. In a comparison to profiles and spot height measurements acquired from large-scale aerial photographs, the difference between photogrammetric canopy height and 1999 LIDAR canopy height measurements

Figure 5 –1999 LIDAR canopy surface model.

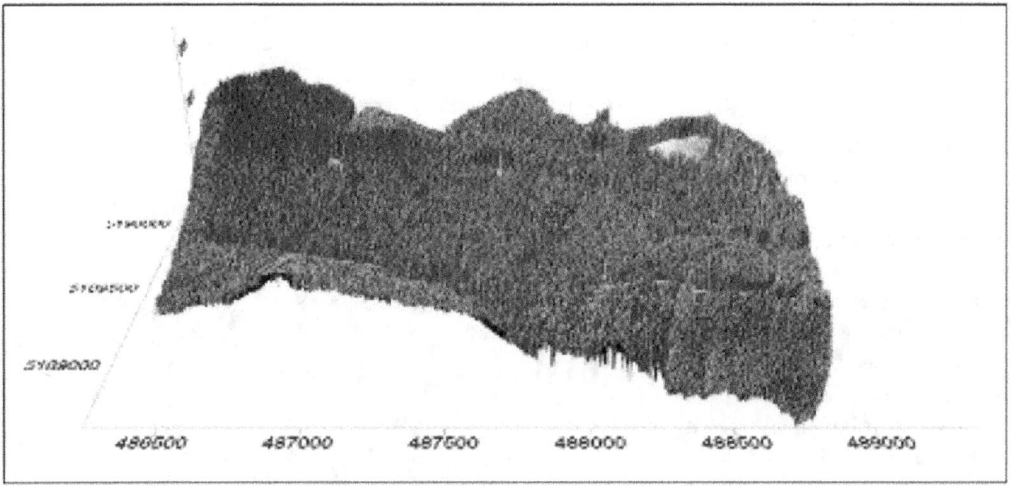

Figure 6—2003 LIDAR canopy surface model.

(after accounting for tree growth) was found to be within approximately 1 m (Andersen et al. 2003). The detailed LIDAR-derived canopy surface model provides a rich description of overstory canopy structure, including information on canopy cover, gap distribution, and individual tree dimensions (Andersen, 2003).

Species Recognition

Several previous studies have shown that the intensity information provided for each LIDAR reflection can be used to classify by species type (Andersen et al., in prep., Brandtberg et al. 2003, Holmgren and Persson, 2004). Brandtberg and others used summary statistics of the height distribution and intensity values within individual tree crown segments to classify tree species within an eastern deciduous forest in West Virginia (Brandtberg et al. 2003). In another study carried out in Sweden, LIDAR-derived metrics describing structural and reflectance characteristics of individual tree crowns were used to discriminate between spruce and pine trees (Holmgren and Persson 2004). In leaf-off conditions, the near-infrared reflectance from hardwood tree crowns (and dead trees) is significantly lower than that from coniferous crowns (fig. 7). Preliminary results indicate that leaf-off LIDAR can be used to accurately classify tree crowns into hardwood-softwood classes (Andersen et al., in prep.). This capability may be particularly important in determining species composition for riparian zone management.

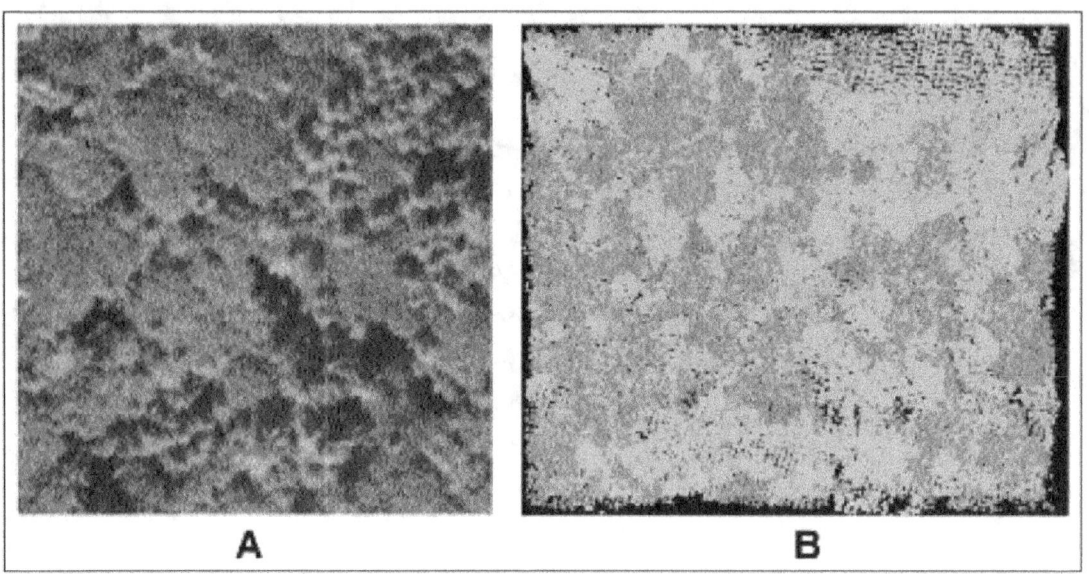

Figure 7—Species classification using LIDAR intensity data a) leaf-on orthophoto, b) leaf-off hardwoods and dead trees (brown), conifers (green).

Plot-Level Measurement

The vertical distribution of LIDAR data within a given area provides a detailed description of forest structure (fig. 8). Regression techniques can be used to model the relationship between a set of metrics describing the vertical distribution of LIDAR canopy returns within a plot area (e.g., 0.1 ha) and stand structure variables derived from a plot tree list. Given the allometric relationships between canopy dimensions and biomass, governed by the laws of proportional growth, there is a strong physical basis for the quantitative relationship between the distribution of LIDAR measurements, which are essentially characterizing the density of canopy foliage, and stand variables such as biomass, stem volume, and basal area (West et al. 1997). The metrics used to characterize the vertical distribution of LIDAR measurements within a plot include various height quantiles (e.g., 10th, 20th, …, 90th percentile heights), as well as other metrics such as mean height, maximum height, coefficient of variation of height, and a LIDAR-derived measure of canopy cover (calculated as the percentage of LIDAR first returns that reflect from the canopy level [i.e., more than 2 m above the ground]). Once these regression models are developed to establish the quantitative relationship between the LIDAR metrics and the inventory parameters, these predictive models can be used to generate maps of various stand parameters over the entire extent of the LIDAR coverage. With this approach, however, it is important to collect plot-level inventory data over the full range of stand conditions present in the mapped area. If stand conditions exist that fall outside of the plot types used to generate the predictive models, the estimates are in effect

Figure 8—Distribution of LIDAR returns within a 0.8 ha (0.2 ac) plot area, Capitol Forest study area)

extrapolations outside the range of data and will be unreliable. Because this approach relies only on the vertical distribution of LIDAR returns and is not dependent on accurate measurement of individual tree crowns, it is particularly useful when the LIDAR data density is relatively low (<1 return/m^2). This approach uses LIDAR data acquired throughout the full depth of the forest canopy, including the understory layer, and therefore provides a more comprehensive estimate of stand parameters than the individual-tree approach described in the next section, which is

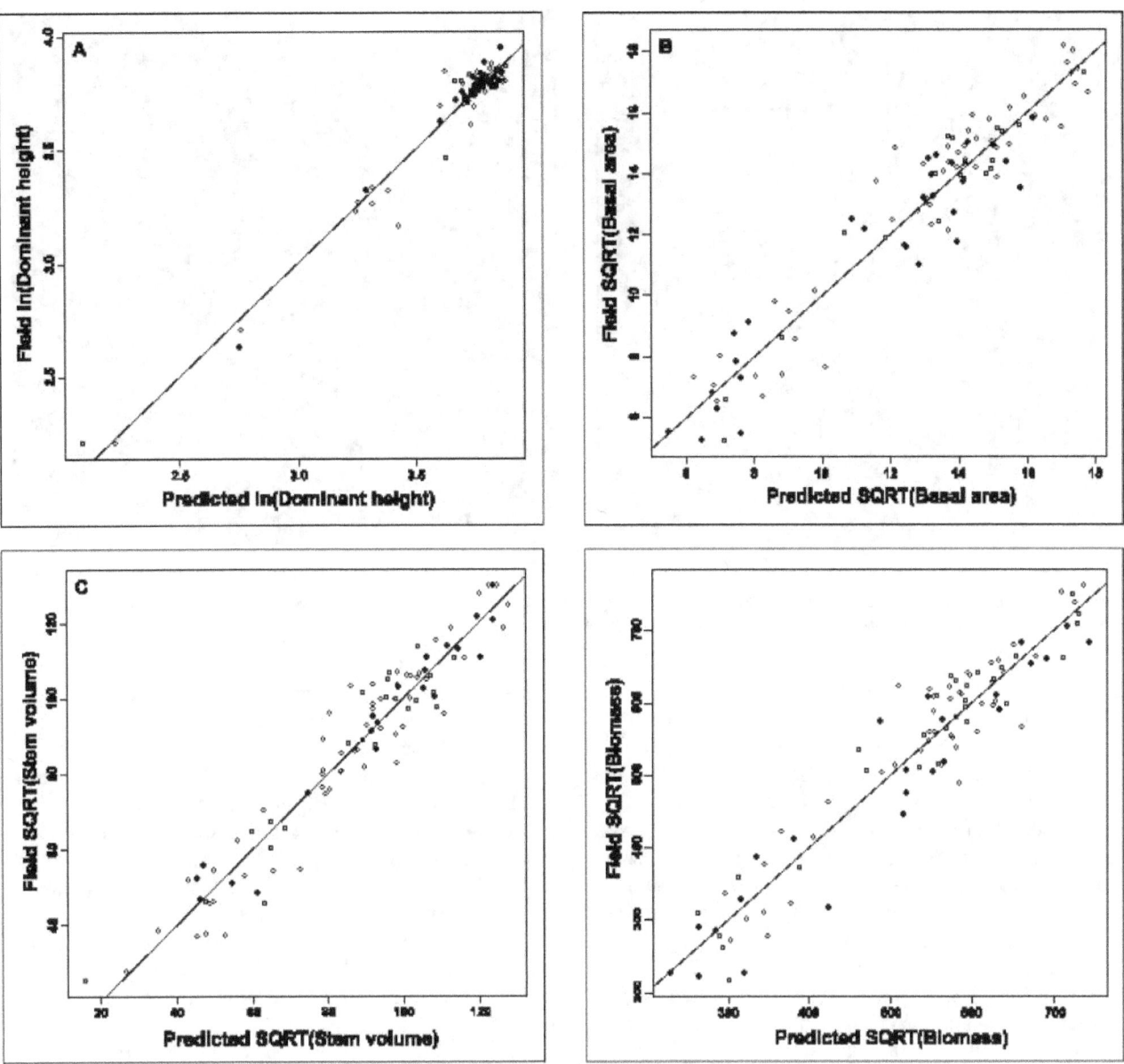

Figure 9—Results of plot-level LIDAR-based estimation of forest inventory parameters at Capitol Forest study site. Scatterplots represent relationship between predicted (*x*) and field-based (*y*) estimates at the individual plots for a) dominant height, b) basal area, c) stem volume, and d) biomass. Lines represent 1:1 relationship.

limited to the overstory layer. This plot-level approach to LIDAR-based forest inventory has been applied across a variety of forest types by researchers in North America and Europe (Means et al. 2000, Naesset 2002, Naesset and Okland 2002). In a study done at the Capitol Forest study area, strong regression relationships were found between LIDAR-derived predictor variables and field-measure inventory variables, including basal area ($R^2 = 0.91$), stem volume ($R^2 = 0.92$), dominant height ($R^2 = 0.96$), and biomass ($R^2 = 0.91$) (fig. 9). This plot-level approach has also

been used to estimate canopy fuel variables, including canopy height, canopy bulk density, and canopy base height at the Capitol Forest study site (Andersen et al. 2005).

Individual Tree-Level Measurement

If LIDAR data are acquired at a high enough density, details at the scale of individual tree crowns can be resolved in the LIDAR-derived canopy surface model (fig. 5). A previous study showed that individual tree attributes, including tree height and crown base height, could be accurately

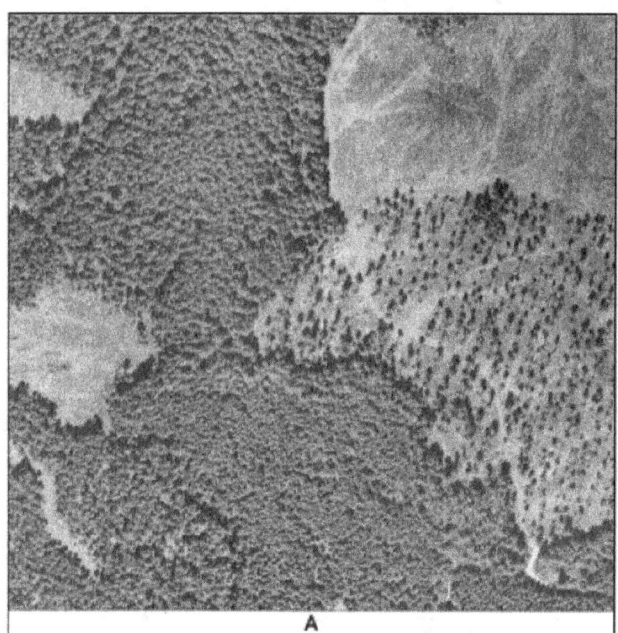 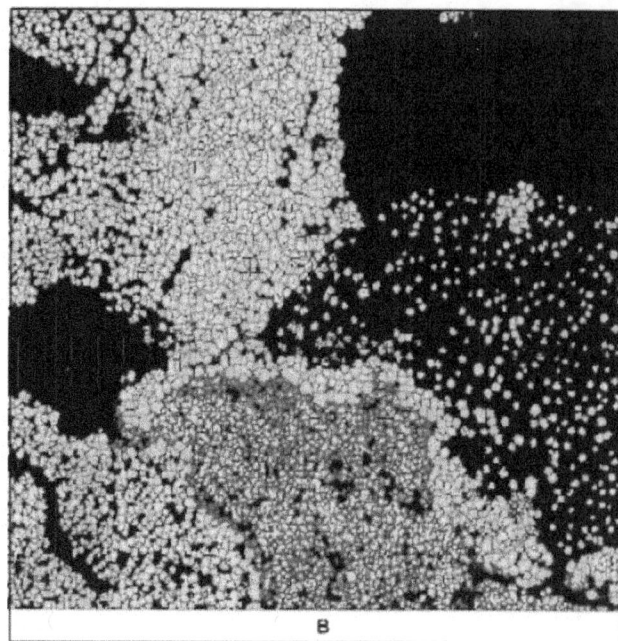

Figure 10—a) Orthophoto of selected area, and b) individual tree-level segmentation of LIDAR canopy height model via morphological watershed algorithm (color-coded by height; black lines indicate boundaries of segments).

measured by using a software system (FUSION) that provides for interactive visualization and direct measurement of the raw LIDAR point cloud (McGaughey et al. 2004). In fact, results from this study indicate that in open stands, individual tree dimensions (especially crown width and crown height) can be measured more accurately with LIDAR than with traditional field methods (by using Criterion laser instruments, etc.). LIDAR-based individual tree measurement can be automated through the application of computer vision algorithms. One of the more effective computer vision algorithms for automated individual tree crown recognition is the morphological watershed algorithm (Soille 1999). Conceptually, this algorithm finds the boundaries of b a s i n s, or watersheds, within a surface model. If the LIDAR- based canopy surface model is inverted, each tree crown is essentially a small basin, and after application of the watershed algorithm, the boundary of each individual tree crown is delineated. The output of this algorithm is a segmented canopy-height model, where each segment represents the area associated with individual tree crowns (fig. 10). A limitation of this LIDAR individual-tree level measurement approach is that only trees in the overstory can be accurately segmented and measured. However, in practice this is not a serious limitation because overstory trees are typically of most interest in the context of commercial forest inventory. Several previous studies have shown that this morphological computer-vision approach can be effective

in identifying tree crown structures and measuring individual tree crown dimensions (Andersen et al. 2001, Persson et al. 2002, Schardt et al. 2002). Once the canopy height model has been segmented into individual tree crowns, the raw LIDAR data within each crown segment can be extracted to acquire high-resolution measurements of individual tree crown attributes, including tree height and crown base height (fig. 11). If height-to- diameter or crown-diameter-to-stem-diameter regression models are available for the area, these LIDAR-derived crown measurements can be used to estimate other tree attributes, including diameter and stem volume. In addition, because the near-infrared reflectance from hardwood crowns is significantly lower than conifers in leaf-off LIDAR data, the mean (or median) intensity of the LIDAR returns within each crown segment can be used to classify the tree segment into a species type (i.e., hardwood or softwood) (fig. 12).

LIDAR-BASED FOREST MONITORING

Measurement of Individual Tree Growth

When high-density LIDAR data are acquired over the same forest area in different years, the difference in the individual tree height measurements acquired from these multi-temporal LIDAR data sets represents an estimate of the tree height growth over the intervening period. This approach allows for accurate measurement of overstory tree

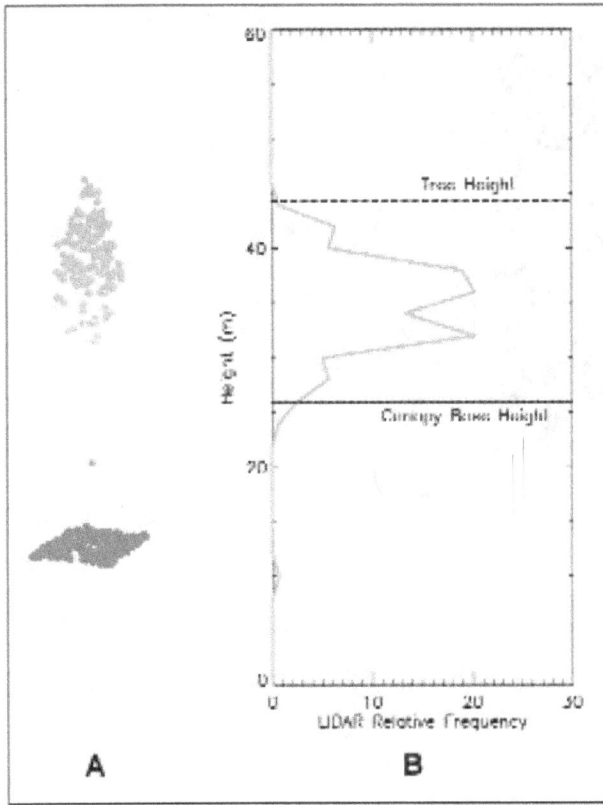

Figure 11—Use of LIDAR to measure individual tree crown dimensions: a) raw LIDAR measurements extracted from tree crown segment, and b) vertical distribution of LIDAR returns for this crown, with estimate of tree height and crown base height shown.

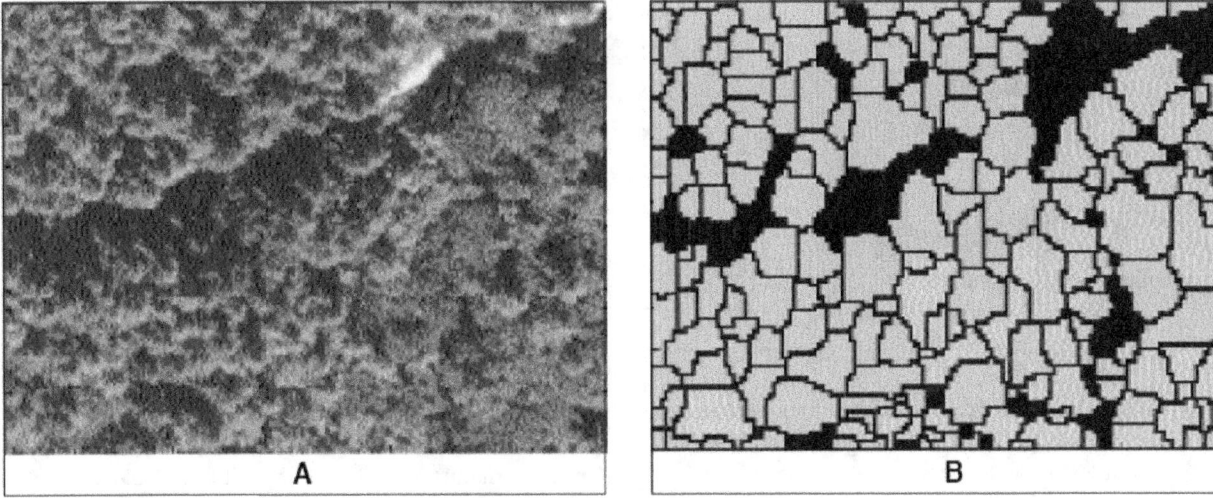

Figure 12—Use of LIDAR intensity to classify species: a) orthophoto of selected area with mixed hardwoods (bigleaf maple), and conifers, and (b) individual tree crown segments classified by species: conifer (green) and hardwoods (brown).

117

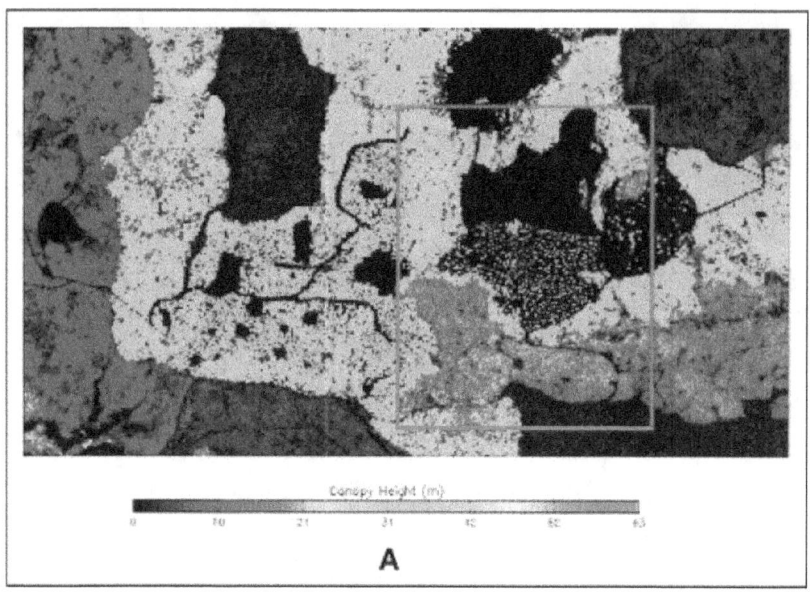

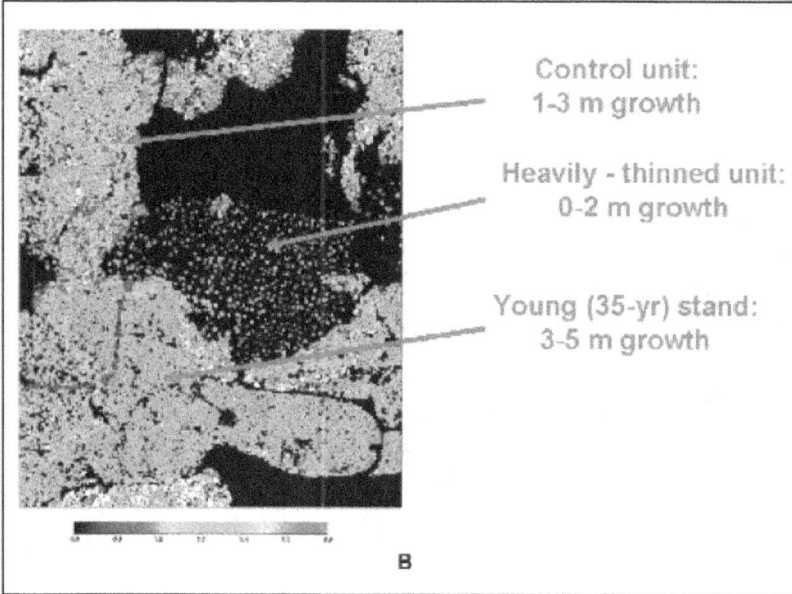

Control unit:
1-3 m growth

Heavily - thinned unit:
0-2 m growth

Young (35-yr) stand:
3-5 m growth

Figure 13—LIDAR-based measurement of individual tree growth, 1999-2003: a) Selected area within Capitol Forest study area shown in LIDAR canopy height model, and b) LIDAR-derived individual tree height growth measurement. A significant difference in height growth between stands is evident [control (70-yr.-old, unthinned stand) ~ 1- to 3-m growth; young (35-yr-old) stand ~ 3 to 5 m; heavily-thinned (70-yr-old stand)~ 0 to 2 m]. Segments colored white indicate hardwoods that were excluded from the analysis.

height growth over an extensive forest area. In a study conducted at the Capitol Forest study area, high-density LIDAR data acquired in 1999 and 2003 were used to extract individual tree height growth measurements. Preliminary results of this analysis showed that small differences in growth between thinning treatments can be detected even over this relatively short period (five growing seasons). As expected, height growth was less pronounced in the heavily-thinned unit (approximately 0 to 2 m), where the primary response to the treatment was increased crown expansion, than in the control unit, where the height growth was in the range of 1

to 3 m (fig. 13). Not surprisingly, the height growth within a younger (35-yr-old) stand was much higher (3 to 5 m) than in the mature stands. The capability of LIDAR to accurately measure the growth rates of individual trees across an entire forest provides an opportunity for much more detailed, and spatially explicit, analyses of site quality and availability, and intertree competition.

CONCLUSIONS

The application of airborne laser scanning to forest survey has the potential to revolutionize our approach to forest

118

inventory and monitoring. LIDAR can provide very accurate measurements of terrain even under dense forest canopy (in both leaf-on and leaf-off conditions), and will support the implementation of more detailed hydrological models and site-specific forest operations. LIDAR also provides highly accurate, high-resolution measurements of forest canopy structure that can be used to estimate important inventory parameters at the plot level (dominant height, basal area, stem volume, biomass) and individual-tree level (height, crown area, crown base height). In addition, the intensity information provided by LIDAR can be used to classify forest species type, an important capability where information regarding forest composition, particularly hardwood-softwood mix, is required. It was also shown that the use of LIDAR data acquired in different years allows for forest-wide analysis of growth at the scale of the individual tree, which can potentially support highly detailed investigations of spatially variable site characteristics and growth potential. Through the analysis of LIDAR data collected before areas are cleared for plot establishment, differences in local site index across plots in the same block could be identified and accounted for in long-term plantation growth-and-yield studies, thus removing a potentially confounding effect that has been impossible to identify in most forest experiments.

ACKNOWLEDGMENTS

The authors thank the Precision Forestry Cooperative at the University of Washington, the USDA Pacific Northwest Research Station, the Washington State Department of Natural Resources, and the Joint Fire Science Program for their support in carrying out this project.

LITERATURE CITED

Andersen, H.-E.; Reutebuch, S.E.; Schreuder, G.F. 2001. Automated individual tree measurement through morphological analysis of a LIDAR-based canopy surface model. Proceedings of the First International Precision Forestry Symposium, Seattle, WA.

Andersen, H.-E. 2003. Estimation of critical forest structure metrics through the spatial analysis of airborne laser scanner data., Seattle, WA: University of Washington. Ph.D. dissertation.

Andersen, H.-E.; McGaughey, R.J.; Carson, W.W.; Reutebuch, S.E.; Mercer, B.; Allan, J. 2003. A comparison of forest canopy models derived from LIDAR and InSAR data in a Pacific Northwest conifer forest. International Archives of Photogrammetry and Remote Sensing. Dresden, Germany: Vol. XXXIV, Part 3/W13.

Andersen, H.-E.; McGaughey, R.J.; Reutebuch, S.E. 2005. Estimating forest canopy fuel parameters using LIDAR data. Remote Sensing of Environment 94: 441-229.

Andersen, H.-E.; Reutebuch, S.E.; McGaughey, R.J. [In preparation]. The use of high-resolution, active airborne remote sensing technologies to support digital forestry. One file with: Hans-Erik Andersen, Precision Forestry Cooperative, University of Washington, College of Forest Resources, Seattle, WA 98195.

Brandtberg, T.; Warner, T.; Landenberger, R.; McGraw, J. 2003. Detection and analysis of individual leaf-off tree crowns in small footprint, high sampling density LIDAR data from the eastern deciduous forest in North America. Remote Sensing of Environment 85: 290-303.

Curtis, R.O.; Marshall, D.D.; DeBell, D.S., eds. 2004. Silvicultural options for young-growth Douglas-fir forests: the Capitol Forest study—establishment and first results. Gen. Tech. Rep. PNW-GTR-598. Portland, OR: U.S. Department of Agriculture, Forest Service, Pacific Northwest Research Station. 110 p.

Golden Software, Inc. 1999, Surfer user's guide. Version 7. Golden CO: Golden Software, Inc.

Harding, D.J.; Lefsky, M.A.; Parker, G.G.; Blair, J.B. 2001. Laser altimetry canopy height profiles: methods and validation for closed-canopy, broadleaf forests. Remote Sensing of Environment 76: 283-297.

Holmgren, J.; Persson, A. 2004. Identifying species of individual trees using airborne laser scanner. Remote Sensing of Environment 90: 415- 423.

Lefsky, M.A.; Cohen, W.B.; Parker, G.G.; Harding, D.J. 2002. LIDAR remote sensing for ecosystem studies. Bioscience 52(1): 19-30.

McGaughey, R.J.; Carson, W.W.; Reutebuch, S.E.; Andersen, H.-E. 2004. Direct measurement of individual tree characteristics from LIDAR data. Proceedings of the annual ASPRS conference. Bethesda, MD: American Society of Photogrammetry and Remote Sensing.

Means, J.; Acker, S.; Fitt, B.; Renslow, M.; Emerson, L.; Hendrix, C. 2000. Predicting forest stand characteristics with airborne scanning LIDAR. Photogrammetric Engineering and Remote Sensing 66(1): 1367-1371.

Naesset, E. 2002. Predicting forest stand characteristics with airborne laser using a practical two-stage procedure and field data. Remote Sensing of Environment 80: 88-99.

Naesset, E.; Okland, T. 2002. Estimating tree height and tree crown properties using airborne scanning laser in a boreal nature reserve. Remote Sensing of Environment 79: 105-115.

Persson, A.; Holmgren, J.; Soderman, U. 2002. Detecting and measuring individual trees using an airborne laser scanner. Photogrammetric Engineering and Remote Sensing 68(9): 925-932.

Reutebuch, S.E.; McGaughey, R.J.; Andersen, H.-E.; Carson, W.W. 2003. Accuracy of a high-resolution LIDAR terrain model under a conifer forest canopy. Canadian Journal of Remote Sensing 29(5): 527-535.

Schardt, M.; Ziegler, M.; Wimmer, A.; Wack, R.; Hyyppa, J. 2002. Assessment of forest parameters by means of laser scanning. Graz, Austria: International Archives of Photogrammetry and Remote Sensing. Vol. XXXIV, part 3A: 302-309.

Soille, P. 1999. Morphological image analysis. New York, NY: Springer-Verlag.

West, G.B.; Brown, J.H.; Enquist, B.J. 1997. A general model for the origin of allometric scaling laws in biology. Science 476: 122-126.

ACOUSTIC TESTING TO ENHANCE WESTERN FOREST VALUES AND MEET CUSTOMER WOOD QUALITY NEEDS

Peter Carter[1], David Briggs[2], Robert J. Ross[3], Xiping Wang[4]

ABSTRACT

Nondestructive testing (NDT) of wood products, such as lumber and veneer, for stiffness and strength evaluation has been proven and commercialized for many years. The NDT concept has been extended and commercialized in the Director HM-200™ tool for testing logs in advance of processing so manufacturers can make more informed log purchases and better match logs to customer needs for product stiffness and strength. Further extension of the NDT concept to standing timber is a logical progression and a new commercial tool, the Director ST-300™, has just been developed for this application. This paper describes operating principles of both tools and presents examples of their use with various species. The potential effects of wood density, moisture content, temperature, and age on results from these tools are also discussed.

KEYWORDS: Nondestructive testing, tree quality, log quality, modulus of elasticity, stiffness.

INTRODUCTION

While a large body of research has focused on understanding and improving the productivity of western forests, improving value in these forests must also consider wood quality. As harvest age decreases and use of intensive silviculture increases, quality of stands, logs, and products is becoming more variable. However, application of intensive silviculture throughout the life-cycle of a stand also presents an opportunity to measure, manage and control quality as well as tree size and volume.

Product markets readily segregate into applications where aesthetic appearance features, such as grain, color and knottiness, predominate in defining quality and applications where mechanical properties, such as stiffness and strength used by architects and engineers in designing structures, predominate in defining quality. In the US, about 52% of the solid-sawn lumber consumed is used in new residential and nonresidential construction and another 30% is used for repair and remodel of existing structures (Eastin 2005). Much of the veneer production is also used in products where stiffness and strength are critical quality characteristics. The dependence of western forests on markets for softwood structural products is illustrated by the state of Washington where 92% of the harvest is softwoods, of which 71% is sawlogs for lumber and 17% is peeler logs for veneer (Smith et al. 2001).

Traditionally, quality of softwood trees, logs and products has been assessed by human visual observation of surface characteristics, such as knots, splits, and rings per inch, and assignment to one of several possible grades based on simple, broad allowable ranges for the characteristics. Although these grades may be sufficient where appearance is the primary consideration, the adequacy of visual grades for applications involving stiffness and strength is questionable since

[1] Peter Carter is manager of resource technology and commercialization, Carter, Holt, Harvey Fibre-Gen, Auckland, New Zealand.

[2] David Briggs is professor and director, Stand Management & Precision Forestry Cooperatives, College of Forest Resources, University of Washington, Seattle, WA.

[3] Robert J. Ross is project leader, Condition Assessment and Rehabilitation of Structures, USDA Forest Service Forest Products Laboratory, Madison, WI.

[4] Xiping Wang is research associate, Natural Resources Research Institute, University of Minnesota Duluth, Duluth, MN and USDA Forest Products Laboratory, Madison WI.

no measure of these properties is actually obtained. Indeed, a concern over reliability and the broad, conservative design values associated with visual grades for structural applications led to the development of machine-stress-rating (MSR) technology for lumber that has been in commercial use since the 1960s. MSR technology non-destructively measures the stiffness of lumber and uses a pre-established relationship between stiffness and bending strength to define a set of strength-based grades. This provides a more refined and flexible approach than visual grading for identifying and sorting lumber into stress grades used in products such as glulam (glued laminated timber) beams and engineered trusses. With the development and rapid growth of new engineered wood products such as laminated veneer lumber (LVL), I-beams and I-joists, there has been a parallel growth in non-destructive testing (NDT) for the stiffness and strength of lumber and veneer used as components of these products. In addition, concerns with design values of structural lumber graded with visual methods is creating momentum for verification testing of visually graded structural materials.

These trends have renewed interest of mills in non-destructive methods. Mills seeking to capture a price premium (Spelter 1996) by producing non-destructively tested lumber and veneer, find that it is very expensive to process logs or purchase timber stands that have low yield of product with the stiffness and strength levels desired by their customers. Consequently, researchers have developed technology for applying NDT to measure stiffness of logs to improve sorting and matching with desired levels of lumber or veneer stiffness (Wang et al. 2002, 2004a). This research has led to development and introduction of the Director HM-200™, a log-stiffness testing tool described later in this paper. A logical and desirable extension is to apply the NDT technique to measure stiffness of wood in standing trees (Wang et al. 2001, 2003), thereby providing timber sellers and purchasers with a means for improved harvest scheduling and timber marketing based on the potential yield of stress-graded products that can be obtained from trees within a stand. A new tool, the Director ST-300™, has been developed for evaluating wood stiffness in standing trees and is also described in this paper.

BASICS OF NDT ASSESSMENT OF STIFFNESS

Stiffness of a piece of lumber, or a log, can be measured by placing it in a suitable static bending test apparatus, recording the deflection as load is applied, and calculating the modulus of elasticity (MOE or E), which is a measure of stiffness or resistance to deflection. Although this "static bending" MOE can be measured without testing the piece to failure, it is slow and involves expensive equipment that is not very portable. Consequently researchers have been exploring the use of the "dynamic" MOE, which is well correlated with the static MOE. Dynamic MOE is obtained by measuring the velocity of an acoustic wave through the material and is expressed by the following formula

$$E_d = \frac{\rho}{g} V^2 \qquad (1)$$

where

E_d dynamic modulus of elasticity (in lb/in^2 or Pa)
ρ density of the material (in lb/ft^3 or kg/m^3)
g acceleration due to gravity (in 386 in/s^2 or 9.8 m/ s^2)
V velocity of the wave through the material (in ft/s or m/s)

Recognizing that g is a constant and applying any conversions between units, the constant k can be introduced and the equation becomes

$$E_d = k\rho V^2 \qquad (2)$$

In practice, the density of many materials is relatively constant; hence the velocity of the acoustic wave can be used as a direct indicator of the dynamic MOE, a measure of the material's stiffness.

ASSESSING STIFFNESS OF LOGS WITH THE DIRECTOR HM-200™

Operating the Director HM-200™

Figures 1 and 2 show use of the Director HM-200™ for evaluating logs. The user first enters the log length or selects the length from a pre-loaded list and then presses the Director HM-200™ against the log. A sensor head signals that it has contact and the user strikes the end of the log with a hammer. The sensor picks up the acoustic wave signal as it passes back and forth along the length of the log at a rate of a few hundred passes per second. Software in the Director HM-200™ processes the signal and displays the velocity in either feet or meters per second, depending on whether the unit has been set for metric or imperial units. The same velocity will be displayed regardless of which end of the log is chosen or where on the end the sensor head is placed and the hammer blow is struck. This is because the Director HM-200™ software obtains the weighted average velocity for the log from its analysis of the whole wave signals received. The user can program the Director HM-200™ to recognize up to 3 grade categories based on the displayed velocity. These are signaled to the operator by a color code in the display and by a unique sound signal. The operator can then suitably color spray or otherwise mark the log for subsequent sorting.

122

Figure 1—The Director HM-200™ in use in a log yard.

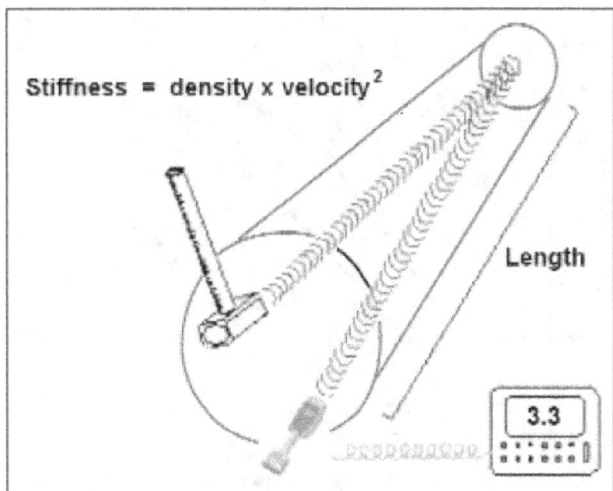

Figure 2—Operating principle of the Director HM-200™.

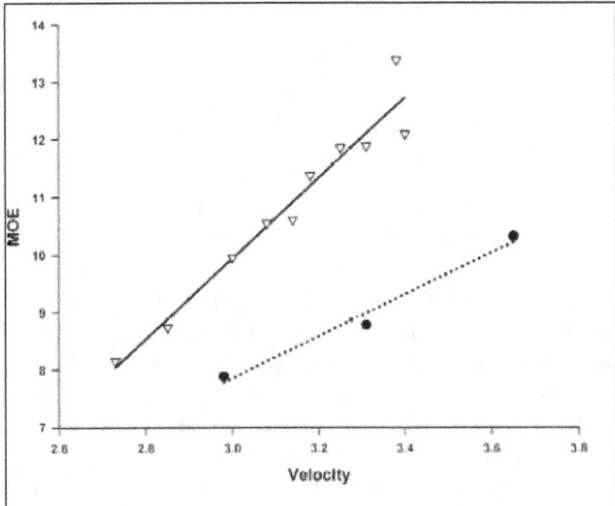

Figure 3—MOE (kPa) of dry lumber from a log verses Director HM-200™ velocity of the log (km/sec) for Southern pine (upper line, R^2 = 0.9779) and radiata pine (lower line, R^2 = 0.9792).

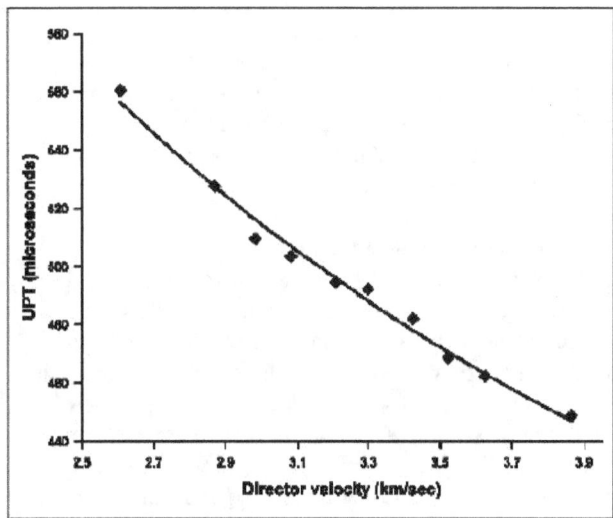

Figure 4—Ultrasound propagation time (UPT) of veneer from a log vs Director HM-200™ velocity of the log (km/sec) 10 percentile log batches from a Southern pine trial.

Velocity, Stiffness of Product Within Log, and Economic Benefit

Figure 3 illustrates the correlation between the acoustic velocity (km/s) of green radiata pine (lower curve) and southern pine (upper curve) logs and static bending MOE of the dry boards sawn from the logs. Each data point represents a log batch. A high correlation (R^2=0.98) was observed for both species. Figure 4 illustrates the relationship between acoustic velocity for log batches (10 percentile groups from log sample) for southern pine and the average ultrasound propagation time (UPT) of veneer from the logs. Ultrasound propagation time is the elapsed time for ultrasound to travel between fixed roller wheel points

on a Metriguard™ veneer tester. Although a linear regression seems adequate to represent the relationship, a power regression model (model in the form of $y = ax^b$) was found to best fit the trend, with a coefficient of determination (R^2) value of 0.99.

Figure 5 shows the increasing yield of structural grades of lumber with increasing acoustic velocity of logs processed, as measured with the Director HM-200™ at two New Zealand radiata pine sawmills. Assuming a price differential of NZ\$200/m³ on lumber, an increase of 0.1 km/s in logs sorted with the HM 200 produces a gain in structural lumber yield of about 5%. This translates into a gain of

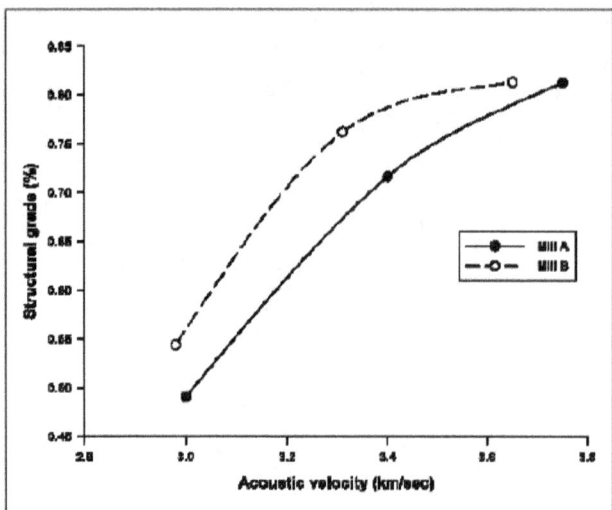

Figure 5—Yield of structural lumber grades verses Director HM-200™ log velocity (km/sec) for two New Zealand radiata pine sawmills.

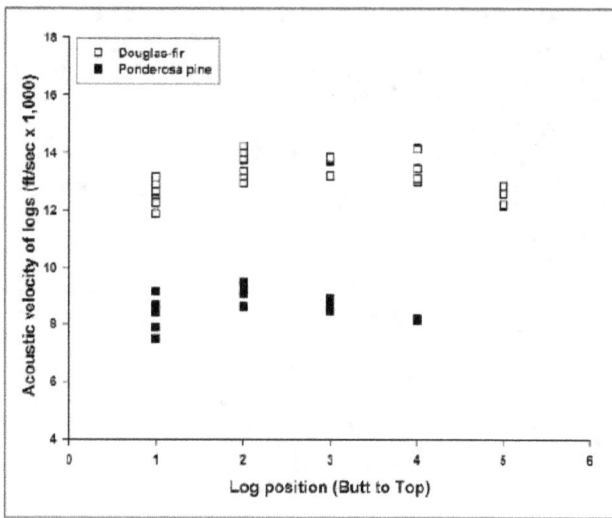

Figure 6—Acoustic velocity of logs in relation to log position in a tree stem.

about NZ$6/m³ on log volume or about NZ$1.8 million for a mill processing 300.000 m³ of logs per year. A similar analysis for veneer for LVL production in the US resulted in a gain of about US$16/m³ on log volume (about $80-$100/MBF Scribner log scale).

Variation With Log Position and Age

As trees grow in height, they produce new cambium along the shoot. This young cambium forms growth rings with low wood density and a large microfibril angle which together result in wood of low stiffness and strength. As the cambium ages, it eventually produces denser, lower microfibril angle wood which then is stiffer and stronger. Thus a tree typically has a core of "juvenile" wood, depending on species from about 7 to 20 or more rings wide, that becomes surrounded by later rings of "mature" wood. More rings, hence more mature wood, occur in the butt log of a tree whereas the top log has fewer rings and has not yet undergone the transition to mature wood formation. Therefore, one can expect that stiffness and acoustic velocity would decrease as the percentage of juvenile wood increases from the butt log to top log position in a tree. With the exception of the butt log, this pattern is borne out as shown in figure 6 for Douglas-fir and ponderosa pine logs (Wang et al. 2004b). It appears that the butt log does not follow the expected pattern. Researchers have found that the lower bole has mature wood with lower density and higher microfibril angles leading to lower stiffness (Megraw et al. 1999).

Since logs in the upper stem of a tree have both fewer rings and a higher percentage of low stiffness juvenile wood, one would expect low acoustic velocity in these low age

logs. This is also borne out and leads to a generally rising trend of average acoustic velocity of logs from a stand as stand age increases (figure 7). Figure 8 shows 21 radiata pine stands in order of increasing average log acoustic velocity as measured by the Director HM-200™. The mean as well as 2 standard deviations is displayed for each stand (log source). This demonstrates that there is much greater variability within, rather than between, stands. Since some younger stands contain logs with much greater velocities than logs in older stands; the Director HM-200™ provides a more reliable means for identifying and sorting the logs with better stiffness characteristics than would be obtained using age or other misleading appearance features. Although sorting logs with the Director HM-200™ at a landing or log yard provides obvious advantages, it would be desirable to have counterpart technology for standing trees to help find the best stands.

ASSESSING STIFFNESS OF STANDING TREES WITH THE DIRECTOR ST-300™

Operating the Director ST-300™

Figure 9 shows the components and set-up of the Director ST-300™. Transmitter and receiver probes are driven through the bark into the outer wood of the lower stem. They are vertically aligned along the stem approximately 1.3 meters apart and it does not matter which probe is the higher or lower unit. A laser guided ultrasound rangefinder measures the exact distance between the probes. An acoustic wave is imparted into the tree stem through the transmitter probe by a hammer blow. The receiver probe picks up the acoustic signal passing through the tree and determines the time-of-flight of the acoustic wave. The distance and time

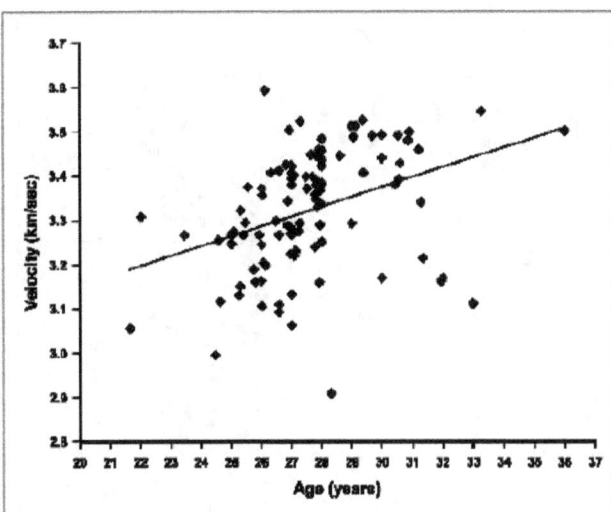

Figure 7—Director HM-200™ velocity (km/s) verses average log age in New Zealand radiata pine stands

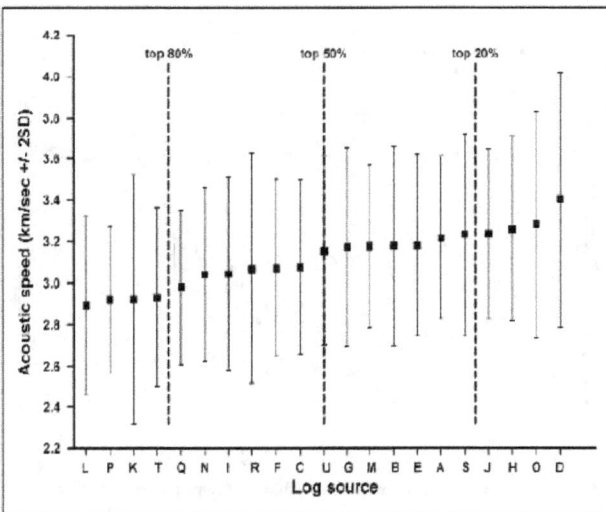

Figure 8—Mean and variation in Director HM-200™ velocity (km/s) for logs from New Zealand radiata pine stands. Log sources (stands) are sorted by mean acoustic speed.

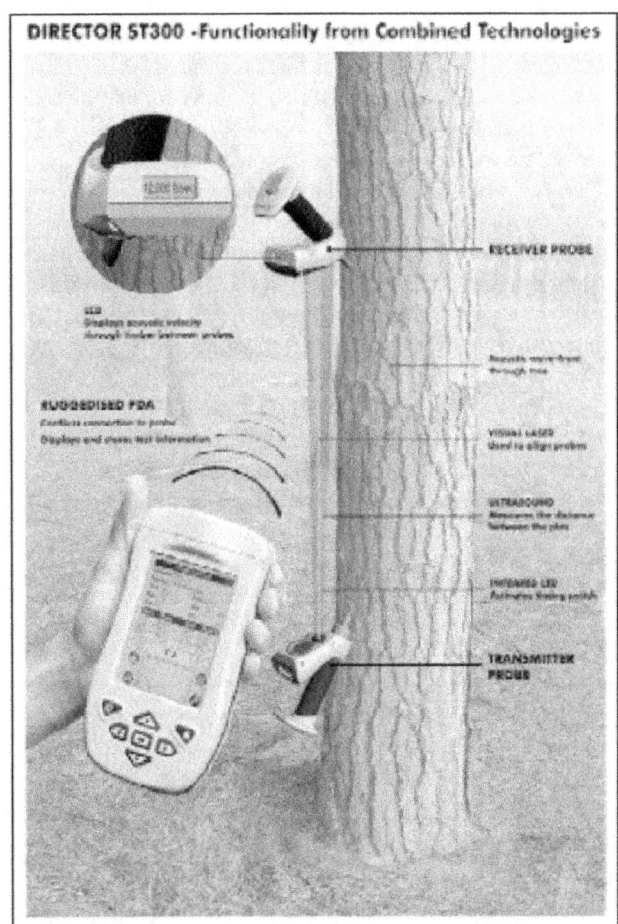

Figure 9—Components of the Director ST-300™.

are sent by wireless communication to a PDA (personal digital assistant) that calculates the acoustic velocity and also allows the user to enter other tree and stand data. Unlike the Director HM-200™, which obtains the weighted average velocity by analyzing whole wave signals transmitted between the ends of a log, the Director ST-300™ measures time-of-flight for a single pulse wave to pass through the outer wood of the tree from transmitter probe to receiver probe. Given this difference in how velocity is measured and the fact that the Director ST-300™ only measures velocity along a short distance along what will become the base of the butt log from the tree, the most obvious and immediate question is: "What is the relationship between velocities obtained with the Director ST-300™ and those from the Director HM-200™?" Figure 10 provides evidence that the answer is there is a very strong linear relationship between acoustic velocity measured in trees and acoustic velocity measured in logs (Wang et al. 2004b).

Figure 11 shows tests in radiata pine of the effect of misaligning the probes, i.e., keeping the receiver probe at X and moving the source probe further and further out of alignment (XA vs. XE). Since time-of-flight is measured through the outer wood between the probes, figure 11 also shows that moving the probes to a different location around the circumference of the stem has a minor effect on velocity (XA vs. YE). Finally, figure 11 shows the effect of lengthening the distance between the probes; including a knot whorl with associated deviant grain slightly lowers the velocity and thus, the predicted value of stiffness. Results shown in figure 11 imply that correlations between Director ST-300™ and Director HM-200™ velocities will be

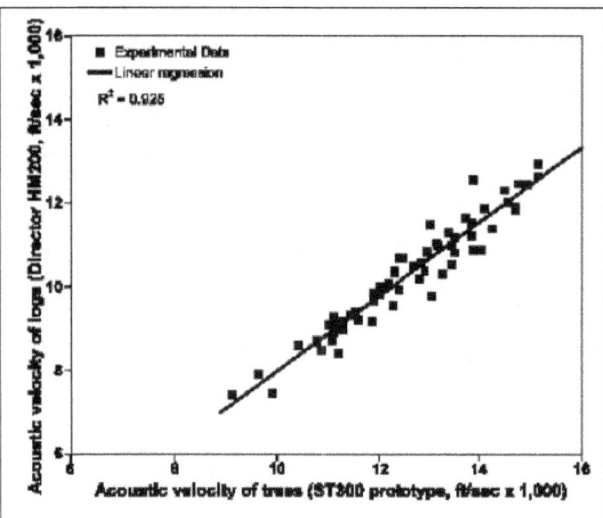

Figure 10—Relationship between measurement of acoustic speed of logs with the Director HM- 200™ and measurement of acoustic speed of parent trees with the Director ST-300™.

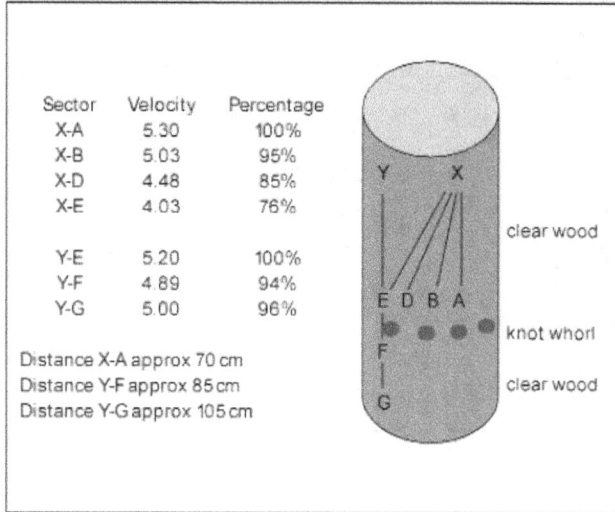

Sector	Velocity	Percentage
X-A	5.30	100%
X-B	5.03	95%
X-D	4.48	85%
X-E	4.03	76%
Y-E	5.20	100%
Y-F	4.89	94%
Y-G	5.00	96%

Distance X-A approx 70 cm
Distance Y-F approx 85 cm
Distance Y-G approx 105 cm

Figure 11—Effects of Director ST-300™ probe location in relation to knot inclusion and displacement from vertical on velocity in a radiata pine stem.

improved as one acquires and averages more samples around the stem circumference with the Director ST-300™. The issue of whether or not one should acquire more samples within each tree or sample more trees within the stand of interest depends on the objective of the assessment project.

EXPERIENCE WITH THE DIRECTOR ST-300™ IN DOUGLAS-FIR

A test of the Director ST-300™ was conducted in September 2004 in an unthinned and a thinned plot in the Stand Management Cooperative's (SMC) Type II Installation 803, Beeville Loop, located near Shelton, WA. This thinning trial was placed in a stand that was planted with 2-0 Douglas-fir seedlings in 1955 on site class II (122 feet based on King 1966). In 1987, the SMC established five plots, a control that had 320 trees per acre and would receive no future treatments and four plots of similar initial stocking that w o u l d undergo thinning regimes. A crew of three measured 63 trees in the unthinned control (plot 2) and 50 trees in a plot that was thinned in 1987 from a Curtis relative density (Curtis 1982) of 55 to a relative density of 35 (plot 1). At the time of the test, breast height age was 43, stand age was 49 and age from seed was 51. Time to locate and walk between trees, set up the test, and measure dbh averaged 1 minute per tree.

Figure 12 presents the cumulative mean and standard error for each plot as more trees were measured; by the time 35 trees were sampled, the difference between the plots became apparent. The thinned plot, with faster growing and larger diameter trees, has higher average acoustic velocity and hence would be expected to produce greater yield of products with higher stiffness. We speculate that this site may experience water stress in summer, thus, the unthinned stand, with more competing trees, may stop growing earlier thereby truncating formation of dense latewood. The reduced production of latewood would result in lower overall wood density, which would translate into slower velocity and lower stiffness. This is atypical of what would be expected on sites where moisture is not limiting. In a wood quality study conducted on young-growth western hemlock and Sitka spruce, Wang examined the effects of thinning treatments on both stress wave velocity and wood stiffness. The results revealed that highest stress wave velocity and stiffness were mostly found in unthinned control stands whereas the lowest values were found in stands that had received heavy and medium thinning (Wang et al. 2001). This indicated that lower density stands exhibited a trend toward decreased stress wave velocity and decreased stiffness.

Figure 13 shows weak negative trends of velocity with tree diameter in each plot. The unthinned plot trend is lower than that for the thinned plot although the trends converge for the larger diameter trees that were presumably in the dominant crown class. Figure 14 shows similarly weak

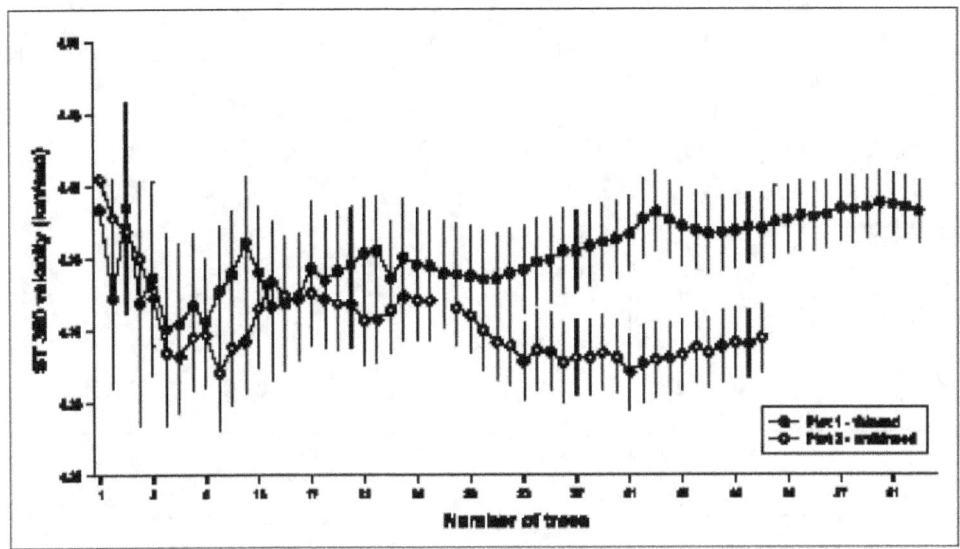

Figure 12—Effect of increasing sample size on mean and standard error of Director ST-300™ acoustic velocity in Douglas-fir trees in thinned and unthinned plots at the Stand Management Cooperative Beeville Loop installation. Shown is cumulative mean plot velocity (±1 standard error) as number of trees sampled increased.

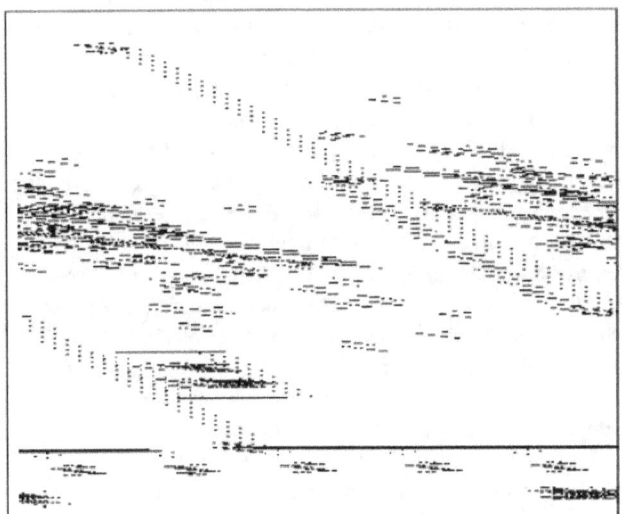

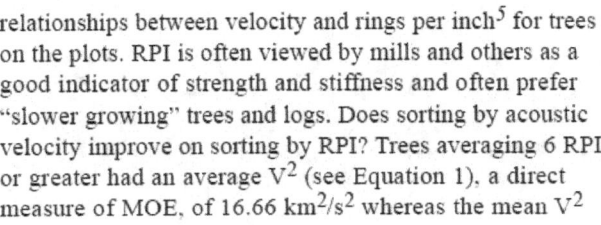

Figure 13—Relationship between tree DBH and Director ST-300™ velocity for Douglas-fir trees in thinned, $R^2 = 0.2527$, and unthinned, $R^2 = 0.0906$, plots at the SMC Beeville Loop installation.

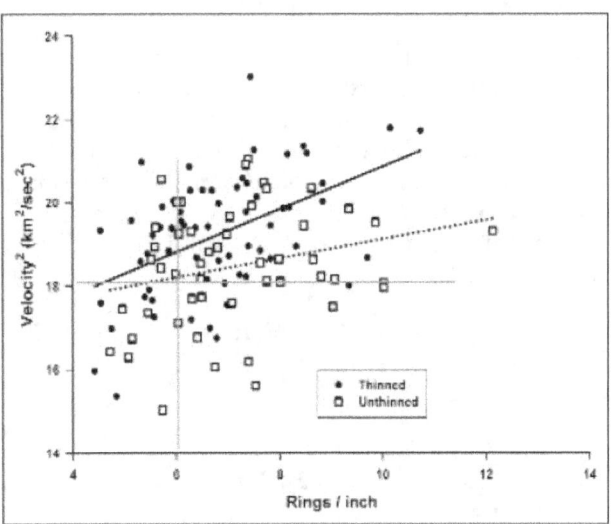

Figure 14—Relationship between rings/inch and Director ST-300™ velocity for Douglas-fir trees in thinned, $R^2 = 0.2333$, and unthinned, $R^2 = 0.0604$, plots at the SMC Beeville Loop installation.

relationships between velocity and rings per inch[5] for trees on the plots. RPI is often viewed by mills and others as a good indicator of strength and stiffness and often prefer "slower growing" trees and logs. Does sorting by acoustic velocity improve on sorting by RPI? Trees averaging 6 RPI or greater had an average V^2 (see Equation 1), a direct measure of MOE, of 16.66 km²/s² whereas the mean V^2

of all of the trees in both plots was 18.09 km²/s², a gain of 2.3%. Note that roughly half of the trees with less than 6.0 RPI have V^2 greater than 18.09 km²/s² and many trees with more than 6.0 RPI have V^2 less than 18.09 km²/s². Using the preceding economic analysis data, this 2.3% gain from acoustic sorting would translate to about $8/m3 ($40-48/MBF Scribner).

---

[5] RPI = rings per inch, which is calculated as breast-height age divided by stem radius in inches (radius = diameter at breast height / 2)

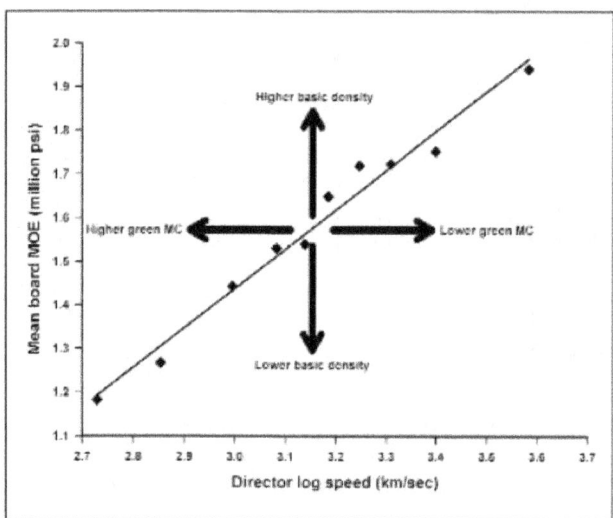

Figure 15—Relationships between 10th percentile classes of average board MOE, and Director log speed for radiata pine. Arrows indicate shift of the relationship with changes in basic wood density and moisture content.

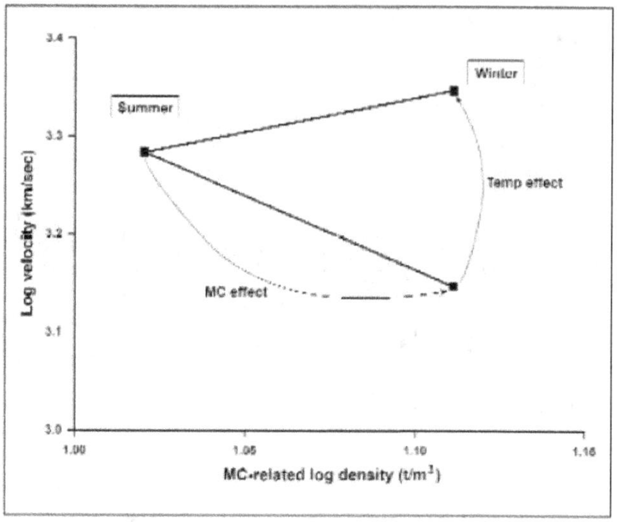

Figure 16—Effect of seasonal change in temperature and moisture content on log density and log velocity in radiata pine. Log density is based on JAS log scale.

OPERATIONAL CONSIDERATIONS

At a given time of year in a given stand, one can assume that the density, ρ in Equation (1), which is simply weight divided by volume, is reasonably constant and that the effect of changes in temperature would be minimal. Although for many materials density is constant, it is variable for wood; hence there may be seasonal and other effects to consider. In the case of fresh, wet "green" wood, density can be calculated as follows:

$$\rho = \rho_{H_20} SG_g \, (1 + MC_{od}) \qquad (3)$$

Where

ρ = density (in lb/ft^3 or kg/m^3)
ρ_{H_20} = density of water (62.4 lb/ft^3 or1000 kg/m^3)
SG_g = wood basic density[6] (also referred to as specific gravity or relative density)
MC_{od} = wood moisture content (oven-dry basis, in decimal form)

The basic density of wood varies by species and has a systematic pattern of change from pith to bark and from base to top of tree that is associated with the formation processes of juvenile and mature wood. These patterns are part of the explanation of why acoustic velocity changes with log position within a tree (figure 6) and why acoustic velocity is correlated with log age (figure 7).

It should be apparent from equation (3) that density increases as wood moisture content increases; this is simply a result of the fact that water in wood cells weighs much more than the air which replaces the water during drying. Consequently, one can expect lower velocities in wet wood as compared to dry wood. In living trees and freshly-cut logs, lumber, and veneer, wood moisture content often varies between sapwood and heartwood. For example, moisture content for softwood species ranges from 98 to 249% for sapwood and from 31 to 121% for heartwood (Forest Products Laboratory 1999). The moisture content of a log whose velocity is being measured by the Director HM-200™ is a weighted average of sapwood and heartwood moisture contents. The moisture content of the outer wood of a tree whose velocity is being measured with the Director ST-300™ will be that of sapwood. Fortunately, it has been found that when moisture content is above 40%, there is little effect on acoustic velocity (Ross et al. 2004). However, for logs from species with low heartwood moisture contents, for dead timber, and for logs that may have undergone some drying since harvest, an adjustment for the effect of moisture content may be needed. Continuous monitoring of moisture content of a sample of logs will be useful to gain an understanding of the effect of moisture content and make appropriate adjustments, if necessary. Figure 15 illustrates the typical directions that changes in moisture content and basic density have on deviation of samples from an established trend line.

---

[6] Based on oven dry weight and green volume.

In addition to the effects of basic density and moisture content, large seasonal changes in temperature may also require the user to make an appropriate adjustment on acoustic measures. Figure 16 illustrates the effects of seasonal changes in temperature and moisture content on acoustic velocity of radiata pine. In-depth research is still needed to further explore the influence of seasonal weather change on acoustic measurements on trees and logs.

CONCLUSIONS

Nondestructive testing of logs for stiffness with the Director HM-200™ offers a new reliable and flexible approach for sorting and matching logs to manufacturer and customer demands for stiffness and strength of products they contain. It may also provide a new means by which landowners and loggers can grade and market logs.

The nondestructive testing concept has been extended to standing trees with Director ST-300™ which provides an indicator of stiffness over an approximate 1.3 m distance in the lower stem; lower portion of the butt log. This will provide a new means for assessing mature stands for marketing, for harvest planning and scheduling, and has the potential for assisting in planning silvicultural operations in immature stands.

LITERATURE CITED

Curtis, R.O. 1982. A simple index of stand density for Douglas-fir. Forest Science 28: 92-94.

Eastin, I. 2005. Does lumber quality really matter to builders? In: Harrington, C.A.; Schoenholtz, S.H., eds. Productivity of Western Forests: A Forest Products Focus. Proceedings of a meeting held June 20-23, 2004, Kamilche, WA. Gen. Tech. Rep. PNW-GTR-642. Portland, OR: U.S. Department of Agriculture, Forest Service, Pacific Northwest Research Station: 131-139.

King, J.E. 1966. Site index curves for Douglas-fir in the Pacific Northwest. Weyerhaeuser Company Forestry Paper No. 8. Centralia, WA.

Megraw, R.A.; Bremer, D.; Leaf, G.; Roers, J. 1999. Stiffness in loblolly pine as a function of ring position and height, and it's relationship to microfibril angle and specific gravity. In: Proceedings of the 3rd Workshop Connection Between Silviculture and Wood Quality Through Modeling Approaches. La Londe-Les-Maures, France: IUFRO Working Party S5.01-04: 341-349.

Ross, R.J.; Brashaw, B.K.; Wang, X.; White, R.H.; Pellerin, R.F. 2004. Wood and timber condition assessment manual. Madison, WI: Forest Products Society. 73 p.

Smith, W.B.; Vissage, J.S.; Darr, D.R.; Sheffield, R.M. 2001. Forest resources of the United States, 1997. Gen. Tech. Rep. GTR-NC-219. St. Paul, MN: U.S. Department of Agriculture, Forest Service, North Central Research Station. 190 p.

Spelter, H.; Wang, R.; Ince, P. 1996. Economic feasibility of products from Inland West small-diameter timber. Gen. Tech. Rep. FPL-GTR-92. Madison, WI: U.S. Department of Agriculture, Forest Service, Forest Products Laboratory. 17 p.

Forest Products Laboratory. 1999. Wood handbook: wood as an engineering material. Gen. Tech. Rep. FPL-GTR-113. Madison, WI: U.S. Department of Agriculture, Forest Service, Forest Products Laboratory.

Wang, X.; Ross, R.J.; McClellan, M. [et al.] 2001. Nondestructive evaluation of standing trees with a stress wave method. Wood and Fiber Science 33: 522-533.

Wang, X. Ross, R.J.; Mattson, J.A. [et al.] 2002. Nondestructive evaluation techniques for assessing modulus of elasticity and stiffness of small-diameter logs. Forest Products Journal 52(2): 79-85.

Wang, X.; Ross, R.J.; Punches, J. [et al.] 2003. Evaluation of small-diameter timber for value-added manufacturing - a stress wave approach. In: Proceedings, The Second International Precision Forestry Symposium. Seattle, WA: College of Forest Resources, University of Washington: 91-96.

Wang, X.; Ross, R.J.; Green, D.W. [et al.] 2004a. Stress wave sorting of red maple logs for structural quality. Wood Science Technology 37: 531-537.

Wang, X.; Ross, R.J.; Carter, P. 2004b. Assessment of standing tree quality – from baseline research to field equipment. In: Forest Products Society 2004 Annual Meeting – Technical Forum. Grand Rapids, Michigan, USA.

DOES LUMBER QUALITY REALLY MATTER TO BUILDERS?

Ivan L. Eastin[1]

ABSTRACT

Understanding the ways in which residential builders perceive and use softwood lumber and substitute structural materials is essential to the success of any forest products manufacturer. This research represents the third in a longitudinal study and describes trends in material substitution in the residential construction industry in 2001. This study looks at material substitution in structural framing applications and provides a benchmark for structural panel usage in exterior wall sheathing, sub-flooring and subroofing applications. The results of this research suggest that the pace of material substitution in the residential construction industry has moderated since 1998. To a large degree this might be attributed to lower lumber prices, less volatility in lumber prices, and the fact that builders have become more accepting of the perceived decline in softwood lumber quality that has been attributed to the younger, faster grown plantation resource and improved scanning and processing technologies in the sawmill industry. The exception to this trend is in floor framing applications where wood I-joists continue to expand their market share at the expense of softwood lumber. The most troubling result is the continuing misperception among residential builders that when compared to alternative (non-wood) materials, softwood lumber is the least environmentally friendly material. This result could have serious implications for the forest products industry in the future as green building programs become more prevalent and home buyers become more assertive in demanding that environmentally friendly materials be used in building their homes. This misperception suggests that further research is needed to determine the basis for the misperception and that strategies need to be developed to ensure that information regarding the positive environmental benefits of using wood relative to non-wood substitutes is effectively communicated to home builders and home buyers.

KEYWORDS: Material substitution, softwood lumber, marketing, attributes, residential construction.

INTRODUCTION

Historically, residential housing has been the single largest market for softwood lumber in the United States (Joint Center for Housing Studies 2001). While there has been a close relationship between housing starts and softwood lumber consumption and production in the past, domestic supply constraints and the emergence of the repair and remodel market in the late 1980s have tended to relax this relationship (fig. 1). Currently about 40 percent of U.S. lumber consumption can be attributed to residential construction while the repair and remodeling sector accounts for an additional 30 percent of lumber consumption (fig. 2).

Following the imposition of timber harvest constraints in the Pacific Northwest in the late 1980s, the price volatility of softwood lumber increased dramatically, figure 3. The timber harvest constraints occurred just as the residential construction industry entered a period of dramatic growth. The combination of sustained growth in the housing industry, declining lumber production, timber harvest constraints and the softwood lumber trade dispute between the US and Canada all contributed to increased price

[1] Ivan L. Eastin is professor of forest products marketing and the Acting Director of the Center for International Trade in Forest Products (CINTRAFOR), College of Forest Resources, Box 352100, University of Washington, Seattle, WA 98195.

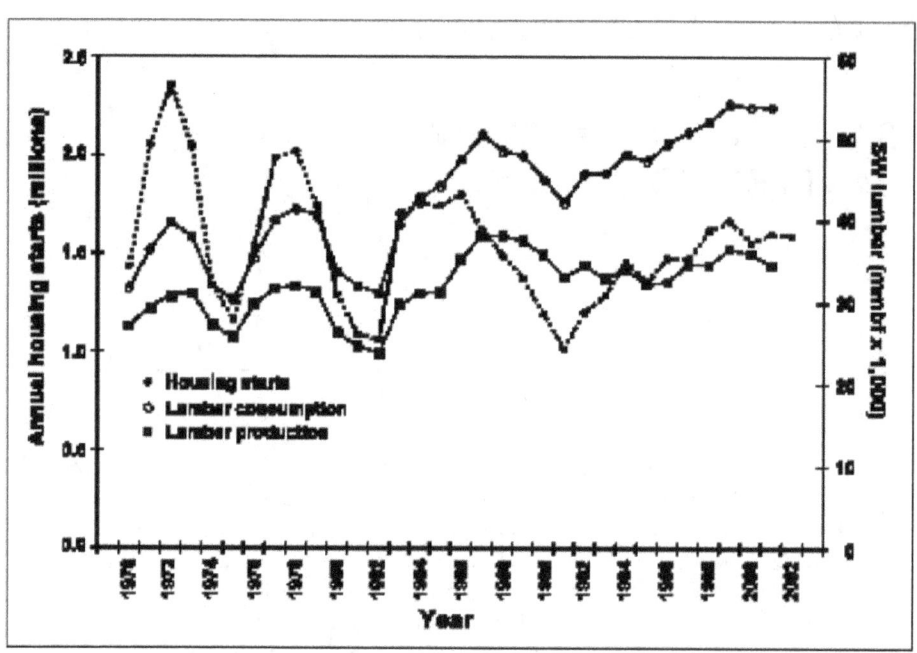

Figure 1—The relationship between housing starts and the consumption and production of softwood lumber in the US.

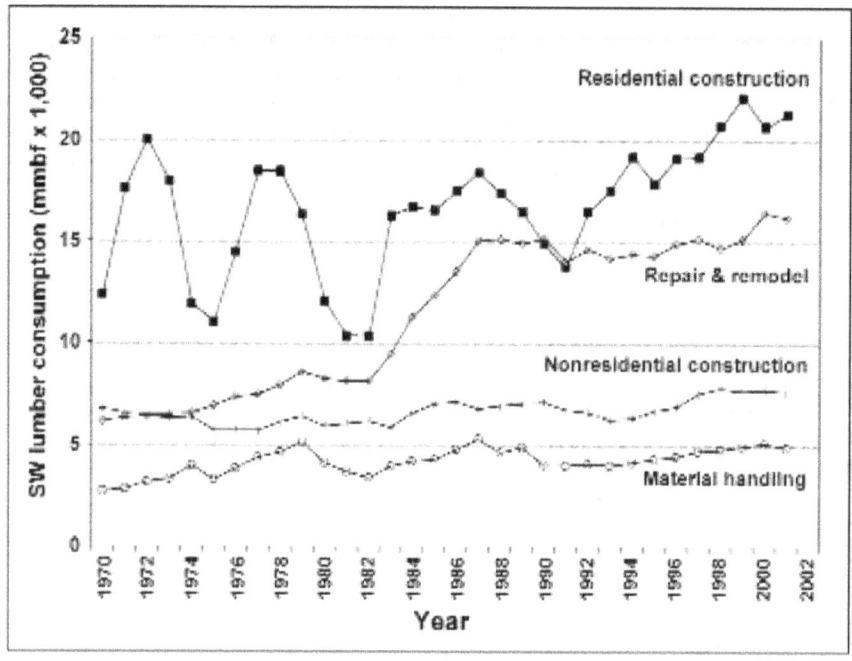

Figure 2—Major end-use markets for softwood lumber (Western Wood Products Association 2002).

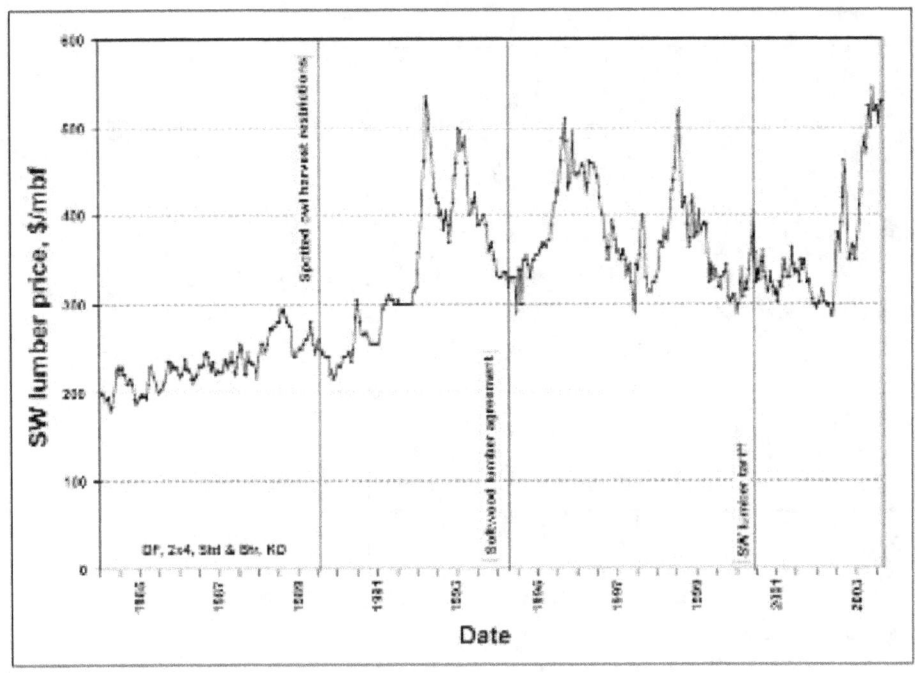

Figure 3—Price changes for softwood lumber dimension lumber over time.

volatility. Sensitive to the dramatic effect that volatile lumber prices can have on their profit margins, builders began to look at using more price-stable materials as substitutes for softwood lumber (Shook et al. 1998; Fell 1999; Eastin et al. 2000; Eastin et al. 2001; Shook and Eastin 2001; Fell 1999).

Understanding the ways in which residential builders purchase and use softwood lumber and lumber substitutes is essential to the success of any forest products manufacturer. The Center for International Trade in Forest Products (CINTRAFOR) completed its first study on material substitution in 1995 (Eastin et al. 1996), providing a benchmark for softwood lumber use in structural applications in residential construction. In 1998, a second study by CINTRAFOR found that softwood lumber was slowly losing market share to engineered wood products and non-wood substitutes (Fleishman et al. 2000). The 1998 CINTRAFOR study also provided a benchmark for material usage in residential decking applications (CINTRAFOR Working Paper No. 78). A third study conducted in 2002 describes the trends in material substitution in the residential construction industry in 2001 (Garth et al. 2004).

STUDY METHODS

Studies in this field rely primarily on survey instruments. The sample population for this survey consisted of 2,400 single-family homebuilders as well as the top 100 homebuilders in the United States. A stratified, random sample of 2,400 homebuilders was obtained from a database of US homebuilders maintained by Cahners Direct Marketing Services located in Des Plaines, IL while a census of the top 100 homebuilders was obtained from Builder Magazine (May 2001 edition).

The database obtained from Cahners was specifically designed to include an equal number of builders (600 builders) in each of the four regions in the US. In addition to the regional specification, the sample frame was further stratified to include an equal number of small, medium and large sized firms within each region.

A cover letter was mailed to each survey recipient stating the goals and purpose of the survey. In addition, each homebuilder received an eight page survey and a self addressed stamped envelope in which to return the completed survey. The results of this survey were offered free to any builder that participated in the survey. As an additional incentive, the names of all survey respondents were entered into a drawing for five Porter Cable 10-AmpQuick Change Reciprocating Saws. Two follow up letters were sent to non-respondents at intervals of two and four weeks following the initial mailing. A total of 189 valid responses were received which correlates to a final response rate of 9.0% (taking into account undeliverable surveys).

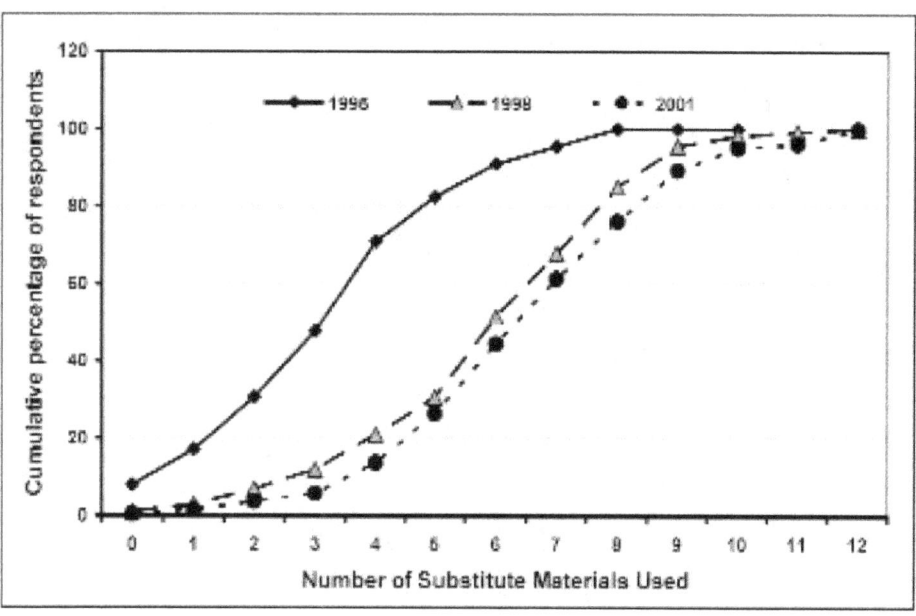

Figure 4—Number of substitute products used by residential builders.

SURVEY RESULTS

Builders Use of Substitute Materials

The total number of substitute materials used by residential builders in 2001 was very similar to that found in the 1998 survey. A cumulative percentage graph comparing the three survey results of 1995, 1998, and 2001 is presented in figure 4. Almost half of the respondents in 2001 have used seven or more substitute materials; this is very similar to results in 1998. In addition, almost a quarter of the respondents have used nine or more substitute materials. In 1998, only 15% of builders had tried nine or more substitutes. The further shift of the usage curve to the right indicates that builders are using more substitute materials over time.

As was mentioned in previous survey results, the trend of higher substitute usage can be partially explained by builders' dissatisfaction with several softwood lumber attributes, particularly with respect to overall price, price stability, and softwood lumber quality. As a traditionally conservative group, particularly with respect to the trial a n d adoption of new substitute materials, the shift by builders toward using a broader range of structural materials should be seen as an indication of their continued dissatisfaction with softwood lumber. This shift should also be seen as an indication that builders are more willing to try new products as a result of their past experiences with substitute materials. This explains why the aggregate use of substitute materials

continues to grow even as the prices of softwood lumber have moderated in recent years.

Material Use in Specific End-Use Applications

Survey participants were asked to estimate the percentage (on a volume basis) of material usage during the past year in specific structural end-use applications (tables 1 and 2). These structural applications included wall framing (including both load bearing and non-load bearing walls), floor joists, roof framing and headers. The designation of non-load bearing wall and load bearing wall applications were a new addition to the 2001 survey. Material use in header applications was also a new category in the 2001 survey.

The softwood lumber usage changes since 1998 are minor but interesting. Softwood lumber used in wall framing and wood I-joists in used flooring both gained ground slightly. The change in wall and roof uses was less than 1 percentage point. This differs from the results of the 1998 survey when softwood lumber lost considerable ground to virtually every other substitute material identified in the survey. Low and stable softwood lumber prices appear to be a major factor in explaining the stabilization of the market share of softwood lumber between 1998 and 2001.

Steel has seen a moderate decline across all structural end-use applications. Table 1 provides a clearer picture of steel use in wall framing. The underlying message is that steel, though used by builders in some applications in some

Table 1—Product usage in specific framing applications in 1995, 1998, and 2001. LVL = laminated veneer lumber.

	1995	1998	2001
	- - - - - - - -Percent - - - - - - - -		
Wall framing			
Softwood lumber	93.0	83.1	83.4
Finger-jointed stud	4.0	5.3	5.5
Steel framing	0.0	8.8	6.6
LVL	0.0	0.8	1.6
Wood truss	0.0	1.1	1.1
Wood I-joist	0.0	0.4	0.4
Floor framing			
Wood I-joist	23.0	38.8	43.2
Softwood lumber	59.0	41.8	38.6
Wood truss	16.0	10.4	12.7
LVL	0.0	3.0	2.3
Steel framing	2.0	2.2	1.7
Finger-jointed stud	0.0	0.3	0.3
Roof framing			
Wood truss	46.0	47.7	49.7
Softwood lumber	51.0	40.0	40.9
Wood I-joist	2.0	3.4	3.0
LVL	0.0	2.7	2.7
Steel framing	1.0	2.9	1.7
Finger-jointed stud	0.0	1.3	0.1
Headers			
Softwood lumber	n/a	n/a	71.9
LVL	n/a	n/a	20.4
Steel framing	n/a	n/a	3.8
Wood truss	n/a	n/a	1.6
Wood I-joist	n/a	n/a	1.2
Finger-jointed stud	n/a	n/a	0.2

Table 2—Material use in load bearing and non-load bearing walls in 2001

	Wall Framing End-Use Application	
	Load bearing	Non-load bearing
	- - - - - - Percent- - - - - -	
Softwood lumber	83.4	83.9
Finger-jointed stud	5.5	5.5
Steel framing	6.6	8.5
LVL	2.7	0.4
Wood truss	1.1	0.8
Wood I-joist	0.4	0.4

Table 2 segments the wall framing data into load bearing and non-load bearing wall applications. Steel framing is used significantly more in non-load bearing walls than in load bearing walls. LVL shows the opposite trend and is used significantly more in load bearing walls than in non-load bearing walls. Interestingly, the use of softwood lumber is relatively consistent between both types of wall applications, suggesting that most builders prefer to use a single structural material rather than switch between materials depending on the end-use application.

Builder Importance Ratings for Softwood Lumber Attributes

Builders were asked to rate the importance of a broad range of structural softwood lumber attributes in their material purchase decisions. The average importance ratings summarized in table 5 are virtually identical to those obtained in the two previous CINTRAFOR surveys and there are two important inferences to be made regarding this observation. First, attitudes of builders toward the importance of specific structural lumber attributes have remained relatively constant since 1995. Second, the builders surveyed in 2001 are similar to those surveyed in the 1995 and 1998 studies. These results are notable because, given the fact that residential construction framing technology has remained fairly constant over time, we would not expect the relative importance of specific purchase criteria to change much over time.

Builder Satisfaction Ratings for Softwood Lumber Attributes

The satisfaction ratings for the softwood lumber attributes are summarized in table 6. It is important to note that although the satisfaction scores have generally increased, straightness and lack of defects in softwood lumber continue to be the material attributes with the lowest satisfaction

regions of the US, has not been successful in offering a total framing system that builders are willing to adopt. Builders remain reluctant to use steel to frame the entire house and as a result, its overall market share has declined. In addition, low softwood lumber prices are seen as a significant factor in the declining use of steel framing.

The share of softwood lumber used in header applications is less than that observed in wall framing, although it still exceeds 70%, table 2. Builders reported using LVL (laminated veneer lumber) for about 20 percent of header construction. The survey data indicates that builders reported large increases in their use of LVL and while some LVL is used in wall, floor and roof framing applications, the largest volume was used in header applications which often require the higher stiffness of LVL to bridge large window, door and garage door openings.

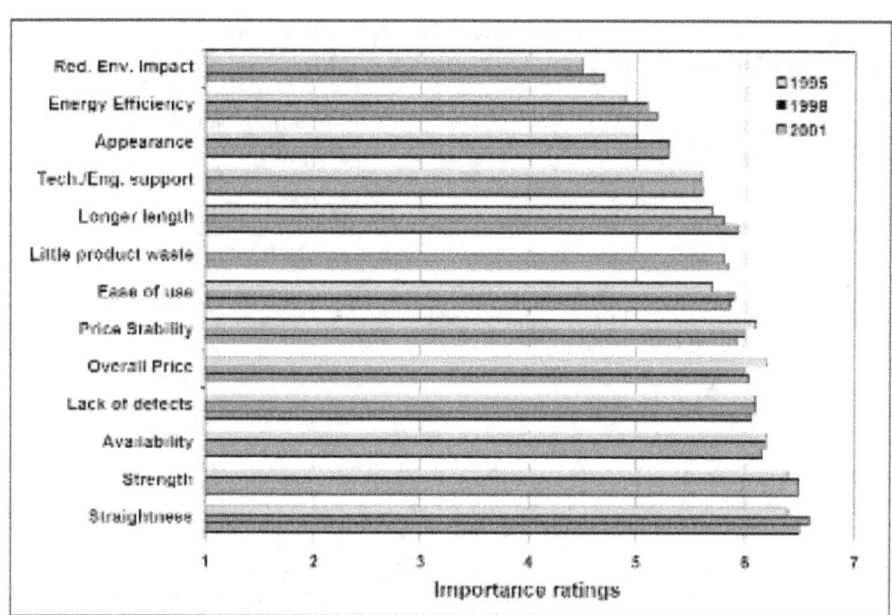

Figure 5—Survey respondents average importance ratings for softwood lumber attributes.

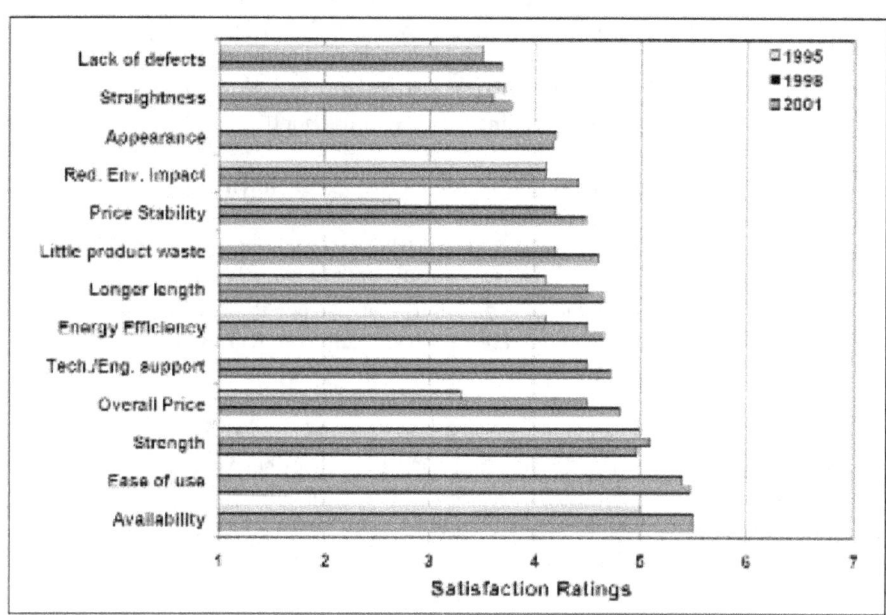

Figure 6—Survey respondents average satisfaction ratings for softwood lumber attributes.

ratings. Straightness and lack of defects are reported to be two of the most important lumber attributes and yet they are the two attributes with the lowest satisfaction ratings. Considering the low satisfaction ratings provided for the straightness and lack-of-defects attributes of softwood lumber, it appears clear that builders remain critical of the quality of softwood lumber, a result that has remained fairly consistent over the 1995-2001 period. In contrast, the satisfaction ratings for price and price stability continue to increase as softwood lumber prices and price volatility continue to moderate.

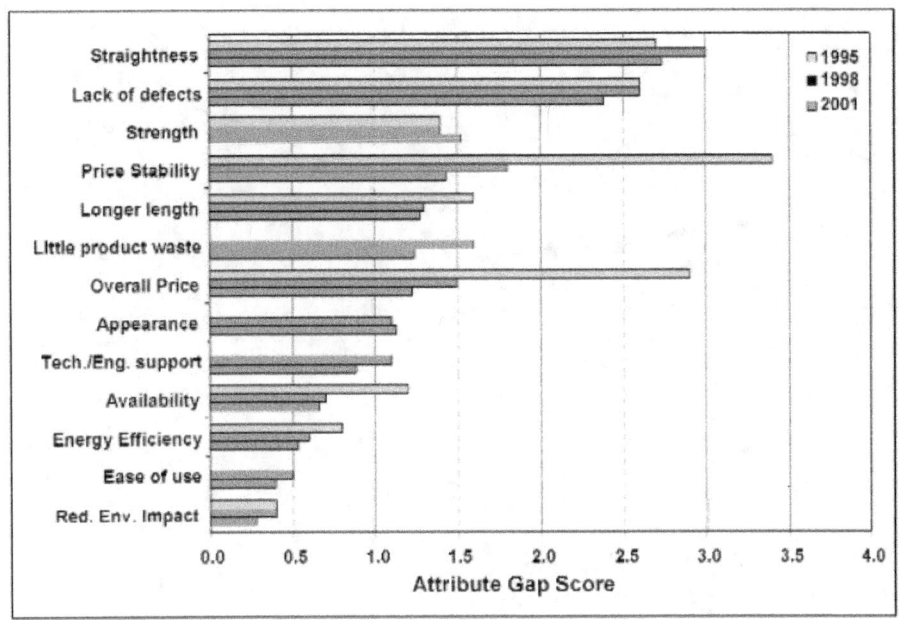

Figure 7—Average gap score between the importance and satisfaction attribute ratings.

Comparison of Importance and Satisfaction Attribute Rating Scores

A gap analysis highlights the observation that builders appear to be more satisfied with softwood lumber. Table 7 quantifies the difference between the importance and satisfaction ratings for each of the 13 softwood lumber attributes. These gaps were calculated by subtracting the satisfaction rating from the importance rating for each material attribute. Strength was the sole attribute for which an increase in the importance-satisfaction gap was reported. For the remaining 12 attributes, either a decrease in the gap or no change was reported. This is certainly good news for softwood lumber manufacturers. However, substantial gaps were observed for the straightness and lack of defects attributes and, although the magnitude of these gaps was slightly lower than observed in the previous surveys, this gap remains problematic for softwood lumber manufacturers. Similar to the 1998 survey, builders were asked to list the three most important lumber attributes that they consider when purchasing softwood lumber. The softwood lumber attributes of strength, price, and straightness remained the top three attributes.

Perceptions of Environmental Performance for Substitute Building Materials

Another objective of this research was to assess builders perceptions of the environmental impacts associated with the use of each substitute material relative to softwood lumber. Survey respondents were asked to compare each substitute material to softwood lumber with respect to its impact on the environment using a Likert-like scale where a rating of 1 indicated that the substitute material had a much less favorable impact on the environment relative to softwood lumber, a rating of 4 indicated that it had the same impact and a rating of 7 indicated that the substitute material had a much more favorable impact on the environment relative to softwood lumber. The average scores for this and previous surveys are summarized in figure 8. All of the materials identified in the survey saw an increase in average ratings with the exception of wood I-joists. The biggest increase was seen in steel, followed by concrete blocks, SIPs (structural insulated panels) and wood/steel trusses.

Clearly builders still perceive softwood lumber as having a poor environmental image, which may be due to recent efforts to position substitute materials as being environmentally friendly. For example, much of the marketing effort for steel has been to position steel as an environmentally friendly product relative to wood and this message seems to have taken hold. However, environmental performance currently ranks the lowest in importance during the purchase decision as seen in figure 5. While there have been several efforts to improve the environmental perception of wood recently, it appears that these have been too limited in scale and scope to have had any substantial impact on builders' perceptions of wood.

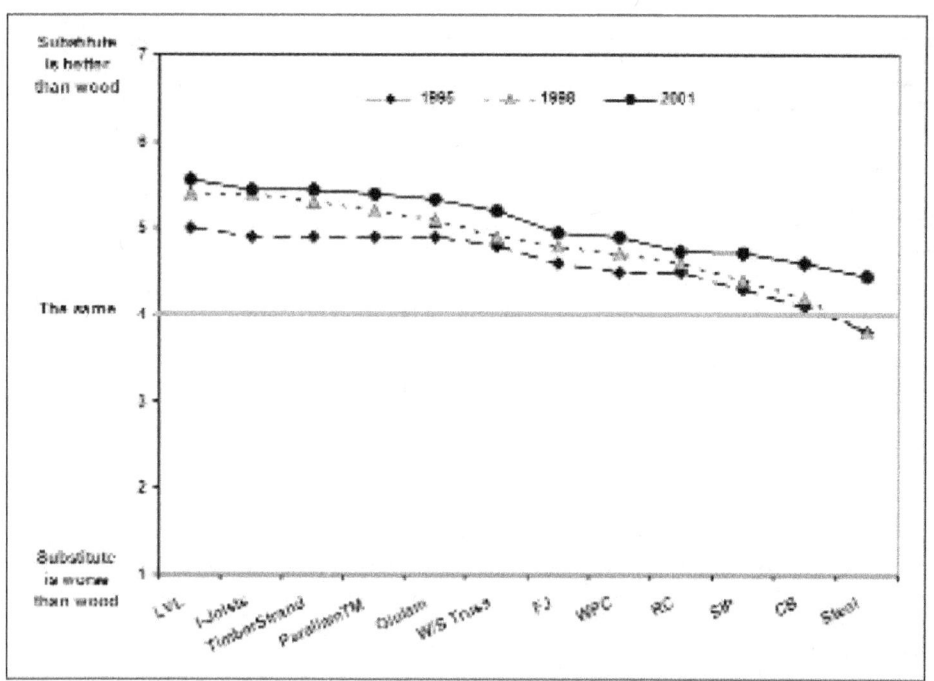

Figure 8—Respondent's perceptions of environmental performance of substitute materials relative to softwood lumber. LVL = laminated veneer lumber, TM = trademark, W/S = wood or steel, FJ = finger-jointed lumber, WPC = wood-plastic composite lumber, RC = reinforced concrete, and CB = concrete block.

CONCLUSIONS

The results of this research suggest that the pace of material substitution in the residential construction industry has moderated since 1998. To a large degree this might be attributed to lower lumber prices, less volatility in lumber prices, and the fact that builders have become more accepting of the decreased softwood lumber quality that has been attributed to the younger, faster grown plantation resource. The exception to this trend is in floor framing applications where wood I-joists continue to expand their market share at the expense of softwood lumber. The 2001 survey results clearly show that material quality remains the most important set of attributes and that the largest gap between importance and satisfaction is observed with the material quality attributes. However, a closer review of the survey data suggests that builders may be more concerned with the overall value of structural materials (defined as the ratio of quality over unit price) as opposed to simply material quality.

The most troubling result is the continuing misperception among residential builders that softwood lumber is the least environmentally friendly material. This result could have serious implications for the forest products industry in the future as green building programs become more prevalent and homebuyers become more assertive in demanding that environmentally friendly materials be used in building their homes. This misperception clearly shows that further research is required to determine the basis for this misperception and to identify strategies to ensure that information regarding the positive environmental benefits of using wood relative to non-wood substitutes is effectively communicated to home builders and home buyers.

LITERATURE CITED

Eastin, I.L.; Fleishman, S.; Shook, S.R. 2001. Softwood lumber substitution in the residential construction industry: 1998. Forest Products Journal 51(9): 30-37.

Eastin, I.L.; Fleishman, S.; Shook, S.R. 2000. Change of plans: material substitution in the residential construction industry. Engineered Wood Journal. 2000(Fall): 34-37.

Eastin, I.L.; Simon, D.D.; Shook, S.R. 1996. Softwood substitution in the US residential construction industry. CINTRAFOR Working Paper No. 57. Seattle, WA: University of Washington. Center for International Trade in Forest Products. 54 p.

Fell, D. 1999. Target engineered products to builders most likely to innovate. Wood Technology. 126(4): 22-25.

Fleishman, S.J.; Eastin, I.L.; Shook S. 2000. Material substitution trends in residential construction, 1995 vs. 1998. CINTRAFOR Working Paper No. 73. Seattle, WA: University of Washington. Center for International Trade in Forest Products. 76 p.

Garth, J., Eastin, I.L.; Edelson, J. 2004. Material Substitution Trends in Residential Construction, 2001 vs. 1998 and 1995. CINTRAFOR Working Paper No. 93. Seattle, WA: University of Washington. Center for International Trade in Forest Products.

Joint Center for Housing Studies. 2001. The state of the nation's housing. Cambridge, MA: Harvard University.

Shook S.R.; Eastin, I.L. 2000. A characterization of the US residential deck market: 1998. CINTRAFOR Working Paper 78. Seattle, WA: University of Washington. Center for International Trade in Forest Products. 45 p.

Shook, S.R.; Eastin, I.L. 2001. A characterization of the US residential deck material market. Forest Products Journal 51(4): 28-36.

Shook S.R.; Turner, W.R.; Eastin, I.L. 1998. Adoption, diffusion, and substitution of structural wood panels. CINTRAFOR Working Paper 65. Seattle, WA: University of Washington. Center for International Trade in Forest Products. 32 p.

Western Wood Products Association. 2002. 2001 Statistical yearbook of the western sawmill industry. Portland, OR.

ASSESSING AND MANAGING STANDS
TO MEET QUALITY OBJECTIVES

David Briggs[1]

ABSTRACT

Process capability analysis (PCA) is a statistical quality control technique which managers can use to assess the degree of nonconformance of individual timber stands to specifications for quality properties such as knot diameter, rings per inch, and wood stiffness (MOE). Examples from Douglas-fir (*Pseudotsuga menziesii* Mirb. Franco) plantations demonstrate application of PCA to a single property or a combination and show how PCA can be used to monitor nonconformance over time. Managers can use the PCA information to assist in harvest planning and marketing mature stands and to assist in planning silvicultural planning in immature stands. Purchasers can use PCA to assist in determining if a stand has sufficient conformance to their log quality requirements to justify a bid.

KEYWORDS: Log quality, tree quality, silviculture, statistical quality control, process capability analysis.

INTRODUCTION

For a long time relatively simple, economical field tools have allowed forest managers to measure geometric properties of trees in a stand for inventory, and growth and yield analysis. This has also led to the development and use of growth and yield, harvest scheduling and other forest planning models. Unfortunately, counterparts for measuring quality properties of trees have lagged, hence quality has not received as detailed treatment in inventories, analyses, and models. If quality is treated at all, it is often through assuming an implied relationship of increasing quality with increasing tree diameter. Although a general association of higher quality with increasing tree diameter may have been reasonable for natural stands and minimally managed plantations, it breaks down in intensively managed plantations where different cultural regimes can produce similar size trees with great differences in knot size, percentage of juvenile wood, ring width, and other characteristics. An alternative to the diameter association is to estimate the log grade composition or tree grade of trees in a stand. Unfortunately, these grading systems provide only broad, generalized indications of quality and may not be consistent with, or at the resolution needed by, current and emerging markets. For example the official log grades for Douglas-fir in the Pacific Northwest do not discriminate knot size until knot diameter is at least 2.5 inches (NWLRAG 1998). Furthermore, these grades have sometimes been found to produce illogical results when applied to managed plantations. For example, Sonne et al (2004) found that No. 3 Sawlogs from a 70-year-old Douglas-fir stand that had been thinned and treated with biosolids had greater yield of high grade lumber than from No. 2 Sawlogs; a reversal of customary expectations from these grades. Forest product manufacturers have become more specialized in their log quality preferences as evidenced by an unofficial system of logs sorts (Bowers 1997) that largely replaced the official system. The principal feature of the log sorts is use of a finer resolution of log properties present in the official rules; primarily log diameter; rings per inch, knot diameter, and number of knots per log face. Manufacturer concerns with juvenile wood, wood strength and stiffness, dimensional stability, and other properties are not addressed by the current log grading systems and little has been done to formally translate desired log characteristics into counterparts that can be assessed in trees and stands.

[1] David Briggs is professor and director, Stand Management Cooperative; College of Forest Resources Box 352100; University of Washington; Seattle, WA. 98195.

Forest managers need improved approaches for quantifying relevant quality characteristics both for marketing and managing quality in intensively managed plantations. Techniques for rapid and economical field measurement of key tree quality properties exist, including tools that use acoustic wave transmission to non-destructively assess potential modulus of elasticity (MOE) of products from logs and trees (Carter et al. 2004). Techniques of statistical quality control have been successfully implemented in many industries and manufacturing settings where properties of the product from a process are measured and monitored with the objective of maximizing conformance of properties to specifications supplied by a customer, product designer, or management. Combining these field and statistical techniques provides an opportunity to develop analytic methods for assessing quality of trees and stands that can assist silviculturists, managers and planners with silvicultural and marketing decisions.

This paper reviews a statistical quality control technique, process capability analysis (PCA), useful for assessing the degree of conformance of product properties to specifications issued by a customer or stated as quality objectives. Next, some important log quality properties that can be readily measured or estimated in standing trees for application of PCA are discussed. Several examples illustrating the use of PCA on some of these properties, singly and in c o mbination, are presented for some intensively managed Douglas-fir plantations. Finally, management implications of applying PCA to quality of timber stands are discussed.

PROCESS CAPABILITY ANALYSIS

Process capability analysis refers to techniques for studying "process capability" or the uniformity of a process at either a single point in time or over time through repeated sampling (Montgomery 2001). More specifically, a sample of product from the process is measured for a specific property and process capability is usually estimated by using a probability distribution with the shape, center (mean, μ) and spread (standard deviation, σ) appropriate for the property. If no suitable probability distribution model can be found, process capability can be estimated from the actual frequency histogram. Two contexts for expressing process capability are presented in the following paragraphs.

First, process capability can be stated without reference to external specifications for the property of interest. In this case, process capability is stated as the six-standard-deviation spread of the distribution of the product property, expressed as the upper and lower natural tolerance limits (UNTL, LNTL);

$$UNTL, LNTL = \mu \pm 3\sigma$$

If a normal distribution is assumed for the property, process capability can be stated by noting that 0.27% of the product, or 2700 product items per million, will be outside the UNTL – LNTL range for the property.

Second, process capability can be stated as the percentage of product falling outside, or not conforming to, external specifications for the property. Upper and lower specification limits (USL, LSL) may be one sided or two sided and may originate from product designers and engineers, management directives, product standards, or customers. A manager can compare USL and LSL with the probability distribution of the product property. Nonconformance is the percentage of the distribution outside the bounds defined by USL and LSL. Assuming that the property is normally distributed, that the process is in statistical control as evidenced by control charts for the process, and that the mean is centered between USL and LSL, process capability can be expressed as a process capability ratio (C_p), formed from the external specification limits and the natural limits of the process as follows:

$$C_p = \frac{USL, LSL}{6\sigma}$$

Correct use and interpretation of C_p is dependent on the validity of the assumptions. C_p will not be used here; more experience with the distributions of timber quality properties and the effect of cultural practices on these distributions will be needed to determine if the assumptions underlying C_p are valid.

If the assumptions underlying Cp are not met, an alternative is to compare USL and LSL directly with the probability distribution or frequency histogram of the property. Process capability can be stated as the percent non-conforming as estimated from the portions of the distribution or histogram outside the specification limits. This approach, using actual frequency histograms based on sampling trees from the stand of interest, will be used in the following examples. Future research will be needed to discover probability distribution models that are adequate for quality properties of interest and can reflect impacts of cultural practices that could radically alter the distribution of the property. Developing the frequency histogram of a quality property requires sampling a sufficient number of trees from the stand. In constructing histograms, Montgomery (2001) suggests using between 4 and 20 bins, "choosing the number of bins approximately equal to the square root of the sample size." Thus to have six bins describing a quality property of trees in a stand, one should measure the property on at least 36 trees from the stand. This seems reasonable considering the typical number and size of plots one would place in a stand for inventory or appraisal.

WHAT IMPORTANT LOG PROPERTIES CAN BE EASILY MEASURED IN TREES FOR USE IN PCA?

Consider a mill peeling logs into veneer for plywood and laminated veneer lumber (LVL). Its log specifications may include a maximum and minimum diameter, a growth rate limit expressed as a lower bound on rings per inch, and an upper bound on knot diameter. It may also pay a premium for logs exceeding a lower bound on modulus of elasticity (MOE), a measure of stiffness and a key characteristic for veneer to qualify for LVL manufacture. Can these log quality properties be easily translated into measurements that can be easily obtained from standing trees and subsequently used in PCA?

Log Diameter Range

The dbh of the sample trees, combined with a taper curve to predict diameters inside bark, can be used to estimate log diameters. Since dbh is customarily measured in an inventory, measuring this property adds no new cost. If forest growth models are used, most project the dbh of individual trees and some produce log stock tables that would provide a means for finding nonconformance to log diameter range specifications. Additional accounting may be necessary before a model could automate calculation of nonconformance to user-defined log diameter specifications.

Rings Per Inch (Rpi)

On permanent plots where trees are tagged and periodically measured for dbh, the change in dbh can be used to estimate periodic rpi without new cost. One can expect that rpi at breast height (bh) is highly correlated with rpi of the first log in the tree, since bh is within that log, and should be well correlated with rpi of upper stem logs. Increment cores could be used as an alternative but this would add expense in collecting the cores and measuring the rpi. If forest growth models are used, rpi can be readily inferred from dbh changes between projection periods. It may be necessary to add some accounting procedures in the models to automate and report rpi and to produce log stock tables according to user-defined rpi specifications.

Knot Diameter

Typically, each log grade or log sort has a maximum knot diameter (Bowers 1997) and product recovery researchers have found that largest limb average diameter (LLAD, Fahey et al. 1991) also known as branch index (bix, Barbour & Parry 2001), defined as the average of the largest diameter knot in each of the four quadrants or faces of the log surface, is a good predictor of product grade recovery from a log. One can hypothesize that the diameter of the largest knot or LLAD, measured with a caliper on the lower bole, would be highly correlated with the largest knot diameter or LLAD of logs within the tree. The Stand Management Cooperative and others (Ingaramo 2003) have measured diameter of branches within a region centered on BH and have found that this adds little to field time and cost. Examination of the hypothesized relationship between BH and log knot diameter measures will be presented later in this paper. Some growth models can estimate the diameter of branches at each whorl position along the boles of trees (Hann et al. 1997, Mitchell 1975). With some further accounting, this information could be used to estimate nonconformance to a knot diameter specification.

Modulus of Elasticity (MOE)

The relationship between the MOE of a material, its density and the speed of an acoustic wave through the material forms the basis for a method of nondestructive testing of logs for MOE (Wang et al. 2000). This acoustic method measures the "dynamic" MOE in contrast with the MOE obtained by static bending. Researchers have demonstrated excellent relationships between the dynamic and static bending MOE of logs, and between the average static bending MOE of products obtained from a log and the dynamic and static bending MOE of the parent log (Ross et al. 1999, Wang et al. 2004). This research has led to commercial tools for nondestructive testing and sorting logs using acoustic signals and a related tool for nondestructive testing in standing trees has just become available (Carter et al. 2005; this proceedings). This new tool, which is used on the lower bole of a tree, provides the opportunity for assessing the degree to which trees in a stand conform to a specification for MOE. Further research is underway to develop relationships along the chain from tree to product and to optimize use of these tools in the field.

This review indicates that properties important to product and log quality and value can be readily measured on standing trees and many can be inferred from growth and yield models, although this may require some refinements in summary programming. During a stand inventory, sufficient trees are likely to be present on plots to gather these data and pooled if necessary to develop frequency histograms for use in PCA.

PCA OF DOUGLAS-FIR STANDS AT A SINGLE POINT IN TIME

A spacing trial located on the Pilchuck Tree Farm near Stanwood, Washington will be used as an example. In May of 1983, six acres of former cattle pasture was divided into fifty square plots, each 73 ft x 73 ft covering 0.08 acres. Site index is medium to high: 140 ft at 50 years (King 1966), corresponding to 98 ft at 30 years, using the new curves for planted Douglas-fir stands (Flewelling et al. 2001). The plots were planted with two-year-old, unimproved, local origin Douglas-fir seedlings over six densities ranging from 194 to 681 trees per acre; two densities had a rectangular spacing, while the rest were square. The outermost row of trees in each plot was regarded as a buffer to avoid edge effects from contiguous plots. On each plot, trees inside the buffer were tagged and measured for DBH in 1990 and 1998. In the winter of 2001-2002, six plots, chosen at random from each spacing, forming a completely randomized design with six replications of six stocking treatments, were measured for detailed growth, yield, and quality attributes (Ingaramo 2003). Using the 1998 DBH distribution, 12 trees were sampled on each plot; the smallest, the largest, and 10 others selected at random. All sample trees were measured for dbh and divided into N, S, E and W quadrants or faces. In each quadrant, the diameter of all branches greater than or equal to 1/3 inch, located within one-foot above and below breast height (4.5 ft), was measured with a caliper. Branch diameter was measured perpendicular to the branch axis, in the direction of stemcircum ference, just beyond the branch collar. Restricting branch measurement to those that were at least 1/3 inch diameter excluded many small 'whiskers' that tend to self-prune very rapidly, and have little, if any, effect on grading. A random sample of four of the study trees was measured for total height and height to the live crown defined as the average of the height to live branches in the four quadrants. Table 1 summarizes the tree characteristics according to stand density; at age 18 (20 years from seed).

In May 2003, the four height trees were climbed to 17.5 feet using a ladder and the largest diameter branch in each of the N, S, E and W faces of the 16-foot butt log was measured. It was assumed that the stump was 1 foot high and that the log had 0.5 feet of trim allowance. The 16-foot butt log was chosen since it is a preferred length for lumber, closely approximates two peeler bocks for making veneer, and is relatively fast and easy to measure with the ladder method; a crew of five located and measured 136 trees in about four hours. The owner had initiated thinning in some plots and if the sample tree had been removed in the thinning, the standing tree most similar in DBH was used as a replacement. Two plots had been heavily thinned and were inaccessible for sampling due to the amount of felled material on the ground. With the exception of a single branch on the southern aspect of one tree at the lowest density, all branches in the BH region of the sample trees were dead. Furthermore, live crowns had receded above the top of the log and during climbing it was noted that there were only a very small number of living but severely suppressed branches within the 16-foot butt log. It is assumed that there will be negligible additional growth on these few branches.

The hypothesis that there would be a reasonably good correlation between branch diameters in the BH region and on the 16-foot butt log was mentioned earlier. Figure 1 presents regressions between largest diameter branch and LLAD in the BH region and on the 16-foot butt log. LLAD of the 16-foot log produced a better regression than the largest diameter branch of the log. Also, the regressions were poorer using LLAD of the BH region. Over the short two-foot BH region, some quadrants had no branches (zero branch diameter), which increased variation in BH region LLAD and reduced its correlation with the log measures. This is fortunate since it is easier for field personnel to find and measure the largest branch in the BH region rather than spend time locating quadrants and measuring the largest branch in each quadrant.

Applying PCA To Knot Diameter

A timber seller or purchaser would use one of the regressions to translate a log specification for knot diameter into a counterpart BH specification for standing trees. For example, if a sawmill places a 1.5-inch upper limit on LLAD of logs, the equation in figure 1A yields a largest BH knot diameter of 1.5 inches. After translating the log specification to a tree specification, the frequency histogram of largest BH branch diameters from the trees in a stand can be compared with the translated specification. Figure 2 shows such a comparison for the 194 tpa (15 ft x 15 ft) density and shows that about 52% of the trees are nonconforming. A mill may decide to not make a purchase bid for a stand with such high nonconformance. The seller, aware of this poor non-conformance, can focus marketing efforts on those who accept trees with relatively large knots. Some may prefer to create cumulative frequency distributions that may be visually easier for comparing multiple stands with the specification limits in the same graph. Figure 3 shows cumulative frequency distributions for knot diameter for all of the densities in the 18-year-old trial; the percentage of trees nonconforming to the BH knot-diameter specification ranges from only 3% in the 681 (8 ft x 8 ft) density, to 52% for the 194 tpa (15 ft x 15 ft) density.

Table 1—Mean (and standard deviation) of tree characteristics by spacing in the Pilchuck Tree Farm spacing trial at age 18

Charachistic	Density, trees/acre Spacing ft x ft					
	194 (15 x 15)	218 (20 x 10)	302 (12 x 12)	340 (16 x 8)	435 (10 x 10)	681 (8 x 8)
Quadratic mean	11.1	10.7	9.8	9.4	8.8	7.5
diameter, in	(0.56)	(0.37)	(0.36)	(0.26)	(0.21)	(0.18)
Total height, ft	52.5	50.8	53.5	53.2	56.1	54.1
	(1.67)	(4.69)	(4.82)	(3.19)	(2.26)	(2.07)
Crown ratio	.68	.67	.56	.58	.52	.47
	(0.015)	(0.021)	(0.046)	(0.054)	(0.022)	(0.031)
Crown base, ft						
(calculated)	16.8	16.8	23.5	22.3	26.9	28.7
Largest b.h.	1.54	1.41	1.25	1.24	1.21	1.01
diameter, in	(0.26)	(0.23)	(0.23)	(0.21)	(0.28)	(0.22)

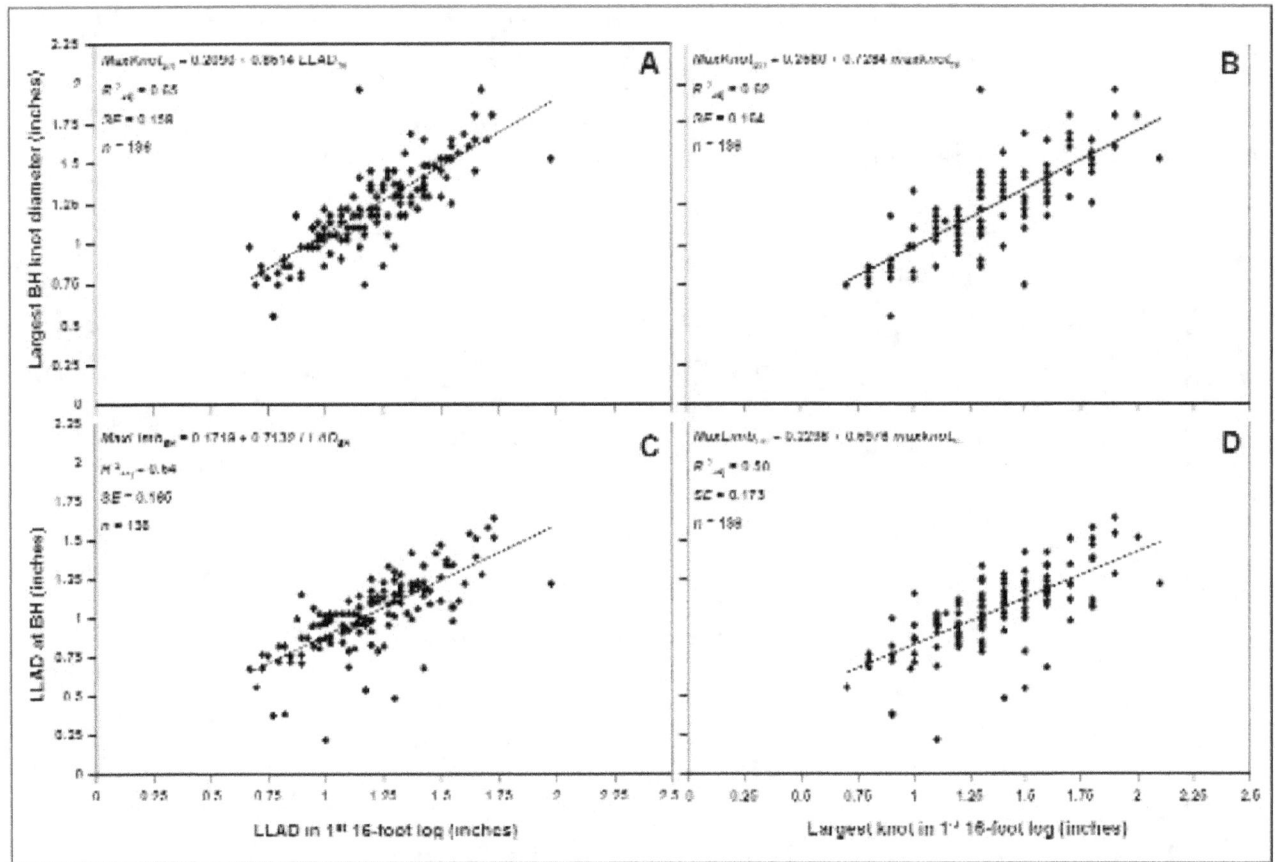

Figure 1—Knot diameter measures in the BH region of a tree verses knot diameter measures in its 1st 16-foot log.

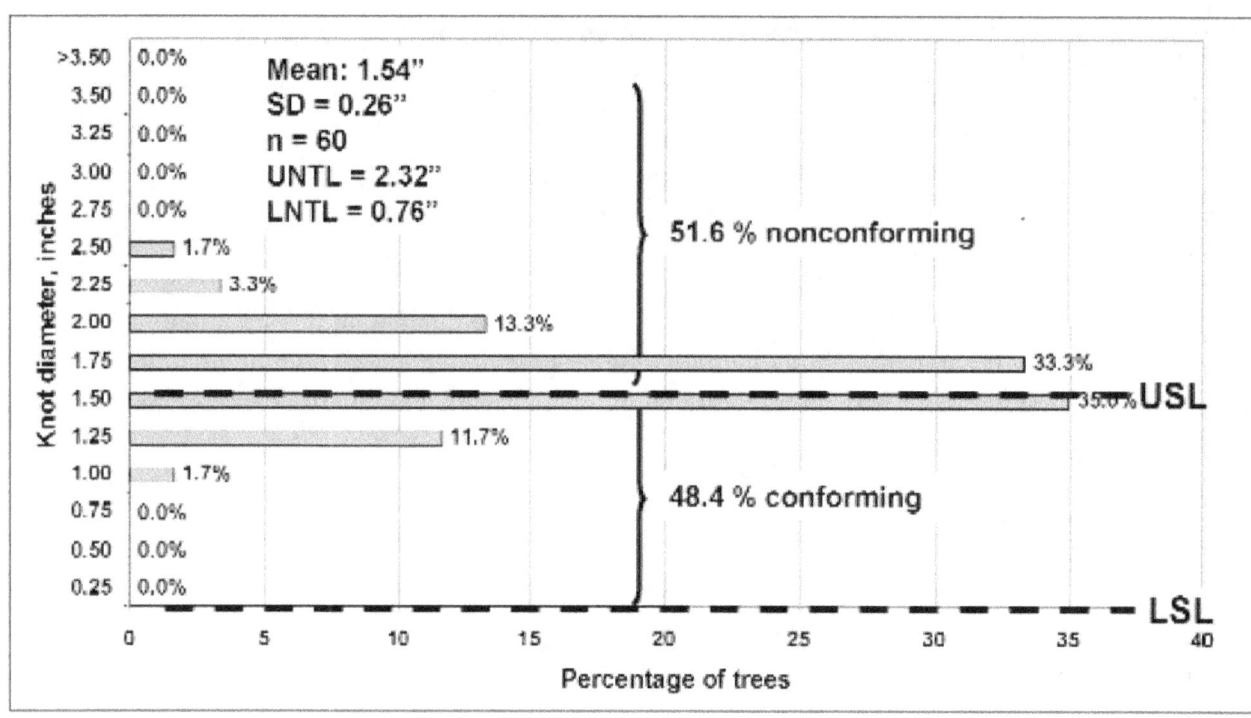

Figure 2—Distribution of the largest diameter knot in the BH region of 18-year-old trees in a plot planted at 15-ft x 15-ft spacing.

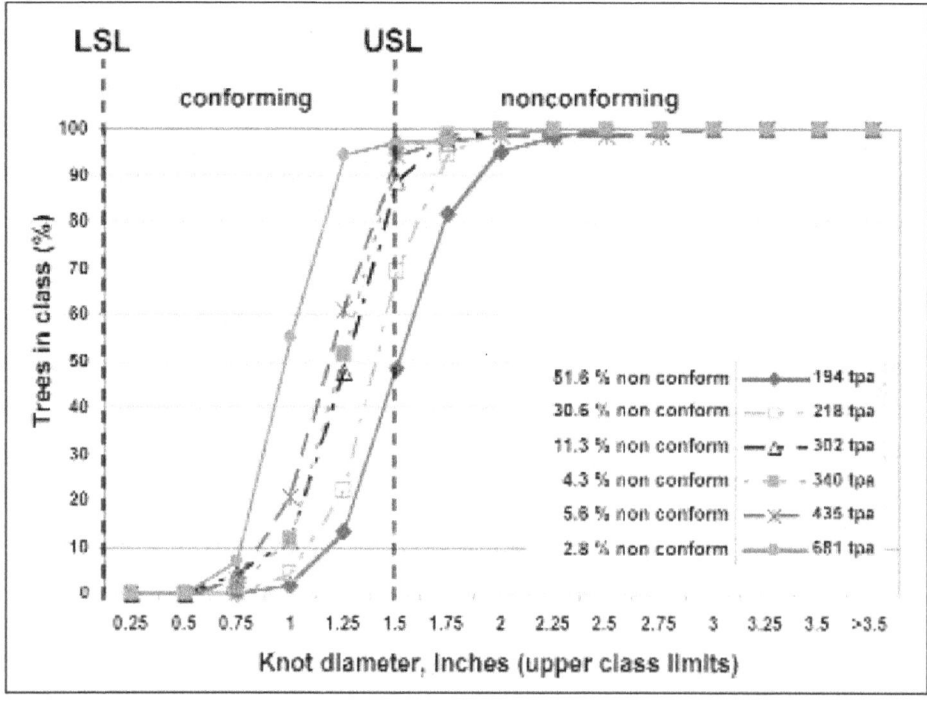

Figure 3—Cumulative distributions of the largest diameter knot in the BH region of Pilchuck Tree Farm spacing trial at age 18.

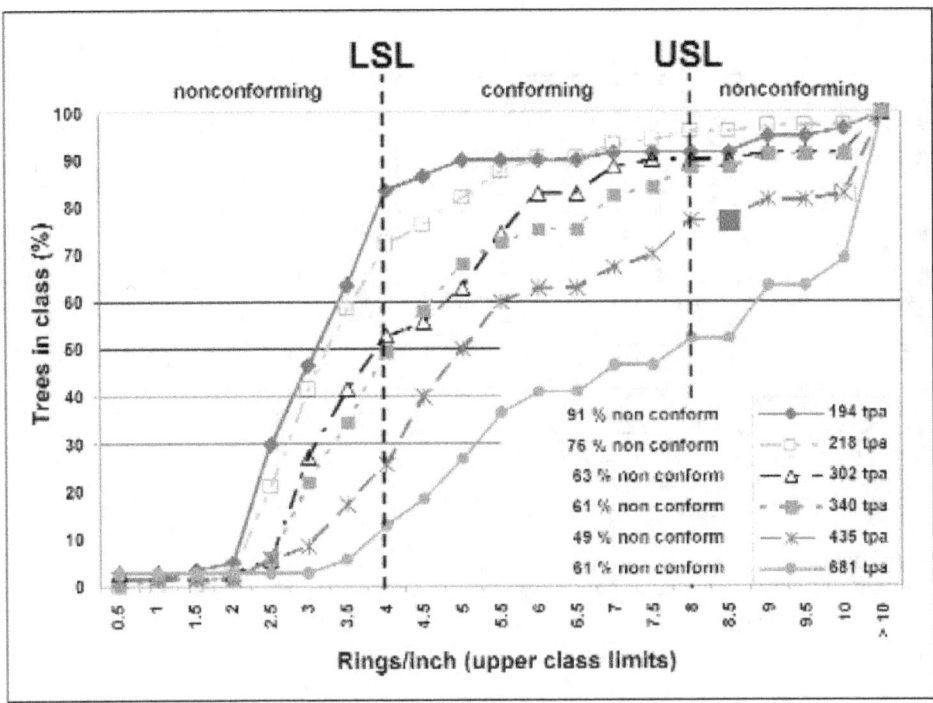

Figure 4—Cumulative distributions of rings/inch of the Pilchuck Tree Farm spacing trial at age 18.

Applying PCA To Rings Per Inch

Mills often find that extremely fast growth is an undesirable characteristic for their products while tree growers find that extremely slow growth is undesirable from a financial perspective. Suppose a mill's log specification excludes growth rates faster than four rpi while a landowner does not wish growth slower than eight rpi. Figure 4 shows an LSL of four rpi and a USL of eight rpi overlaid on the cumulative frequency distributions of rpi for the 18-year-old spacing trial, calculated from the 1998 and 2001 dbh measurements; nonconformance ranges from 49% at 435 tpa (10 ft x 10 ft) to 91% at 194 tpa (15 ft x 15 ft).

Applying PCA To Knot Diameter and Rings Per Inch Simultaneously

Specifications must usually be considered jointly rather than independently; trees must simultaneously satisfy having the largest BH branch diameter not greater than 1.5 inches and rpi not less than four and not greater than eight. Joint specifications can be readily treated by a data plot or two-variable histogram. Figure 5 plots largest BH branch diameter vs rpi for the 194 tpa (15 ft x15 ft) density along with specification limits for both quality characteristics; 98.3% of the trees are nonconforming to both specifications. Figure

6 summarizes the results across all densities. Nonconformance to the joint specification ranges from 98% at 194 tpa (15 ft x 15 ft) to 56% at 435 tpa (10 ft x 10 ft).

PCA OF DOUGLAS-FIR STANDS AT MULTIPLE TIME POINTS

Consider a 0.5-acre plot planted at 100 trees per acre (21 ft x 21ft), one of the spacings in Stand Management Cooperative (SMC) Type I Installations. This plot is part of Installation 925 located near Belfast, WA on a moderately poor site (SI 107). The installation was planted in 1990 with 2-0 Douglas-fir seedlings and has been measured every two years starting in 1997. The SMC developed a BH branch/ knot assessment protocol that was first applied to the installation in 1999 hence this is one of few that has been measured with this procedure three times. The SMC BH knot protocol for Douglas fir locates the first whorl of branches above BH and the region from the point midway to the next lower and next higher whorl. In this region, the diameter of the largest branch is measured and the number of branches that are at least 50% of this largest diameter are counted. This procedure is applied to those trees on the plot that are measured for crown and total heights. Table 2 summarizes the plot at ages 9, 11, and 13. The base of the live crown is below BH hence branches at BH are alive and growing in

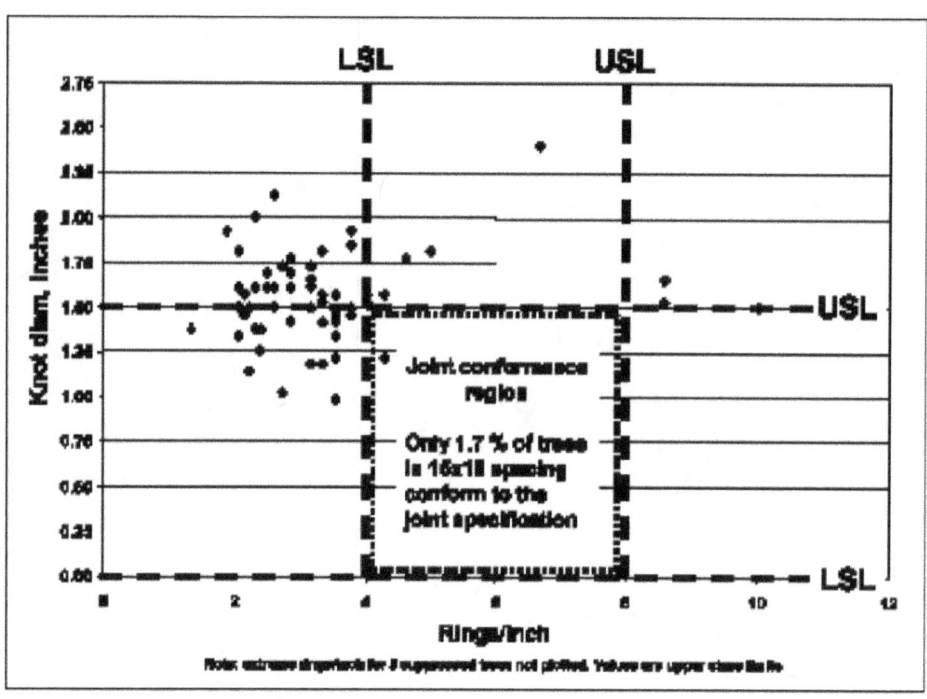

Figure 5—Largest diameter knot in the BH region at age 18 verses rings/inch of the 15-ft x 15-ft (194 tree/acre) spacing at the Pilchuck Tree Farm.

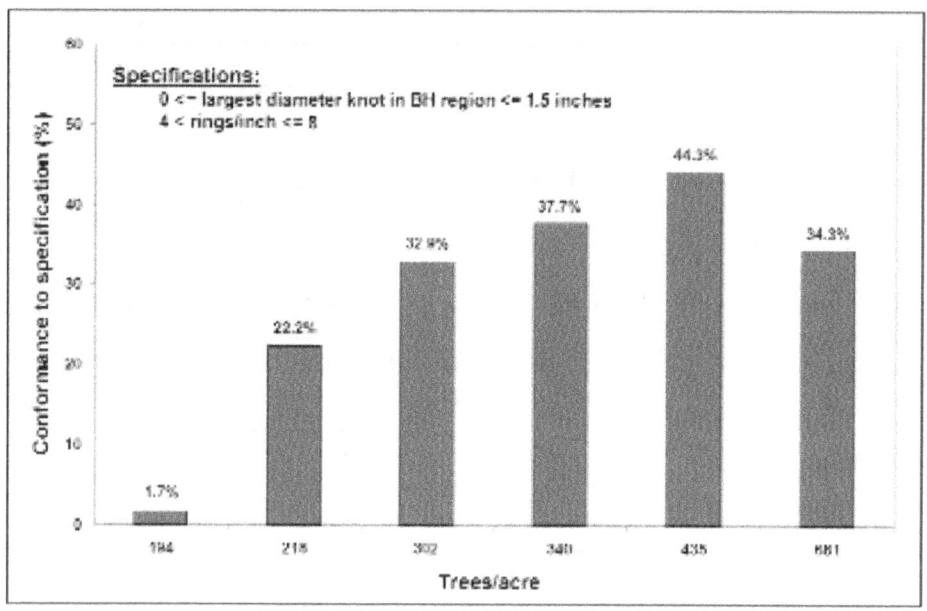

Figure 6—Conformance of Pilchuck Tree Farm spacing trials to joint specifications at age 18 .

Table 2—Trees charasteristics by stand age at SMC installation 925, 21 ft x 21 ft (100 tpa) planting

| Charasteristics | Stand age | | |
	9	11	13
D.b.h., in.	1.6 (0.54) N=49	2.6 (0.82) N=49	3.8 (0.89) N=49
Total height, ft	12.0 (2.72) N=49	15.6 (5.81) N=49	20.8 (7.31) N=49
Height to crown, ft	1.2 (0.54) N=49	1.2 (0.62) N=49	1.3 (0.91) N=49
Largest b.h. branch diameter, in	0.51(0.14) N=47	0.63(0.17) N=45	0.80(0.18) N=45

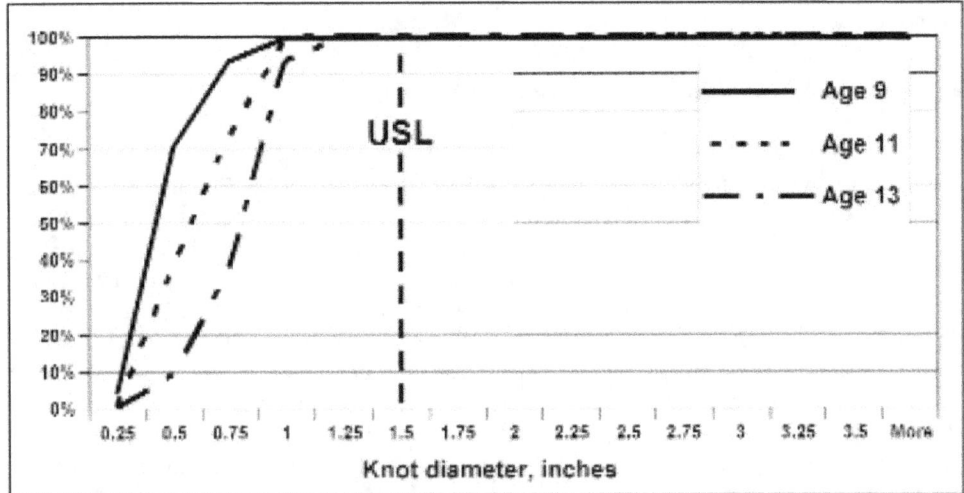

Figure 7—Cumulative distributions of largest diameter BH knot verses age for 21-ft x 21-ft (100 tree/acre) spacing at Stand Management Cooperarative Installation 925.

diameter. Figure 7 presents cumulative distributions of largest BH branch diameter as this plot has aged. It is easy for management to monitor the progression of the stand relative to a target specification for largest BH knot diameter and consider actions that may be taken to prevent excessive nonconformance.

Discussion and Management Implications

The examples presented above illustrate how producer and consumer desires for quality properties can be converted into specifications for trees. For some properties such as rings per inch, developing an acceptable tree specification may involve trade-offs between the desires of the parties that define a range of mutually acceptable values. PCA allows managers to combine these specifications with sample-based frequency distributions from stands of interest to estimate nonconformance. This provides important information on marketability of a stand and information that can assist in choosing future management actions. Process capability and conformance to specifications can be improved by taking actions to shift the process mean and/or reduce

variation. Managers can monitor changes in process capability and the effectiveness of actions taken over time through repeated sampling. The following paragraphs provide two examples.

First, consider nearly mature or mature stands that are being considered for harvest scheduling or are already scheduled for sale. A producer, aware of the log specifications of potential consumers, can use PCA as part of sale development to assess which consumers are more likely to be interested in a stand and focus marketing efforts accordingly. Similarly, consumers can use PCA when they assess a stand to decide if it is worthy of a bid. Organizations with large timberland holdings may use PCA as a method for assessing conformance of stands to alternative market specification sets. These market conformance options could be included in harvest planning models to improve decisions as to which stands should be harvested and when in order to meet mill and other customer demands. For example, if a company has a laminated veneer lumber (LVL) plant, it

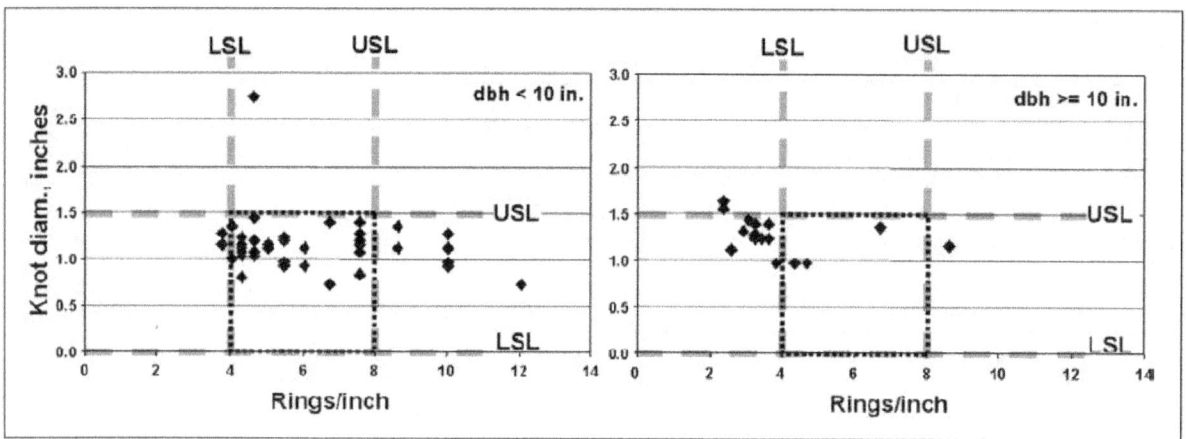

Figure 8—Largest diameter knot in the BH region at age 18 verses rings/inch by DBH of the 10-ft x 10-ft (435 tree/acre) spacing at the Pilchuck Tree Farm.

would like assurance that it's harvest plan provides an adequate supply of timber with high potential to meet the needs of the LVL plant product line.

Second, in immature stands, there are many ways that PCA could assist in silvicultural planning. For example, consider figure 8 where the plot of largest-diameter BH knot and rings per inch has been segregated for trees larger and smaller than 10 inches in dbh. This new detail shows how well larger and smaller trees conform to the joint specification. This could assist in planning future silvicultural activities such as deciding if a thinning should be done and, if so, which trees to remove. A goal might be to try to identify, retain and manage trees that maximize conformance of the final stand. As a different example, figure 7 showed the progression of largest diameter BH knot with age in the SMC 100-tree-per-acre plot. Since the crown base is very low on these trees, will the crown recede before too many trees develop large branches and become nonconforming? If this is likely, is pruning justified? These examples imply the need for a mechanism for projecting the results of such actions and providing feedback. If growth and yield models are being used to project the effects of alternative actions, are they capable of tracking quality properties and providing feedback in a PCA format? Silviculturists could use such models to simulate various options and eliminate those with poor conformance with anticipated future market specifications.

Although the applications of PCA presented in the examples focused on knot diameter and rings per inch, the techniques could be easily extended to other properties such as data gathered with the new Director ST-300™ technology

for non-destructive testing trees for MOE (Carter et al. 2005; this proceedings). Figure 9 presents frequency histograms of acoustic velocities obtained from an unthinned (n = 63 trees) and a thinned (n = 50 trees) plot in SMC Type II Installation 803 at bh age 43 (Carter et al. 2005; this proceedings). If a mill specification stated that it prefers stands with trees with velocities exceeding 4.3 km/sec, the thinned stand, with 48% of trees above this threshold, is preferable to the unthinned stand with only 27% exceeding this threshold. Furthermore, the mill may pay a premium for trees exceeding 4.5 km/sec; 25% of trees in the thinned stand meet this premium whereas only 12% of the unthinned trees qualify. Combining tools such as the Director ST 300™ with PCA can provide landowners and mills with an improved and more flexible method for matching timber quality with market needs.

When using regression models to translate log values to tree values as done earlier with the conversion of LLAD of logs to largest BH knot diameter, a consumer would note that using the direct equation prediction of largest diameter BH knot would result in a tree specification where some trees with an acceptable largest diameter BH knot would contain logs with an excessive LLAD (fig. 10). The consumer's risk can be reduced by calculating a lower prediction limit, say 95%, which would reduce the largest diameter BH knot specification from 1.5 to about 1.25 inches. The use of lower limits is used in setting grades for machine-stress-rated lumber. Note that this lower limit increases the producer's risk, as more trees with acceptable logs will be rejected. Ultimately, the parties involved would negotiate a solution that strikes a balance between producer and c o nsumer risks.

150

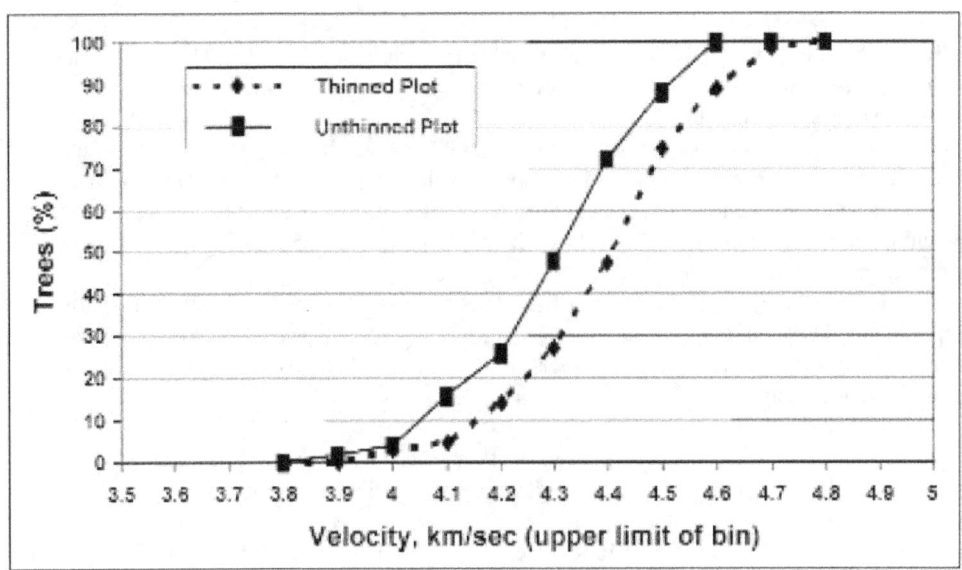

Figure 9—Cumulative frequencies of acoustic velocities measured by the Director ST-300™ in thinned and unthinned plots at Stand Management Cooperative Installation 803.

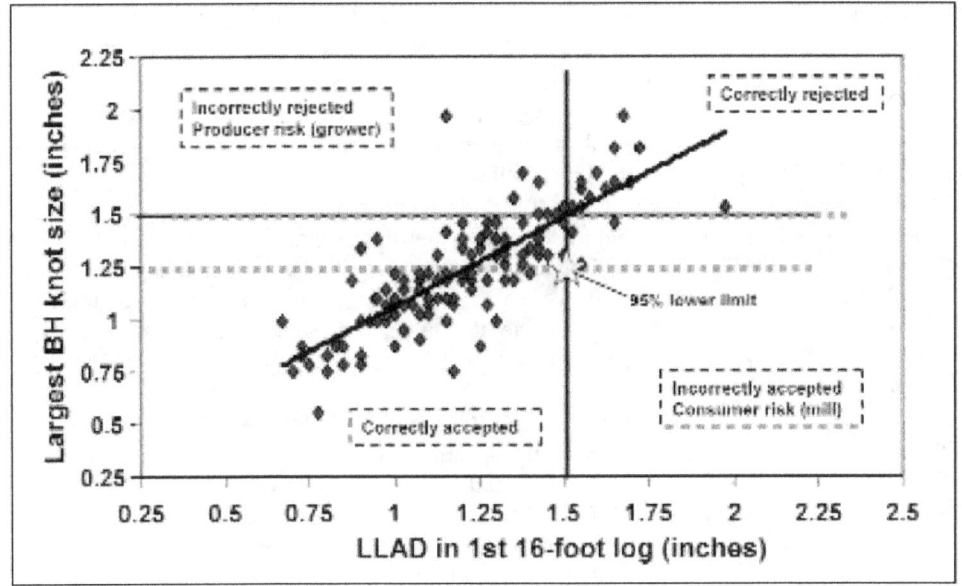

Figure 10—Producer (grower) and consumer (mill) risks as influenced by maximum BH knot size and the largest-limb average diameter in the 16-ft butt log.

CONCLUSIONS

Process capability analysis has been shown to be a useful technique for quantifying conformance of a variety of quality properties of trees that are important to log consumers. Several important properties can be easily estimated at or near BH with little additional cost. Requirements for many log properties specified by consumers can be translated into counterpart values that can be easily measured on the lower bole of trees in the field; these values appear to be well correlated with the butt log. Sample size requirements appear to fit reasonably within the number of trees that would be found in commonly used inventory plots.

Given specifications for one or more tree properties, management can use a suitable individual tree growth model to make projections and estimate the degree of nonconformance when the stand becomes ready to harvest. Armed with this information, cultural options such as density mana g e-ment, fertilization, and pruning can be forecast and evaluated in the context of how these options would influence the proportion of the stand that would be nonconforming. These projections would provide management planners and harvest schedulers with improved insights concerning t h e potential marketability of developing stands in their portfolio and provide feedback with respect to the degree to which remedial silvicultural options can reduce non-conformance.

LITERATURE CITED

Bowers, S. 1997. Key to Douglas-fir log grades. Forestry Extension. Corvallis, OR: Oregon State University.

Barbour, R.J.; Parry, D.L. 2001. Log and lumber grades as indicators of wood quality in 20- to 100-year-old Douglas-fir trees from thinned and unthinned stands. PNW-GTR-510. Portland, OR: U.S. Department of Agriculture, Forest Service, Pacific Northwest Research Station. 22 p.

Carter, P.; Briggs, D.; Ross, R.J.; Wang, X. 2005. Acoustic testing to enhance western forest values and meet consumer wood quality needs. In: Harrington, C.A.; Schoenholtz, S.H. eds. Proceedings—Productivity of Western Forests: A Forest Products Focus. Gen. Tech. Rep PNW-GTR-abc. Portland, OR: U.S. Department of Agriculture, Forest Service, Pacific Northwest Research Station: GTR-642. 121-129.

Fahey, T.D.; Cahill, J.M.; Snellgrove, T.A.; Heath, L.S. 1991. Lumber and veneer recovery from intensively managed young-growth Douglas-fir. Res. Pap. PNW-RP-437. Portland, OR: U.S. Department of Agriculture, Forest Service, Pacific Northwest Research Station. 25 p.

Flewelling, J.; Collier, R.L.; Gonyea, B. [etal.]. 2001. Height-age curves for planted stands of Douglas fir, with adjustments for density. SMC Working Paper 1. Seattle, WA: Stand Management Cooperative, College of Forest Resources, Universiy of Washington. 25 p.

Hann, D.W.; Olsen, C.L.; Hester, A.S. 1997. ORGANON user's manual: Edition 6.0. Corvallis, OR: Department of Forest Resources, Oregon State University.

Ingaramo, L. 2003. Effect of initial density and planting design on growth and quality of young Douglas-fir: a case study. Seattle, WA: College of Forest Resources, Univesity of Washington. M.S. thesis. 87 p.

King, J.E. 1966. Site index curves for Douglas-fir in the Pacific Northwest. Weyerhaeuser Company Forestry Paper No. 8. Centralia, WA: Weyerhaeuser Company, Western Forestry Research Center.

Mitchell, K.J. 1975. Dynamics and simulated yield of Douglas-fir. Forest Science Monogram 17. 39 p.

Montgomery, D.C. 2001. Introduction to statistical quality control, 4th ed. Wiley. 796 p.

NWLRAG. 1998. Official log scaling and grading rules. Northwest Log Rules Advisory Group. 8th ed.

Ross, R.J.; Willits, S.W.; von Segen, W. [et al.]. 1999. A stress wave based approach to NDE of logs for assessing potential veneer quality. Part 1. Small diameter ponderosa pine. Forest Products Journal 49(11/12): 60-62.

Sonne, E.; Turnblom, E.; Briggs, D.; Becker, G. 2004. Log and lumber quality and value from a low site, 55 year old Douglas-fir stand in western washington 20 years after thinning and biosolids fertilization. Western Journal of Applied Forestry. 19(1): 1-8.

Wang, X., R. Ross, J.; McClellan, M. [et al.]. 2000. Strength and stiffness assessment of standing trees using a nondestructive stress wave technique. Res. Pap. FPL-RP-585. Madison, WI: U.S. Department of Agriculture, Forest Service, Forest Products Laboratory. 9 p.

Wang, S.; Ross, R.J.; Green, D.W. [et al.] 2004. Stress wave sorting of red maple logs for structural quality. Wood Science and Technology 37: 531-537.

PAPERS BASED ON POSTERS

CARBON SEQUESTRATION IN DOUGLAS-FIR STANDS OF THE COASTAL CONIFEROUS FOREST REGION OF WASHINGTON STATE

A.B. Adams, R.B. Harrison, M.M. Amoroso, D.G. Briggs, R. Collier,
R. Gonyea, B. Hasselberg, J. Haukaas, and M.O. O'Shea[1]

ABSTRACT

Quantifying the effects of urea fertilization on carbon (C) in the solid and solution phases of soils can aid forest management. We evaluated the effect of urea fertilization on pure second-growth Douglas-fir [*Pseudotsuga menziesii* (Mirb.) Franco] stands growing in four soil series of the coastal coniferous forest region of Washington State. Our major objective was to determine the range of carbon flux and sequestration for this region. This paper covers our results for soil organic carbon (SOC) sequestration. Our soils were selected to give a range of texture from coarse-grained glacial to fine-textured volcanic. We compared soil types, soil depths and fertilization treatments over 20-year intervals. There was no difference in soil C in a coarse glacial outwash soil. By contrast, in a glacial sandy outwash soil all mineral horizons had more soil C and the forest floor less C compared with the paired unfertilized plot. In two volcanic soils our results provide evidence that DOC from the forest floor and A horizons was sequestered in both the epipedon and lower horizons. Differences between glacial and volcanic soils suggest that mechanisms of C were different in the coarse-textured materials than the fine-textured volcanic material. Urea fertilization added nitrogen to soils at all installations with differences ranging from 1-3 Mg N ha^{-1}. The 2 glacial soils had lower site indices. They had less SOC (mean of 87 versus 348 Mg ha^{-1}) but greater increases in aboveground C (mean increase of 41 versus 8 Mg ha^{-1}). Although fine-textured sites were more productive overall, the aboveground response to urea was limited in comparison to differences found in fertilized plots of the glacial sites. In contrast, SOC did increase with urea applications in fine-textured sites in excess of increases solely attributable to DOC.

KEYWORDS: Carbon sequestration, urea fertilization, managed Douglas-fir stands.

INTRODUCTION

There exist several ecosystem management strategies directed toward enhancing carbon (C) sequestration through forest management: 1) to partition C into longer-lived pools; 2) to increase the physical, chemical and biochemical protection of soil C; and, 3) to enhance C storage in living tree biomass. The overall theme of our work is to relate management practices to soil organic carbon (SOC) partitioning among alternative pools including dissolved organic carbon (DOC) production and transport. Specifically, in this paper we report on the storage of soil organic carbon (SOC) based on texture, horizon, depth and fertilization with urea. Gains in forest productivity have been shown with Douglas-fir stands in the Pacific Northwest (Stegemoeller and

Chappell 1990). Increased aboveground biomass may (Johnson 1992) or may not (Harding and Jokela 1994, Canary et al. 2001) be accompanied by a gain in soil C. Urea fertilizer can increase the movement of SOM (Kelly 1981). Our initial hypothesis was that total C accumulation would exceed C accumulation in wood plus roots in response to nutrient management of fine-textured soil, but not on coarse-textured soils. This paper includes sequestration of SOC and aboveground C, but does not cover root C.

The Regional Forest Nutritional Research Project (RFNRP) (Stegemoeller et al., 1990) established installations in the Pacific Northwest to evaluate the response of coastal Douglas-fir to urea-N fertilization. In 1991, this project was combined with the Stand Management

[1] A.B. Adams, R.B. Harrison, M.M. Amoroso, D.G. Briggs, R. Collier, R. Gonyea, B. Hasselberg, J. Haukaas, and M.O. O'Shea are faculty and staff of the College of Forest Resources, University of Washington, Box 352100, Bloedel Hall 292, Seattle, WA 98195.

Cooperative (SMC) in order to include research on integrated studies (SMC 1999). For this study we utilized the stand database created by RFNRP and currently maintained by the SMC at the University of Washington. The sites [arranged in order from coarsest textured soil (Site 1) to finest textured soil (Site 4)] used were Cedar River [RFNRP #159 (a coarse glacial outwash soil)], Port Gamble [#196 (sandy outwash)], Radio Hill [#247 (coarse silty loam over a compacted duripan)] and Mud Mountain [#235 (deep, silty loam)]. These soils represent a regional association of parent material types from a very coarse skeletal matrix, to outwash sand and then to deep, silty loam. The skeletal matrices of Sites 1 and 2 were derived predominantly from glacial parent material and Sites 3 and 4 from tephra. The RFNRP permanent plots revealed that following fertilization, the periodic increment increased due to the N treatment, resulting in 49.9, 31.3, 6.4, and 9.7 Mg ha^{-1} additional C in the four sites, respectively, for an average of 24.3 Mg ha^{-1} additional C from a 16-year growth period (Adams et al., submitted). The largest aboveground tree responses were in the glacial soils. This paper focuses specifically on the SOC in relation to the aboveground live tree C compartments of these stands.

METHODS

When the four installations were established (1972 to 1980), 224 kg ha^{-1} elemental N as urea fertilizer was added to treatment plots. The same amount of fertilizer was then again added at 8 and 16 years. In addition, Sites 1 and 2 received 224 kg ha^{-1} urea 12 years after installation. One pit was dug and soils collected at each 0.1 ha plot (2 pits per installation). Soil collections were made from the face of pits using a hand trowel. Sampled layers were delineated and measured based on color, texture and structure breaks. All soils with texture < 25 mm and rocks ≥ 25 mm were weighed as two separate components in the field. A 1 kg sub-sample of the < 25 mm component was taken from each field identified layer and used to determine field moisture, particle size distribution (standard sieve procedures with dried samples), C and N content and pH. Mineral soil was air-dried to constant weight. Forest floor material was dried for 7 days at 70°C. The amount of C and N (in Megagrams ha^{-1}) were calculated for each layer based on thickness, percent soil C or N, and bulk density (Db); then, values for all layers were summed within each horizon. Adams et al. (in prep.) contains a more detailed explanation of the sites and methods.

RESULTS

The range of soil textures present was a function of parent material. Although volcanic and glacial activity both impact soils in the Pacific Northwest, the soil skeletal matrix of the parent material is usually dominated by one of the two processes. Our study found (fig. 1) that the two coarse-textured installations (Sites 1 and 2) were dominated by glacial outwash with mixed mineralogy, whereas Sites 3 and 4 were volcanic in nature (ashy, silty loam). Rocks dominated Site 1, while sand dominated Site 2. Tephra dominated Sites 3 and 4. Clay (which can play a role in C stabilization and sequestration) (Brady and Weil 2002) was almost absent from Site 1, but present on the other three sites where it ranged from 5% to 9% by dry weight.

There was a marginally significant difference in total SOC between unfertilized and fertilized paired plots (p < 0.1, paired Student's t-test analysis, n = 4 (fig. 2). There was a significant difference in N between fertilized and unfertilized plots (p < 0.05) and both N and C in glacial soil were significantly less than N and C of volcanic soils (p < 0.05, ANOVA, n = 8). A regression of the means of soil C from the two pits at each site compared with percent silt was significant (R^2 = 0.91, F = 19.2, P < 0.05; Y = 4.3X +20.2, n = 8).

When profiles for these soils are compared with respect to C (fig. 3), forest floor C is less in fertilized compared to unfertilized plots. In the sandy glacial outwash plots (Site 2), C is higher in all horizons; interestingly, the E and B horizons show two or three times as much C as the same horizons in the unfertilized plot. In the volcanic installations, the higher soil C content is due to larger amounts of C in the A and AB (Site 3) or just the AB (Site 4) horizons. Much of the SOC is found below the A horizon. This difference is due to larger volumes of soil included in the calculations to a one m depth as well as the increase in Db of the < 2 mm fraction that was measured.

At all installations fertilized plots have less C in the forest floor than paired unfertilized plots (fig. 4), but this difference was negligible (< 1 Mg ha^{-1}) at Site 1. In contrast, mineral soil of fertilized plots at Sites 2, 3, and 4 had more soil C relative to paired unfertilized controls. The differences in C sequestration between paired plots were mainly attributable to larger amounts of soil C in fertilized plots between 10 and 60 cm depths (Adams et al. in prep.). The three sites with greater mineral soil C were more acidic and had higher C/N ratios than paired unfertilized plots. The greatest increases in C sequestration occurred between 5 and 60 cm and at C/N ratios between 20 and 35.

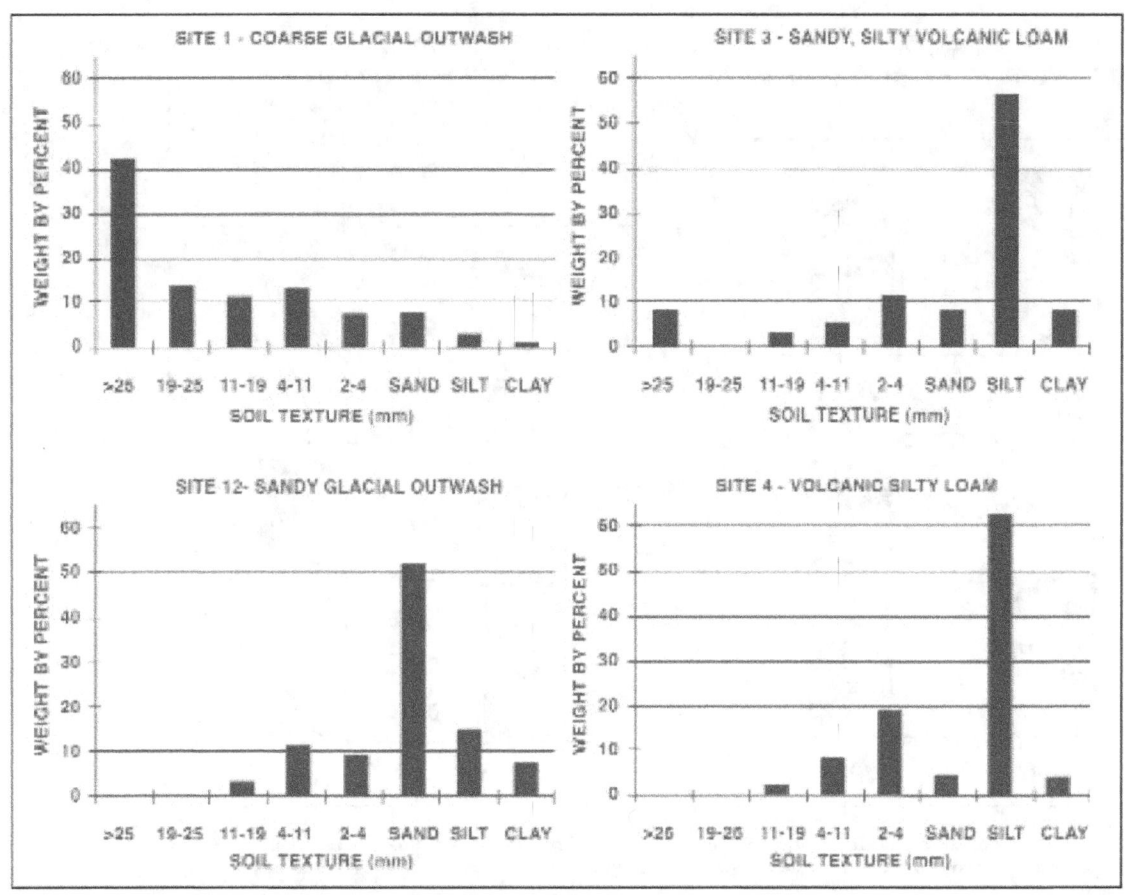

Figure 1—Particle size distribution taken at 25 cm mineral soil depth for each site. Site 1 (Cedar River) had many large rocks and gravel with only 12% < 2mm. Site 2 (Port Gamble) was mostly sandy outwash. Site 3 (Radio Hill) was coarse loamy silt with some rocks and Site 4 (Mud Mountain) was mostly silty loam with no rocks.

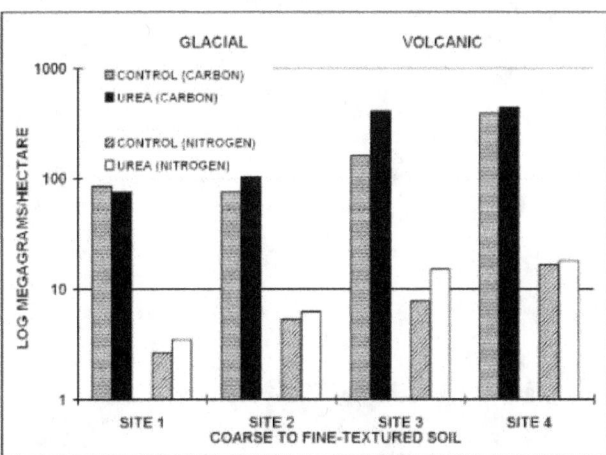

Figure 2—Distribution of C and N by site and treatment in 2001. All previously fertilized plots still had more nitrogen several years after cessation of urea applications. Volcanic soils and treated soils had more carbon, but this difference was only significant with volcanic versus glacial soils. Please note that the Y axis is a log scale.

DISCUSSION AND CONCLUSIONS

Our results provide evidence that in fertilized coarse-textured soils (as manifested in glacial parent materials) C sequestration is mostly in aboveground living trees, whereas fine-textured soils (in this case, products of volcanic parent materials) have more C sequestered in soils. The mechanisms for coarse-textured soils appear to be different than those of fine-textured ones. The idea of mechanistic differences is supported by lower pH values, higher C/N ratios and solubilization of fertilized forest floors. In the Central Puget Sound, the proportion of silt in soil may play a major role in the amount and nature of C sequestered. Besides texture, mineralogy is undoubtedly playing a role in shaping the results because the silt source in our study area is volcanic as opposed to the mixed mineralogy from the glacial parent material. The benefit to using texture as a criterion of C sequestration and forest productivity is that it can be easily and quickly determined in the field. Mineralogy, on the

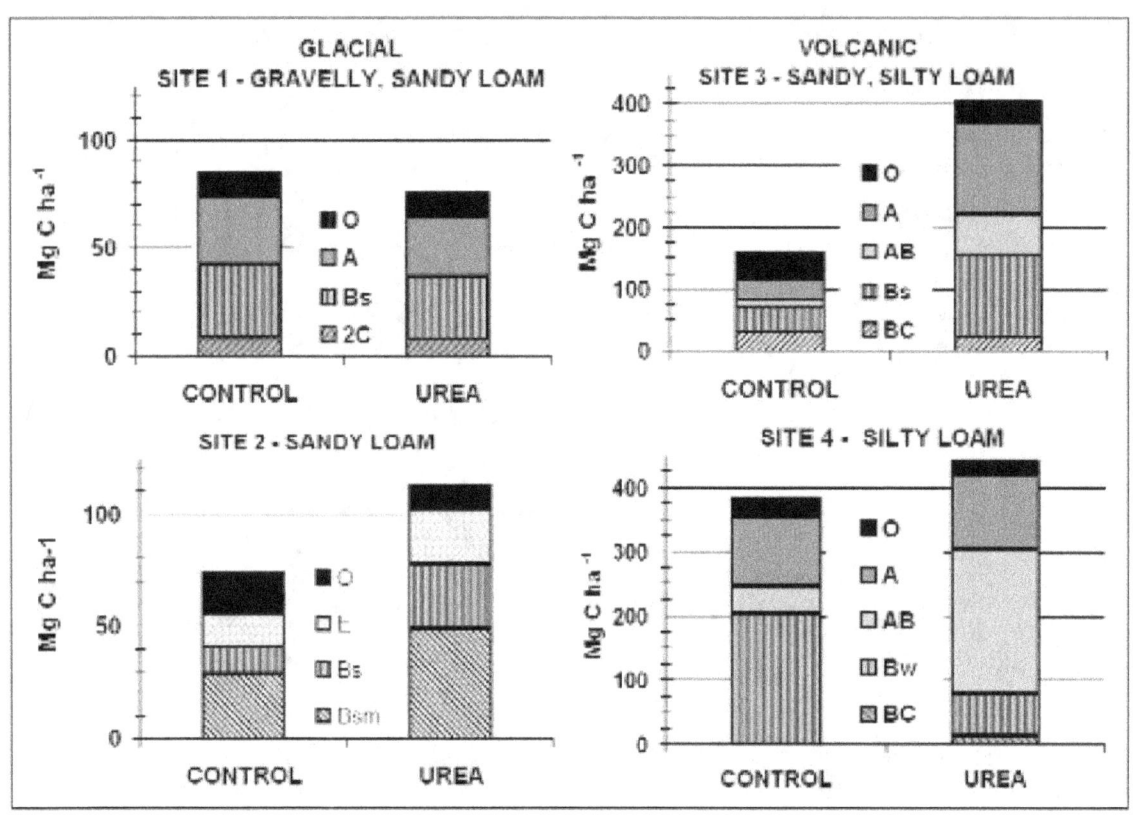

Figure 3—Distribution of C by site and soil profile. In all cases the fertilized O horizon had less C than did the unfertilized plot. There was no difference between treated and control of Site 1, but the A, E and B fertilized horizons of Sites 2, 3 and 4 had much more C than did their respective controls.

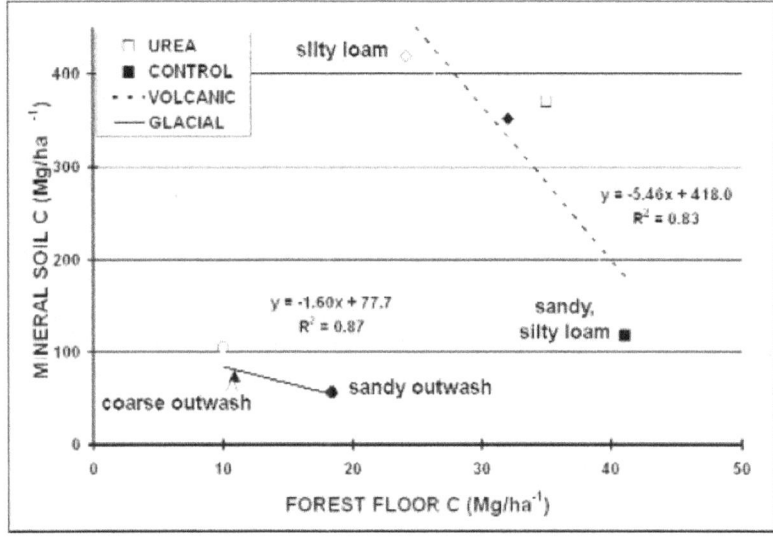

Figure 4—Forest floor (O horizon) C versus mineral soil C. Fertilized plots have more C in the mineral soil, but less C in the forest floor relative to paired controls.

other hand, requires complicated analyses that are expensive in terms of time and money. The fact that volcanic soil holds more C is not surprising. What is interesting is the idea that C sequestered above ground varies with soil type; in particular, the less productive sites sequester more C in trees when N fertilizer is applied.

ACKNOWLEDGMENTS

Research supported by the U.S. Department of Energy's Office of Science, Biological and Environmental Research funding to the Consortium for Research on Enhancing Carbon Sequestration in Terrestrial Ecosystems (CSITE). Oak Ridge National Laboratory is managed by UT-Battelle, LLC for the U.S.Department of Energy under contract DE-AC05-00OR22725. Additional support came from the PRISM program (Jeff Richey, University of Washington). C.T. Garten and Bob Luxmoore helped to initiate and supervise the project. We are grateful to Weyerhaeuser Company, The Campbell Group, The Hancock Co., Champion Pacific Timberlands, Inc. and the City of Seattle for access to their property.

LITERATURE CITED

Adams, A.B.; Harrison, R.B.; Sletten, R.S.; Jensen, C.M.; Strahm, B.D.; Turnblom, E.C. [in preparation]. Carbon movement and sequestration in managed Douglas-fir stands in the coastal coniferous forest region of Washington State.

Brady, N.C.; Weil, R.R. 2002. the nature and property of soils. 13th ed. [city unknown], NJ: Prentice Hall. 960 p.

Canary, J.D.; Harrison, R.B.; Compton, J.E.; Chappell, H.N. 2001. Additional carbon sequestration following repeated urea fertilization of second-growth Douglas-fir stands in western Washington. Forest Ecology Mangement 138: 225-232.

Crane, W.J.B. 1972. Urea-nitrogen transformations, soil reactions, and elemental movement via leaching and volatilization in a coniferous forest ecosystem after fertilization. Seattle, WA: University of Washington. Ph.D. dissertation. 250 p.

Harrison, R.B.; Adams, A.B.; Licata, C.; Flaming, B.; Wagoner, G.W.; Carpenter, P.; Vance, E.D. 2003. Quantifying deep-soil and coarse-soil fractions: avoiding sampling bias in estimating carbon in Pacific Northwest forest soils. Soil Science Society of America Journal 67: 1602-1606.

Johnson, D.W. 1992. Effects of forest management on soil carbon storage. Water, Air,and Soil Pollution 64: 83-120.

Kelly, J.M. 1981. Carbon flux to surface mineral soil after nitrogen and phosphorus fertilization. Soil Science Society of America Journal 45: 669-670.

Stand Management Cooperative [SMC]. 1999. What is the Stand Management Cooperative? SMC Fact Sheet, No. 1. Seattle, WA: College of Forest Resources, University of Washington. 10 p.

Stegemoeller, K.A.; Chappell, H.N. 1990. Growth response of unthinned and thinned Douglas-fir stands to single and multiple applications of nitrogen. Canadian Journal of Forest Research 20: 343-349.

Stegemoeller, K.A., Chappell, H.N., Bennett, W.S., 1990. Regional forest nutrition research project analysis history: objectives and achievements. RFNRP Report No. 12. Seattle, WA: College of Forest Resources, University of Washington. 33 p.

VOLUMETRIC SOIL WATER CONTENT IN A 4-YEAR-OLD AND A 50-YEAR-OLD DOUGLAS-FIR STAND

Warren D. Devine[1], Constance A. Harrington[1], and Thomas A. Terry[2]

ABSTRACT

We compared growing-season soil water content in a young Douglas-fir [*Pseudotsuga menziesii* (Mirb.) Franco] plantation (established in 2000 with no vegetation control) to that of an adjacent 50-year-old conifer stand on a highly productive site in southwestern WA. Soil water content in the older stand was slightly greater than that of the younger stand at soil depths of 10 and 30 cm during the 2003 and 2004 growing seasons. At 100 cm, soil water content was similar between stands. During the 2003 growing season, when precipitation was below average, soil water content declined by a similar amount in both stands.

KEYWORDS: Soil water, Douglas-fir, regeneration, evaporation, transpiration.

INTRODUCTION

Silvicultural practices can influence soil water in forest stands (Langdon and Trousdell 1972). For example, modification of the forest canopy affects stand evapotranspiration rates, which in turn may affect soil water content. In the Pacific Northwest, removal of overstory conifers will quickly result in increases in soil water (Keppeler and Ziemer 1990; Adams et al. 1991; Gray et al. 2002). Thus, in compared to that available in an unharvested area, clearcutting will increase the amount of soil water available to the subsequently regenerated stand. Our objective in this study was to compare growing-season volumetric soil water content (VSWC) in two conifer stands: a young Douglas-fir plantation established after a clearcut and an adjacent 50-year-old Douglas-fir/western hemlock [*Tsuga heterophylla* (Raf.) Sarg.] stand.

METHODS

We investigated two adjacent stands, one established in 1953 and one in 2000, on a highly productive site in the Coast Range of southwestern WA, USA. Mean annual precipitation is 2260 mm, but an average of only 241 mm occurs from 1 June through 30 September (USDA 1999). Topography is gently sloping, and soil is of the Boistfort series (medial over clayey, ferrihydritic over parasesquic, mesic Typic Fulvudands), with a silt loam A horizon (12- to 17-cm thick) underlain by a silt loam AB horizon (19- to 24-cm thick) and a silty clay loam Bw horizon (to >140 cm)[3]. Soils are derived from basalt, with volcanic ash influence, and are well drained, low in bulk density, and high in available water capacity.

Until 1999, the entire study area was occupied by Douglas-fir planted in 1953 and western hemlock that established naturally (Terry et al. 2001). In 1999, a portion of this stand was harvested, removing a volume of 914 m^3 ha^{-1} (55% Douglas-fir; 45% western hemlock). In the harvested area, the Fall River Long-Term Site Productivity study (LTSP) was established, and 1+1 Douglas-fir seedlings were planted at a 2.5- x 2.5-m spacing in March 2000. Although the LTSP study examines a range of treatments, we collected data from a single treatment: a bole-only harvest of the previous stand and no vegetation control. We

[1] Warren D. Devine and Constance A. Harrington are research foresters, USDA Forest Service PNW Research Station, Olympia Forestry Sciences Laboratory, 3625 93rd Ave SW, Olympia, WA 985122.

[2] Thomas A. Terry is senior scientist, Weyerhaeuser Co., PO Box 420, Centralia, WA 98531.

[3] Textures are apparent field textures as assessed by Darlene Zabowski, University of Washington.

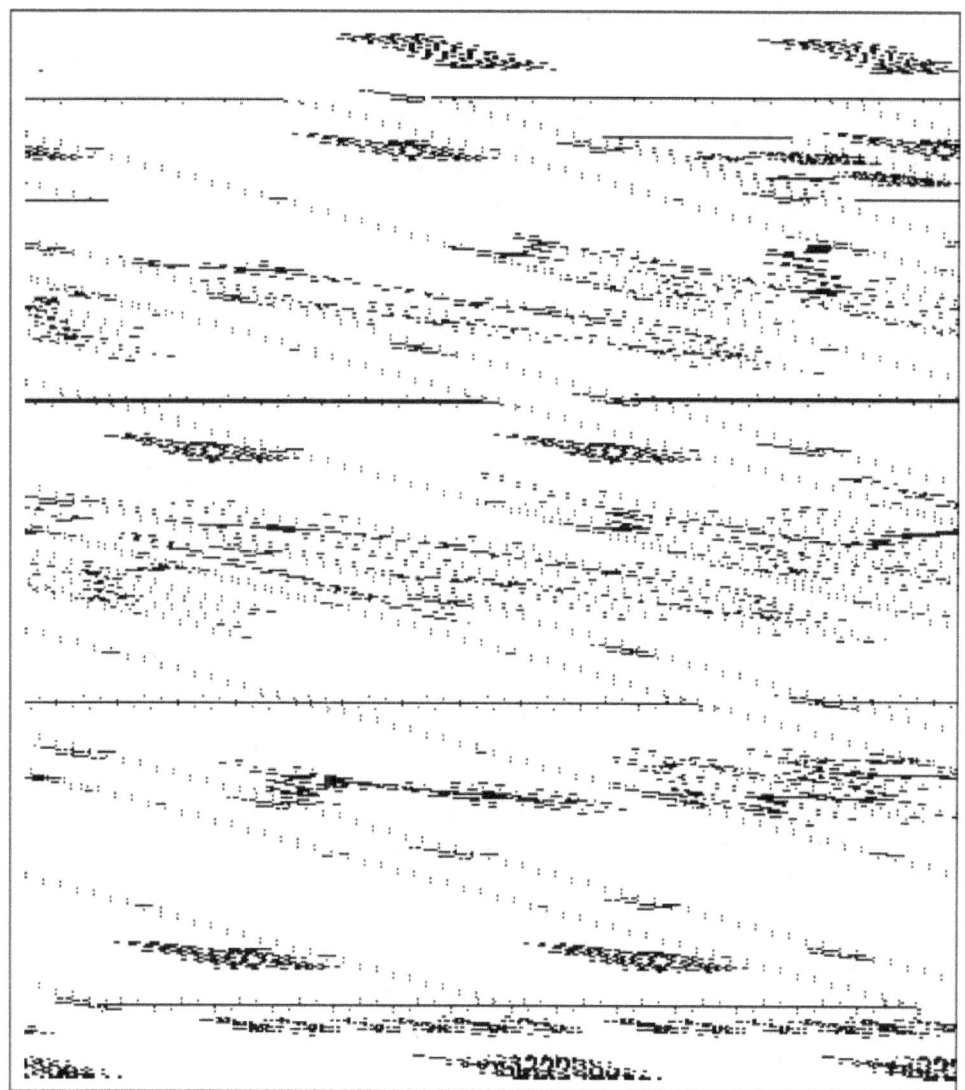

Figure 1—Volumetric soil water content (VSWC, ± standard deviation) at 10-, 30-, and 100-cm soil depths during 2003 and 2004 in two forest stands. Data missing for 25 September 2003 in the 1953 stand.

chose the treatment without vegetation control because we considered it analogous to the understory conditions of the stand established in 1953.

Using a Profile Probe® (Delta-T Devices Ltd., Cambridge, UK), we measured volumetric soil water content (VSWC) at six depths (10-100 cm) at 3- to 4-week intervals during the 2003 and 2004 growing seasons. In 2003, we sampled 12 locations in the 2000 stand and 4 locations in the 1953 stand; in 2004, the number of locations was increased to 21 and 6 in the 2000 and 1953 stands, respectively. Data were recorded in millivolts (mv) and subsequently converted to

VSWC using a soil-specific calibration [% VSWC = (0.057 * mv) + 21.67]. We calculated VSWC loss during the 2003 growing season by subtracting values recorded on 4 September from those recorded on 1 May. Because data presented here were not part of the randomized block design of the LTSP study, we did not use analysis of variance.

RESULTS AND DISCUSSION

Growing-season fluctuations in VSWC varied between 2003 and 2004 due to large differences in precipitation (fig. 1). Precipitation during the 2003 growing season was 50% of the long-term average, while in 2004 it was 134% of

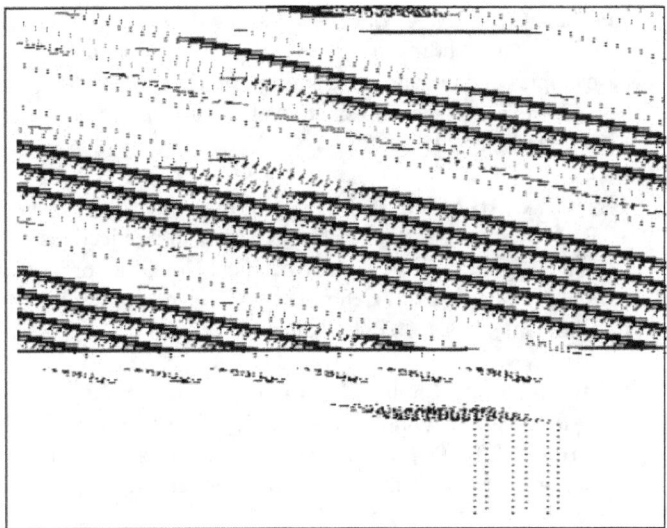

Figure 2—The loss in volumetric soil water content (VSWC, ± standard deviation) from 1 May to 4 September 2003 in two forest stands.

average. In 2003, VSWC decreased from May through early September in both stands at 10- and 30-cm depths. In 2004, VSWC decreased only from June through July at these depths because of above-average precipitation earlier and later in the growing season.

At shallow sample depths, particularly 10 cm, VSWC was generally greater in the 1953 stand than in the 2000 stand. At greater depths, VSWC was similar between the stands. Seasonal fluctuations in VSWC also were similar between stands. There were no differences in VSWC loss between the two stands during the 2003 growing season at any of the sample depths (fig. 2).

The overall similarities in VSWC between the two stands were unanticipated. We had hypothesized that during the growing season, VSWC would decrease by a greater amount in the 1953 stand than in the 2000 stand as a result of greater transpiration by the larger trees. It has previously been shown that growing-season soil water content was lower in a closed-canopy Douglas-fir forest relative to forest openings (Gray et al. 2002; Lindh et al. 2003). However, vegetation regrowth after clearcutting can have a strong, negative effect on soil water content (Adams et al. 1991).

The contribution of understory vegetation to total transpiration was likely greater in the 2000 stand than in the 1953 stand. Total dry biomass of understory vegetation in the 2000 stand (sampled in 2004) was much greater (2940 kg ha^{-1}) than that in the 1953 stand (221 kg ha^{-1}). Much of this vegetation in the 2000 stand consisted of generally shallow-rooted herbaceous species that may have reduced VSWC near the soil surface. Furthermore, the transpiration rate of the vegetation in the 2000 stand was probably greater than that of the vegetation in the 1953 stand because of microclimate differences caused by the forest canopy. For example, from June through August 2002, the temperature at the forest floor was, on average, 4.8° C higher in the 2000 stand than in the 1953 stand. Increased air temperatures result in greater transpiration rates due to a greater vapor pressure gradient between leaves and air (Kramer and Kozlowski 1979).

Processes other than transpiration may have differently influenced the soil water content of the two stands in this study. Evaporation at the soil surface may have been lower in the 1953 stand relative to the 2000 stand due to less solar radiation reaching the ground as well as the mulching effect of the undisturbed forest floor (Hillel 1998). At a soil depth of 5 cm, summer soil temperatures averaged 4.2° C less in the 1953 stand than in the 2000 stand. Thus, cooler soil temperatures may have led to greater VSWC in the 1953 stand, especially at shallow depths. It is also possible that the soil water content in the measured profile of the 1953 stand was influenced by hydraulic redistribution from deeper soil layers. Elsewhere in the region, it has been shown that water is transported upward in the soil profile as a consequence of water uptake by overstory trees (Brooks et al. 2002; Unsworth et al. 2004); however, the soil water contents in our soils were higher than the levels at which this phenomenon is likely to be operating.

While the final harvest of the previous stand in 1999 probably caused a temporary increase in soil water, soil water content by age four in the 2000 stand was similar to or less than that in the adjacent 50-year-old stand. In the younger stand, transpiration, and possibly evaporation at the soil surface, were reducing soil water to an extent similar to that of the overstory trees in the older stand.

ACKNOWLEDGMENTS

We thank our current and former coworkers at the Olympia Forestry Sciences Laboratory for their field work in this study and Douglas Waldren for instrument calibration. Funding was provided by an American Forest & Paper Association-USDA Forest Service Agenda 2020 grant and the USDA Forest Service PNW Research Station.

LITERATURE CITED

Adams, P.W.; Flint, A.L.; Fredriksen, R.I. 1991. Long-term patterns in soil moisture and revegetation after a clearcut of a Douglas-fir forest in Oregon. Forest Ecology Management 41: 249-263.

Brooks, J.R.; Meinzer, F.C.; Coulombe, R.; Gregg, J.R. 2002. Hydraulic redistribution of soil water during summer drought in two contrasting Pacific Northwest coniferous forests. Tree Physiology 22: 1107-1117.

Gray, A.N.; Spies, T.A.; Easter, M.J. 2002. Microclimate and soil moisture responses to gap formation in coastal Douglas-fir forests. Canadian Journal of Forest Research 32: 332-343.

Hillel, D. 1998. Environmental Soil Physics. San Diego, CA: Academic Press. 771 p.

Keppeler, E.T.; Ziemer, R.R. 1990. Logging effects on streamflow: water yield and summer low flows at Caspar Creek in northwestern California. Water Resources Research 26(7): 1669-1679.

Kramer, P.J.; Kozlowski, T.T. 1979. Physiology of Woody Plants. New York, NY: Academic Press. 811 p.

Langdon, O.G.; Trousdell, K.B. 1978. Stand manipulation: effects on soil moisture and tree growth in southern pine and pine-hardwood stands. In: Balmer, W.E., ed. Soil moisture…Site productivity: Symposium proceedings. Atlanta, GA: U.S. Department of Agriculture, Forest Service, Southern Region: 221-236.

Lindh, B.C.; Gray, A.N.; Spies, T.A. 2003. Responses of herbs and shrubs to reduced root competition under canopies and in gaps: a trenching experiment in old-growth Douglas-fir forests. Canadian Journal of Forest Research 33: 2052-2057.

Terry, T.A.; Harrison, R.B.; Harrington, C.A. 2001. Fall River long-term site productivity study: objectives and design. Forest Research Technical Note, Site productivity paper 01-1. Centralia, WA: Weyerhaeuser Company, Western Timberlands R&D. 10 p.

Unsworth, M.H.; Phillips, N.; Link, T.; Bond, B.J.; Falk, M.; Harmon, M.E.; Hinckley, T.M.; Marks, D.; Paw U, K.T. 2004. Components and controls of water flux in an old-growth Douglas-fir—western hemlock ecosystem. Ecosystems 7: 468-481.

USDA Natural Resource Conservation Service, National Water and Climate Center, and Oregon State University Spatial Climate Analysis Service. 1999. Parameter-elevation regressions on independent slopes model (PRISM). http://www.wcc.nrcs.usda.gov/climate/prism html

FACTORS AFFECTING NITROGEN MOBILITY: ORGANIC MATTER RETENTION AND VARIABLE-CHARGE SOILS

Brian D. Strahm[1], Robert B. Harrison[1], Thomas A. Terry[2],
Barry L. Flaming[1], Christopher W. Licata[1], and Kyle S. Petersen[1]

ABSTRACT

Forest harvesting and organic matter management practices may affect the cycling of nutrients, particularly nitrogen (N), through the removal of different organic matter components (e.g., branches, foliage, coarse-woody debris) from a site, and the associated changes in carbon-source quantity and quality. Such practices may also alter microclimatic conditions that influence N cycling processes, thereby affecting the rates at which N is made available to plants or is leached through t h e profile. This study examined the influence of intensive harvesting and organic matter retention practices on soil N dynamics on a highly productive (Site Index I-II+) coastal Douglas-fir (*Pseudotsuga menziesii* (Mirb.) Franco) site in southwestern Washington; the study results are from a time period when all competing vegetation was controlled. Additionally, this study addresses the ability of the Boistfort soil series (Typic Fulvand) to retain nitrate (NO_3) as a function of soil mineralogy and solution concentration. The specific focus of this investigation was to determine the effects of bole-only (BO) harvesting and total-tree harvesting plus coarse woody debris removal (TP) on soil-solution N concentrations and leaching rates (to a depth of 1.0 m) during the third through fifth year following harvest. Additional comparisons were made between the harvested treatments and the adjacent non-harvested stand (FS) representative of the initial stand condition. Solution concentrations were then related to NO_3^- sorption isotherms generated using batch equilibration techniques to determine the quantity of NO_3^- retained via sorption.

Soil-solution monitoring from April 2001 through March 2004 indicated that the increased organic matter retention associated with BO harvesting treatment increased the total N concentrations and leaching flux to a depth of 1.0 m by roughly two to three times that of TP harvest treatments. Nitrate comprised a majority of the 75, 29 and 4.5 kg ha^{-1} yr^{-1} of total N leached in the BO, TP and FS observations, respectively. The annual nitrogen leaching rates to a depth of 1.0 m however, are a small percentage of the 15 Mg ha^{-1} total soil N pool to a depth of 1.0 m (0.5, 0.2 and <0.03%, respectively). Similarly, the amount of NO_3^- sorbed to the mineral surface represents a small fraction of the total soil N pool, however, it comprises 41, 53 and 152% of the NO_3^- leached from the BO, TP and FS observations, respectively.

KEYWORDS: Nitrogen leaching, nitrate sorption, organic matter retention, soil-solution.

[1] Brian D. Strahm, Robert B. Harrison, Barry L. Flaming, Christopher W. Licata and Kyle S. Petersen are members of a forest soils research team, University of Washington, College of Forest Resources, Box 352100, Seattle, WA 98195.

[2] Thomas A. Terry is research forester, Western Forestry Research, Weyerhaeuser Company, Centralia, WA 98513.

OVERVIEW OF STUDY AREAS VISITED ON FIELD TRIPS

FALL RIVER LONG-TERM SITE PRODUCTIVITY STUDY

Constance A. Harrington[1], Thomas A. Terry[2], and Robert B. Harrison[3]

ABSTRACT

The Fall River Long-Term Site Productivity study is a cooperative project designed to examine factors influencing short- and long-term productivity and how management practices affect both tree growth and soil characteristics. The study was established after the existing Douglas-fir/western hemlock stand was harvested in 1999 and several levels of biomass retention were created as major treatments in the study. The study also includes fertilization, vegetation control, compaction, and tillage. Douglas-fir seedlings were planted in spring 2000 and several tree and soil assessments have been made since then. Early results indicate that biomass removals and compaction/tillage affected physical and chemical soil properties but vegetation control was the primary factor affecting tree growth.

KEYWORDS: Douglas-fir, site productivity, seedling growth, vegetation management, woody debris retention, biomass removal, compaction, soil tillage, nitrogen cycling.

INTRODUCTION

Intensive forest management practices aimed at increasing the production of wood products have raised questions regarding potential detrimental effects to sustained forest productivity. Management practices such as harvesting mechanization, harvesting intensity, and vegetation control can affect tree growth and site productivity by creating soil disturbance, removing nutrients in biomass, changing seedling microclimate, and altering plant community composition and the distribution of nutrients and biomass between trees and non-trees.

How these factors affect forest growth over the short as well as the long term (multiple rotations) is not well understood. In addition, the ameliorative potential of practices such as soil tillage and nitrogen fertilization for maintaining and enhancing forest productivity needs to be evaluated. The Fall River study will begin to fill a data gap that exists in the Pacific Northwest for the management of Douglas-fir forests. Fall River is an affiliate site in the Long-Term Soil Productivity Study coordinated by the U.S. Forest Service in several major forest production regions of the U.S. and Canada. Fall River investigators also coordinate with scientists working on other productivity studies in the Pacific Northwest.

STUDY OBJECTIVES

The overall objective of this study is to examine the impacts of a range of biomass removal/wood retention treatments and forest management practices on long-term productivity. The experiment was installed in 1999-2000 on a highly productive Douglas-fir site on Weyerhaeuser

[1] Constance A. Harrington is research forester, USDA Forest Service, Pacific Northwest Research Station, Olympia Forestry Sciences Laboratory, 3625 93rd Ave SW, Olympia, WA 98512.

[2] Thomas A. Terry is senior scientist, Weyerhaeuser Company, PO Box 420, Centralia, WA 98531.

[3] Robert B. Harrison is professor of forest soils, University of Washington, College of Forest Resources, 218 Bloedel Hall, Box 352100, Seattle, WA 98195-2100.

Company's McDonald Tree Farm in southwestern Washington. Fertile soils such as those present at the study site cover extensive areas in western Washington and are managed intensively for Douglas-fir wood production.

Specific research objectives are:

1) Evaluate effects of four levels of biomass removal on soil and Douglas-fir growth over a 40-year rotation.

2) Develop nutrient budgets for various levels of harvest and biomass removal.

3) Determine the impact of soil compaction and tillage on soil properties and tree growth.

4) Evaluate the need for fertilization and its effects on nutrient supply and tree growth.

5) Assess the effects of vegetation control and fertilization on tree growth, plant community composition, and soil characteristics.

6) Evaluate differences in seedling physiology and microclimate associated with the treatments.

The study addresses one of the priority topics in AF& PA Agenda 2020—Achieve and Sustain the Full Productivity Potential of Forest Soils. The study also addresses the Pacific Northwest Research Station's Priority Research Area: Produce Wood within Sustainable Frameworks.

METHODS

Site Description

The study area is on a 20-ha, very productive, low-elevation (300 m), gently sloping (<10 to 15%) site in the Coast Range Mountains located 60 km southwest of Olympia, WA, USA (Terry et al. 2001). Mean annual precipitation is 2260 mm, falling mostly as rain from September through May. Temperatures are mild (9.2°C mean annual) with mean January low of only -0.1°C (USDA NRCS 1999). The soil is a deep, well-drained silt loam over silty clay loam (Typic Fulvudand in the Boistfort series) developed from highly weathered basalt with ash influences in the upper horizons (Steinbrenner and Gehrke 1973).

Study Treatments

Study treatments were designed to look at factors of interest to both scientists and managers. Some treatments were operational while others were designed to "stretch" the system, that is, to implement treatments that are not operational but would provide valuable information on long-term productivity (table 1). In addition, the study was designed to include treatments that could ameliorate problems if there was a reduction in productivity in one or more

of the treatments. For example, fertilization was included to determine if fertilizer additions could compensate for organic matter removals and a compaction-followed-by-tillage treatment was included to see if tillage could eliminate any deleterious effects on soil characteristics or tree growth induced by compaction.

The overall study design is a randomized complete block with 4 blocks. Treatment plots are 30 X 80 m. Study measurements include: tree size, condition and nutrient content; cover, species composition, biomass, and nutrient content of non-tree vegetation; volumetric soil water by depth; N in soil water; soil and air microclimate; and soil physical properties. A complete meteorological station is maintained onsite (fig. 1).

RESULTS

Seedling growth and non-tree vegetation for years 1-4 (fig. 2)

• Seedling growth was markedly lower in the treatment without vegetation control

• There was no significant difference in tree size associated with amount of biomass removed

• Compaction associated with harvesting was not detrimental to seedling growth

• Cover of non-tree vegetation was negatively correlated with soil moisture content and tree growth (for more information on tree responses, see Roberts et al. 2005).

Microclimate during growing season:

• Soil moisture was a good predictor of seedling volume both across and within treatments

• Without vegetation control, soil moisture was lower (Roberts et al. 2005)

• With removal of residues, soil moisture was lower

• With compaction, soil moisture was higher

• Soil temperature during the growing season increased with intensity of residue removal

• Warmer temperatures were beneficial to tree growth when soil moisture during the growing season was high

Soil physical properties:

Soil compaction in traffic lanes affected soil properties but they did not exceed critical levels (for more information on this topic, see Ares et al. 2005)

Table 1—Plot-level treatments at the Fall River Long-Term Site Productivity study

Biomass Removal[1]	Fertilization[2]	Vegetation control	Compaction	Tillage
Total tree plus	+	+	-	-
Total tree plus	-	+	-	-
Total tree	+	+	-	-
Total tree	-	+	-	-
Bole only, 5-cm top	+	+	-	-
Bole only, 5-cm top	-	+	-	-
Bole only	+	+	-	-
Bole only	-	+	-	-
Bole only	+	-	-	-
Bole only	-	-	-	-
Bole only	+	+	+	-
Bole only	+	+	+	+

[1] Total tree plus = removal of entire tree bole and branches with foliage attached plus removal of legacy woody debris (old-growth logs); Total tree = removal of entire tree bole and branches with foliage attached; Bole only, 5-cm top = removal of the tree bole to a 5-cm top diameter (non-merchantable material that met this diameter limit was also removed); Bole only = removal of tree bole to normal merchantability standards (10-cm top, no removal of broken, rotten or otherwise defective material).

[2] Fertilization treatments have not yet been applied.

Figure 1—The weather station at the Fall River study site records information for many meteorological factors.

• Bulk density in the 0- to 30-cm depth was increased by compaction from 0.63 to 0.82 Mg m^{-3}

• Macroporosity at 10- to 20-cm depth decreased in compacted areas (0.36 to 0.19 m^3 m^{-3}) but did not drop below 0.10 m^3 m^{-3}, the level that is usually considered limiting for tree growth

• Soil strength in traffic lanes increased at all depths < 55 cm but never exceeded 1300 kPa; the critical value for impacting tree growth is usually considered to be >2000 to 3000 kPa

• Available water and early tree growth were both increased in traffic lanes

Nitrogen movement and cycling:

The adjacent uncut forest (50-year-old stand) and two of the biomass removal treatments differed in the amount of total N in soil solution at 100 cm: Bole only (BO) > Total Tree plus (TT+) > Uncut forest (for more information on soil chemistry, see Strahm et al. 2005a and Strahm et al. 2005b)

• Nitrate was the major form of N in soil solution at 100 cm.

• NO$_3$ accounted for 92% of N in BO, 84% in TT+, and 57% in the adjacent uncut forest.

Average annual leaching of total N to 100 cm from April 2001 through March 2004 was: 75 kg/ha/yr for BO, 29 kg/ha/yr for TT+, and 4.5 kg/ha/yr for the adjacent uncut forest.

• Percent N in Douglas-fir foliage was lowest in the treatment without vegetation control (Roberts et al. 2005)

• Percent N in Douglas-fir foliage was similar across biomass removal levels (Roberts et al. 2005)

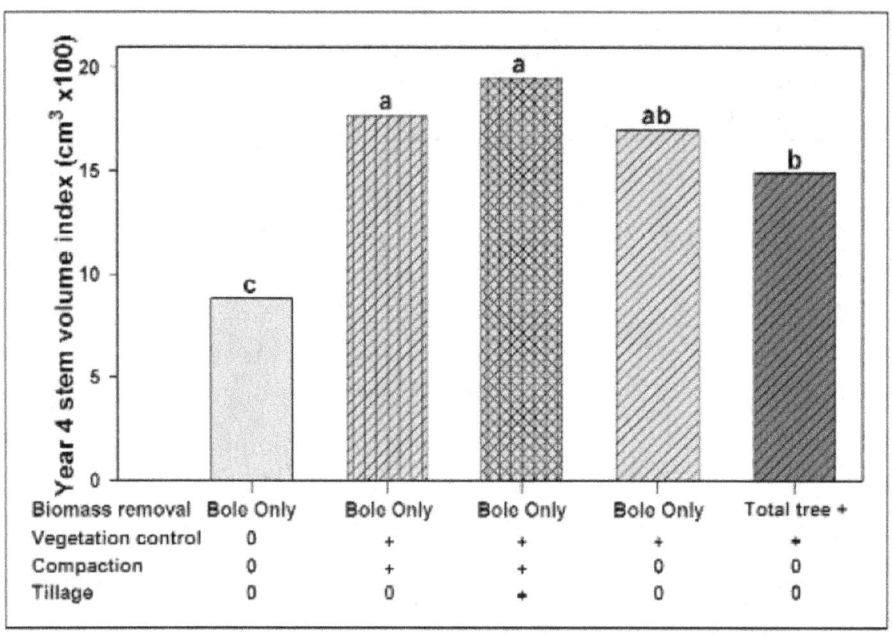

Figure 2—Effects of treatments on year-4 volume index (calculated as basal diameter squared times total height). Bars with the same letter above them do not differ at p < 0.05.

ACKNOWLEDGMENTS

Financial support for this project has been provided by Weyerhaeuser Company, the Northwest Stand Management Cooperative, the National Council for Air and Stream Improvement, the Olympic Natural Resource Center, the Pacific Northwest Research Station, and Agenda2020 (a joint project of the USDA Forest Service, Research & Development and the American Forest and Paper Association).

LITERATURE CITED

Ares, A.; Terry, T.A.; Miller, R.E.; Anderson, H.W.; Flaming, B.L. 2005. [In press]. Ground-based forest harvesting effects on soil physical properties and Douglas-fir growth on a coastal Washington site. Soil Science Society of America Journal.

Steinbrenner, E.C.; Gehrke; F.E. 1973. Soil survey of the McDonald Tree Farm. Tacoma, WA: Weyerhaeuser Company.

Strahm, B.D.; Harrison, R.B.; Flaming, B.L.; Terry, T.A.; Licata, C.W.; Petersen, K.S. 2005a. [In preparation]. Soil-solution nitrogen concentrations and leaching rates as influenced by organic matter retention on a highly productive Douglas-fir site.

Strahm, B.D.; Harrison, R.B.; Flaming, B.L.; Terry, T.A.; Licata, C.W.; Petersen, K. S. 2005b. Factors affecting nitrogen mobility: Organic matter retention and variable-charge soils. In: Harrington, C.A.; Schoenholtz, S.H., eds. Proceedings of Productivity of western forests: a forest products focus. Gen. Tech. Rep. PNW-GTR-642. Portland, Oregon: U.S. Department of Agriculture, Forest Service, Pacific Northwest Research Station: 165.

Terry, T.A.; Harrison, R.B.; Harrington, C.A. 2001. Fall River long-term site productivity study: objectives and design. Paper #01-1, Forestry Research Technical Note, Weyerhaeuser Company, Western Timberlands R&D. 10 p.

Roberts, S.D.; Harrington, C.A.; Terry, T.A. 2005. Harvest residue and competing vegetation affect soil moisture, soil temperature, N availability, and Douglas-fir seedling growth. Forest Ecology and Management 205: 333-350.

USDA Natural Resources Conservation Service, National Water and Climate Center; and Oregon State University Spatial Climate Analysis Service. 1999. Parameter-elevation Regressions on Independent Slopes Model (PRISM). http://www.wcc nrcs.usda.gov/ water/climate/prism/prism html.

FOREST PRODUCTIVITY RESPONSES TO LOGGING DEBRIS AND COMPETING VEGETATION: EFFECTS OF ANNUAL PRECIPITATION AND SOIL TEXTURE

Timothy B. Harrington[1], Constance A. Harrington[1], and Stephen H. Schoenholtz[2]

ABSTRACT

Logging debris and competing vegetation are being manipulated at two sites to determine their potential influences on selected soil factors and productivity of planted Douglas-fir (*Pseudotsuga menziesii* (Mirb.) Franco var. *menziesii*). The sites, located at Matlock WA and Molalla OR, were selected to differ in annual precipitation and soil texture. As part of the field tour for the Forest Productivity Conference, participants visited the Matlock site to observe the various treatments and vegetation responses in the first year since study initiation.

KEYWORDS: Long-term site productivity, soil properties, microclimate, plantations.

STUDY OBJECTIVES AND TREATMENTS

In 1998, the Fall River long-term site productivity (LTSP) study was initiated to examine effects of logging debris removal, competing vegetation control, fertilization, compaction, and tillage on soil characteristics and Douglas-fir growth (Terry et al. 2001). The study is affiliated with the national network of Long-Term Soil Productivity studies (Powers et al. 1990). In 2002, the Agenda 2020 program, members of forest industry, and the USDA Forest Service, PNW Research Station provided financial support to initiate an expansion of the Fall River research. The new research was designed to quantify potential effects of annual precipitation and soil texture on Douglas-fir responses to logging debris manipulation and competing vegetation removal. Six treatments have been replicated at two sites: Matlock WA (Olympic Peninsula) and Molalla OR (Western Cascades). The sites differ from Fall River and from each other in soil texture, precipitation, and temperature (fig. 1). Each site is an independent study.

The research will quantify stand establishment, early (1 to 5 years) and longer-term (5 to 20 years) growth of planted Douglas-fir, and long–term site productivity. A variety of pre-treatment and first-year measurements have been taken at each site, including soil nutrient content, bulk density, *in situ* net nitrogen mineralization and needle decomposition rates, logging debris mass and soil disturbance intensity, competing vegetation abundance, microclimate (air and soil temperatures and soil water content), and Douglas-fir initial size. The specific research objectives are to determine:

1. effects of logging debris abundance (retained vs. removed) and spatial distribution (dispersed vs. piled) and competing vegetation (presence vs. absence) on selected soil factors.

2. influence of soil responses on early growth and nutrition of Douglas-fir seedlings.

3. whether soil and Douglas-fir responses vary between sites differing in annual precipitation and soil texture.

[1] Timothy B. Harrington and Constance A. Harrington are research foresters, USDA Forest Service, PNW Research Station, Forestry Sciences Laboratory, 3625 93rd Avenue, Olympia, WA 98512.

[2] Stephen H. Schoenholtz is associate professor, Department of Forest Engineering, Oregon State University, Corvallis, OR 97331.

The following experimental treatments have been replicated four times at each site in a randomized complete block design:

Logging debris treatment control		Competing vegetation
1. Stem-only harvest: removal of merchantable logs only (i.e., retention of logging debris)	Absent	Present
2. Stem-only harvest + piling: removal of merchantable logs plus moving of tops and limbs into piles (i.e., retention and piling of logging debris).	Absent	Present
3. Whole-tree harvest: removal of merchantable logs plus tops and limbs (i.e., removal of logging debris)	Absent	Present

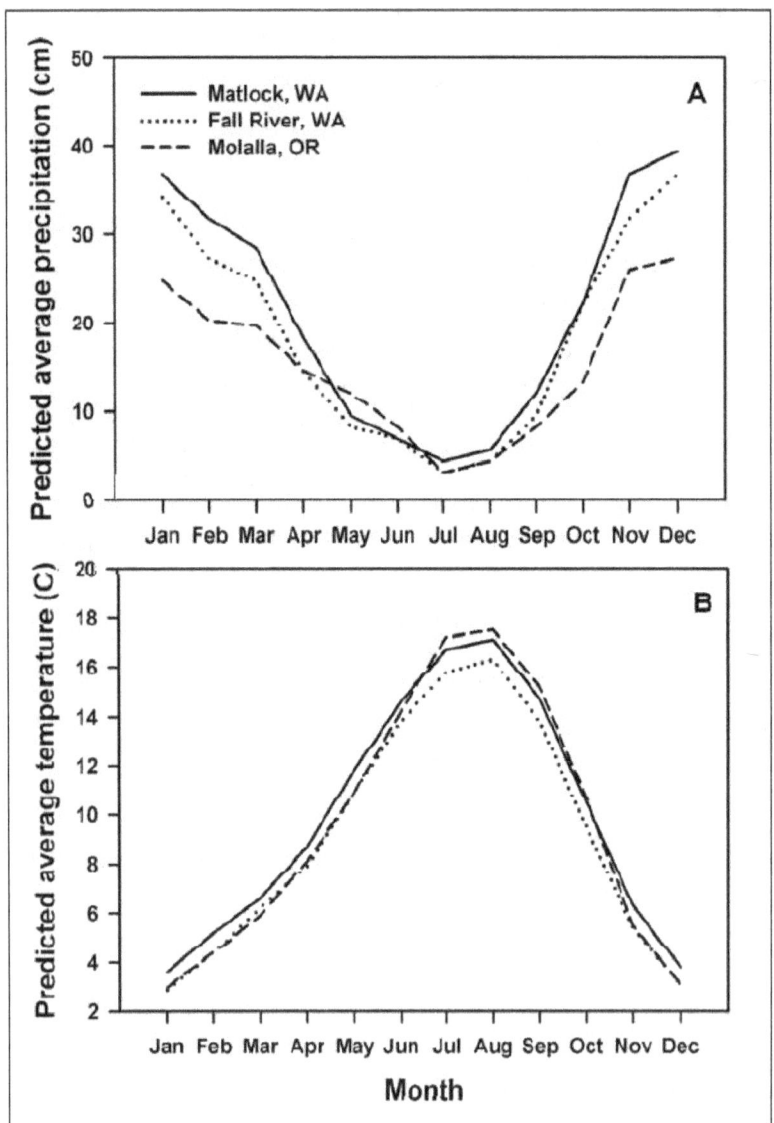

Figure 1—Predicted average monthly values for (a) precipitation and (b) air temperature at three forest productivity study sites in Washington and Oregon. Values were predicted from the PRISM model (Spatial Climate Analysis Service 2005).

CURRENT FINDINGS

In the first 3 or 4 months after treatment, mass of logging debris varied nearly two-fold between the stem-only (20.5 to 20.7 Mg ha^{-1}) and whole-tree (10.9 to 12.3 Mg ha^{-1}) harvesting treatments at each site. In August 2004, first-year cover of competing vegetation differed between herbicide-treated and non-treated plots at Matlock (12% vs. 20%, respectively) but not at Molalla (61% vs. 59%, respectively) where trailing blackberry (*Rubus ursinus* Cham. & Schlecht.) became dominant. The logging debris treatments had no detectable effect on abundance of competing vegetation at either site. Additional herbicide treatments are planned to achieve vegetation-free conditions on 80% or more of the area within treated plots. Although first-year measurements of the planted Douglas-fir have not yet been completed, field observations indicate that survival will be more than adequate for long-term monitoring of forest productivity.

FUTURE DIRECTION

In 2004, additional funding was received from the Agenda 2020 program to begin a new phase of research at Matlock and Molalla. Abundance of logging debris will be varied systematically to quantify the level at which it causes potential effects such as increased soil water conservation and thermal insulation, and shifting roles as a nitrogen source vs. a nitrogen sink. Logging debris will be applied to create 0, 40, or 80% covers (±10%) in 2- x 2-m areas around individual Douglas-fir growing either with or without competing vegetation. This new phase of research will identify some of the mechanisms by which logging debris and competing vegetation influence Douglas-fir productivity. In combination with the Fall River study, the research will contribute to a regional database that will enable forest managers to make more effective silvicultural prescriptions for maintaining or enhancing productivity of Douglas-fir plantations.

ACKNOWLEDGMENTS

This is a product of the Sustainable Forestry component of Agenda 2020, a joint effort of the USDA Forest Service Research & Development and the American Forest and Paper Association. Research partners include Oregon State University (OSU), University of Washington, Port Blakely Tree Farms LP, Green Diamond Resource Company, and Green Crow Ltd. Funds were provided by Pacific Northwest Research Station, USDA Forest Service and OSU (Agreements # PNW-JV-11261993-111 and PNW-CA-11261993-137), and in-kind contributions (e.g., treatment and equipment costs, field assistance, etc) were provided by the members of forest industry cited above.

LITERATURE CITED

Terry, T.A.; Harrison, R.B.; Harrington, C.A. 2001. Fall River long-term site productivity study: objectives and design. Paper #01-1, Forestry Research Technical Note, Weyerhaeuser Company, Western Timberlands R&D. 10 p.

Powers, R.F.; Alban, D.H.; Miller, R.E.; Tiarks, A.E.; Wells, C.G.; Avers, P.E.; Cline, R.G.; Fitzgerald, R.O.; Loftus, N.S., Jr. 1990. Sustaining site productivity in North American forests: problems and prospects. In: Gessel, S.P; Lacate, D.S; Weetman,G.F.; Powers, R.F. (eds.), Proceedings: 7th North American Forest Soils Conference on Sustained Productivity of Forest Soils. Victoria, BC: University of British Columbia: 49-79.

Spatial Climate Analysis Service. Oregon State University, http://www.ocs.oregonstate.edu/prism/, [28 March 2005].

METRIC EQUIVALENTS

When you know:	Multiply by:	To find:
Degrees Fahrenheit (°F)	(F-32) x 0.556	Degrees Celsius (°C)
Inches (in)	2.54	Centimeters (cm)
Feet (ft)	.3048	Meters (m)
Acres (ac)	.4047	Hectares (ha)
Trees per acre	2.471	Trees per hectare
Square feet per acre (ft^2/ac)	.2296	Square meters per hectare (m^2/ha)
Thousand board feet (MBF)	.0024	Cubic meters (m^3)
Fluid ounces	.0296	Liters (L)
Gallons	3.78	Liters (L)

ENGLISH EQUIVALENTS

When you know:	Multiply by:	To find:
Degrees Celsius (°C)	(C*9/5) +32	Degrees Fahrenheit (°F)
Centimeters (cm)	.3937	Inches (in)
Meters (m)	3.2808	Feet (ft)
Kilometers (km)	0.6214	Miles (m)
Square meters per hectare (m^2/ha)	4.3560	Square feet per acre (ft^2/ac)

www.ingramcontent.com/pod-product-compliance
Lightning Source LLC
Chambersburg PA
CBHW080248290526
45790CB00005B/1741